Suzan Hodson

Anthropology and
Contemporary Human Problems

Anthropology and Contemporary Human Problems

THIRD EDITION

John H. Bodley

WASHINGTON STATE UNIVERSITY

Mayfield Publishing Company
Mountain View, California
London • Toronto

Library of Congress Cataloging-in-Publication Data
Bodley, John H.
    Anthropology and contemporary human problems / John H. Bodley.—3rd ed.
      p.   cm.
    Includes bibliographical references (p.   ) and index.
    ISBN 1-55934-522-5
    1. Ethnology. 2. Civilization, Modern—1950– 3. Human ecology.
  4. Social problems. 5. Social prediction. I. Title.
  GN320.B62 1995
  306—dc20 ·
                                                          95-23596
                                                             CIP

Manufactured in the United States of America
10 9 8 7 6 5 4 3 2 1

Mayfield Publishing Company
1280 Villa Street
Mountain View, CA 94041

Sponsoring editor, Janet M. Beatty; production, Proof Positive/Farrowlyne
Associates, Inc.; manuscript editor, Dan Weiskopf; cover designer, Terri Wright; art
director, Jeanne M. Schreiber; cover image © Brian McGilloway; the text was set in
10/12 Janson by Proof Positive/Farrowlyne Associates, Inc. and printed on 50#
Ecolocote by Malloy Lithographing, Inc.

 This book is printed on recycled paper.

Preface

THIS BOOK IS DESIGNED for cultural anthropology courses that focus on world problems and cultural ecology. Using the cross-cultural, evolutionary, and multi-disciplinary perspectives that are unique to anthropology, the text introduces students to the complex problems of contemporary global-scale cultures and helps them better understand their place on the global stage.

In addition to updating the sources, case studies, and statistics in the previous edition, I've used a different lens in this edition to view our contemporary human problems—that of culture scale. What I addressed in previous editions as a contrast between tribal culture and industrial civilization I have now recast as a contrast between small-scale and large- and global-scale cultures. This culture scale analysis is the one I used in my introductory text *Cultural Anthropology: Tribes, States, and the Global System* (Mayfield, 1994). Small-scale cultures are represented by the contemporary "indigenous peoples" and peasants who are so well-known to anthropologists for their reliance on nonmarket subsistence and kin-based support networks.

There are many advantages to the culture scale approach, but most importantly it means that contemporary problems are related to particular cultural processes, especially politicization and commercialization. The role of the transnational global elite and the importance of cultural hegemony are addressed directly. The culture scale perspective emphasizes the long-term survival value of local autonomy, the satisfaction of basic human needs, sustainable resource management, and social equality—all primary goals of small-scale cultures—because these values are often undermined by politically organized large-scale states and global-scale commercial interests. The focus on culture scale suggests that many solutions to contemporary problems may be found by developing local communities supported by regional markets and ecosystems, rather than by making the continuous accumulation of finance capital the dominant cultural process throughout the world.

Chapter 2 argues that the rapid expansion of the global-scale culture over the past 200 years is unlikely to be sustained through the next century without dramatic cultural change. The effects of continuous economic growth—intensified by great social inequality—are reducing the earth's long-term ability to support humanity. In contrast, small-scale cultures are an inherently more sustainable cultural adaptation because they minimize culturally driven incentives to increase pressure on the environment. At the same time these decentralized societies can more equitably provide for all of their people. This argument has important implications for the continuing policy debates about whether environmental dangers are being exaggerated, how much growth can be sustained, and whether a greater emphasis on social justice, human welfare, and wealth redistribution will be needed.

Chapter 2 also includes a reassessment of the famous 1972 *Limits to Growth* study and a "worst case scenario" of environmental disaster using material newly available from the former USSR, which focuses on the human impacts of Chernobyl, industrial pollution, and the shrinking Aral Sea. The rain forest example has been updated and expanded to more broadly cover deforestation. New material is incorporated on the tragic commons, Pleistocene extinctions debates, and the loss of biodiversity. In relation to the "ecologically noble savage" debate, Chapter 2 argues that small-scale cultures do not require self-conscious conservationists, because local self-sufficiency fosters biodiversity even in subsistence crops; globally integrated market exchange systems have historically simplified and degraded ecosystems. In order to provide a more balanced view (at the same time stressing the ecological advantages of small-scale cultures) I've included material in the section on the Pacific that shows extensive ecological modification under the large-scale cultures on Tikopia.

The discussion of food systems notes that the structure of political economies and social inequality are more critical in limiting the availability of food than the ultimate limits to global food production. This discussion also covers the corporate structure of food production, processing, and distribution, especially the degree of economic concentration in these industries. This highlights the contradiction between the ideals of the free market and the realities of oligopoly. Cross-national comparisons of the organization of agricultural production in Great Britain, Norway, and California have been added.

The most significant organizational change in this edition is the merging of the original Chapter 7 on internal order and Chapter 8 on war into a new Chapter 7—"Poverty and Conflict in the Global Culture." This change reflects the end of the Cold War together with the rapid expansion of minimally regulated global markets. It recognizes that the most pressing global concerns are now famines, ecological imbalance, development failures, local wars, and the rich-poor gap. This new chapter discusses the impact of highly concentrated corporate economic power and financial investments by the global elite on households and communities in the United States as well as in the impoverished countries of the world.

The final chapter summarizes the challenge of "sustainable development," posing the problem of how to design a global system that will permit small-scale, community-based cultures to enjoy maximum autonomy within large-scale states interconnected by a global capitalist market system. The conflict between "free-market" capitalism as represented by NAFTA and GATT is considered in relation to the needs of local communities. The UN's Agenda 21 and the Biodiversity Treaty are considered in some detail as important global responses to contemporary problems. The dilemma is that capitalism assumes perpetual economic growth driven by material inequality and profit-seeking individualism, while small-scale cultures emphasize community, stability, and equality.

ACKNOWLEDGMENTS

This edition benefited from the helpful materials and ideas offered by the following students and colleagues at Washington State University: Fekri Hassan, Barry Hewlett, Tim Kohler, Bill Lipe, Frank Myka, John Prater, Margaret Reed, Jim Rotholz, and William A. Warren. I also want to thank Audrey R. Chapman, Ricardo Falla, Thomas Headland, Daniel Salcedo, and Alan E. Wittbecker. The following reviewers helped shape the final product, even though I did not always follow their suggestions: Diane E. Barbolla, San Diego Mesa College; Daniel L. Boxberger, Western Washington University; Michael Chibnik, University of Iowa; Norbert Dannhauser, Texas A&M; Kathleen S. Fine-Dare, Fort Lewis College; Mary Kay Gilliland, Pima Community College; Robert H. Lavenda, St. Cloud State University; Robert Lawless, Wichita State University; Michael Merrifield, Saddleback College; Richard H. Moore, Ohio State University; Francis A. O'Connor, Lehigh University; Emily A. Schultz, Macalester College; and Dianne Smith, Santa Rosa Junior College. Special thanks to Kathleen Bodley for compiling the index.

It has been a pleasure working with my editor Jan Beatty and her Mayfield production staff, especially April Wells-Hayes and Joanne Martin. Thanks also to copy editor Dan Weiskopf, of Proof Positive/Farrowlyne Associates, who worked at the other end of my fax machine.

Contents

Preface   v

1

ANTHROPOLOGICAL PERSPECTIVES ON
CONTEMPORARY HUMAN PROBLEMS   1

Nature and Scope of the Problems   2
Crisis Intensity   5
Crisis Awareness and Response   5
Anthropology's Contribution   8
The Significance of Cultural Scale   10
Our Tribal Superiors   13
The Dangerous Spirit of Rousseau   14
Romanticism: Why Not?   15
The Original Affluent Society   17
The Despicable Savage   17
Understanding Global-Scale Culture   19

2

ADAPTION, CULTURE SCALE, AND
THE ENVIRONMENTAL CRISIS   23

Cultural Evolution and Adaptation   24
Nature and Scope of the Environmental Crisis   26
Biodiversity and the Death of the Tropical Rain Forests   26

Ecocide Soviet Style   28
Environmental Crisis and Cultural Change   31
Global Disequilibrium: Beyond "The Limits to Growth"   32
Environmental Commissions: Global 2000 and
     Our Common Future   35
"Roots" of the Environmental Crisis   40
Ideological Roots   42
Herders, Self-Interest, and Tragic Commons   43
Pleistocene Extinctions   46
Small-Scale Cultures and the Environment   48
Fire and Tribal Resource Management   50
Economics of Small-Scale Cultures   51
Nature in Tribal Ideology   55
The Desana Equilibrium Model   56
Pacific Island Chiefdoms and the Environment   57

3

NATURAL RESOURCES AND THE CULTURE OF CONSUMPTION   **59**

Energy and Culture: Basic Considerations   59
The Culture of Consumption Defined   65
Resource Consumption in America   68
Taking Stock   70
The Economics of Resource Depletion   74
Sustainable Development for the Common Good   75
The Consumption Culture's Environmental Cost: Western Coal   77
Consumption Culture Versus Tribal Culture: Bougainville Copper   79

4

WORLD HUNGER AND THE EVOLUTION OF FOOD SYSTEMS   **83**

The Malthusian Dilemma   84
The Evolution of Food Systems   88
The Domestic Mode of Food Production   95
Technological Advances in Food Production   99
State-Level Food Systems   101
Famine in the Modern World   103
Measuring Hunger   105
Needless Hunger in Bangladesh   110

5

COMMERCIAL FACTORY FOOD SYSTEMS 113

Factory Food Production   114
Factory Potatoes Versus Swidden Sweet Potatoes   120
Social Costs of the Food Production System   123
Energy Costs of the Distribution System   125
Potato Chips and Manioc Cakes   131
Fishing, Global Trade, and "Ghost Acres"   134
The Limits of Food Production   137

6

THE POPULATION PROBLEM 141

Population Pressure, Carrying Capacity, and
    Optimum Population   144
Population Control Among Foragers   146
Population Equilibrium in Aboriginal Australia   149
The Neolithic Population Explosion   151
Population Control Among Tribal Village Farmers   153
The Tsembaga Equilibrium Model   156
The Havasupai Indians   159
Island Population Problems   160
The State Intervenes   162
Policy Implications   163

7

POVERTY AND CONFLICT IN THE GLOBAL CULTURE 165

Violence and Insecurity in America   167
Social Order in Egalitarian Societies   170
Social Order in Large-Scale Cultures   175
Cross-Cultural Perspectives on War   177
"Roots" of the Security Crisis: Overpopulation or Inequality?   182
The Financialization Process and the Debt Crisis   184
Export Sugar, Starvation, and Infant Mortality in Brazil   187
State Terrorism and Investment Risk in Guatemala   190
Opulence and Deindustrialization in America   194

8

THE FUTURE   199

The Dilemma of Scale   200
The Global Free Market Future   202
Agenda 21 and the UNCED Approach   206
Scaling Down: The Small Nations Alternative   208
A Blueprint for Survival   209
Bioregionalism, Sustainable Commerce, and
    Economic Communities   212

Bibliography   215
Index   235

Anthropological Perspectives on Contemporary Human Problems

A knowledge of anthropology enables us to look with greater freedom at the problems confronting our civilization.

FRANZ BOAS,
Anthropology and Modern Life

CULTURAL EVOLUTION, THROUGH PROCESSES that many would label *progress*, has brought humanity to major turning points many times: the adoption of upright posture, the first use of tools, the development of language, culture as an adaptive strategy, food sharing, village life, food production, social stratification, urbanization, state organization, and now the emergence of an industrially based global commercial economy. All of these changes have been decisive ones—crucial developments with critical implications for the future. However, at this point the outlook is suddenly different, because the commercial economy, together with the great inequities of wealth and power that it has fostered, has dramatically intensified all the potential problems created by earlier developments. It is difficult to imagine a continuation of present trends without the global system either breaking down or transforming in any of several ways. In that sense, the world's cultures are at a crisis point. Drastic cultural changes will occur—the questions are what these changes will be, how they will be directed, and whose interests they will serve.

In many respects this book is Volume 2 of my earlier work, *Victims of Progress*, which deals with the destruction of small-scale, independent tribal cultures by the expanding global culture. It is now clear that many of our most serious contemporary problems are inherent in the basic cultural patterns of our global-scale commercial civilization and indeed in civilization

1

itself. Tribal cultures were designed along fundamentally different lines and therefore managed to avoid most of the problems that threaten contemporary civilization. The contrasts between these major types of culture, small- and global-scale, are so great that the two cannot coexist unless the international order is intentionally redesigned to permit significant cultural diversity. What we are now witnessing is perhaps the final irony of cultural evolution—the latecomer, global-scale culture, has suddenly arisen as a clearly dominant and brilliant short-run success. We have conquered the earlier tribal cultures, which were proven long-run successes, and we seem about to become victims of our own evolutionary progress. To avoid such an outcome, we must view our contemporary problems in as wide a context as possible. We must reexamine small-scale cultures and compare their solutions to basic human problems with our own solutions. This is perhaps anthropology's most critical role. People must now take deliberate control over the cultural systems that sustain their households and communities. This approach suggests that many solutions to contemporary problems may be found by developing local communities supported by regional markets and ecosystems rather than by making the continuous accumulation of financial capital the dominant cultural process.

NATURE AND SCOPE OF THE PROBLEMS

What we face is a *global* crisis. The entire species is in jeopardy; more is at stake now than the existence of individual tribes or nations. A further complication is that we face not one but *multiple* crises in many areas; and, as they multiply, we may suddenly be confronted with an overwhelming "crisis of crises" (Platt 1969). The pace of cultural change is now so rapid that new, unforeseen problems, each of crisis proportions, appear even before the earlier problems have been adequately identified. In effect, crises are now bigger (that is, they bring greater potential for disaster), there are more of them, and they are arising more rapidly than ever before.

We are undergoing an accelerating rate of cultural change that strains our ability to adapt and threatens to leave us in the vulnerable condition that Alvin Toffler (1971) aptly labeled "future shock." This pace of cultural change is apparent when the ages of the major archaeological periods are compared. The Paleolithic period lasted perhaps 3 million years. During that time, early humans and their immediate hominid ancestors remained hunter-gatherers, foraging in the small, thinly scattered bands that produced small-scale cultures and modern humans through a process that could be called *sapienization*. This adaptive process produced *culture*, the learned and shared symbolic ways of life and thought that *Homo sapiens* used to improve their survival. When culture was produced, the sapienization process continued to optimize human well-being by minimizing the cost of cultural activity while maximizing long-term sustainability. The human problem now is that sapienization has been superseded by two other cultural processes, politicization and commercialization, which have dramatically raised the cost of cultural activity and threatened sustainability.

The transition through the Mesolithic period into food production and to the brink of political centralization by the end of the Neolithic period required perhaps 8,000 years. Nearly 5,000 years more were required to reach the beginnings, barely 200 years ago, of the commercially driven, industrially based, global-scale culture. As Toffler (1971:14) and others point out, much of the material culture that now dominates our daily lives appeared in the twentieth century, much of it within the space of a single lifetime. Many of the most significant technological innovations, including antibiotics, TV, computers, satellite communications, nuclear energy, mass-produced organic compounds, and jet propulsion, appeared during the last half of the twentieth century. The present generation is experiencing the most profound changes humanity has ever seen. Whereas earlier "crises" such as the Neolithic transition were certainly "revolutionary" in their long-run impact, they would have been virtually imperceptible to the individuals involved because they occurred over millenia, and their outcomes in particular communities would not have been obvious for hundreds or even thousands of years. Cultural institutions were able to adjust gradually, but today we are often totally unprepared to deal with the unexpected impact of such rapid change.

The most critical qualitative difference in the organization of contemporary cultural change is that change is now primarily commercially driven. New technologies, information, and other cultural "products" that affect the daily lives of billions of people are produced by corporate business enterprises controlled by a relative handful of people. This *commercialization* process has produced a global-scale culture that is staggeringly different from anything preceding it. Its impact on the biosphere, the process of cultural evolution, and humanity itself is impossible to predict with precision.

Not only has the pace of change increased, but its scope has dramatically widened. The early evolution of human beings was not a global crisis. Humans have occupied all of both hemispheres for only perhaps 15,000 to 30,000 years, barely .005 percent of humanity's existence. The Neolithic "crisis" produced by the global climate changes, rising sea levels, and changes in plant and animal communities that accompanied the end of the last Ice Age changed the way many human communities organized their daily lives. These cultural changes, especially the shift to village life and farming, ultimately made it possible for the social inequality and political centralization of large-scale cultures to arise under very specific conditions in certain parts of the world. This *politicization* process created governments that took control over households and autonomous tribal communities. These local changes had ominous long-range implications. The most rapid and dramatic global level changes began when commercialization suddenly became a dominant cultural process at the beginning of the industrial era at the end of the eighteenth century. As recently as 200 years ago, perhaps 50 million people continued to live in politically autonomous small-scale cultures. These independent tribal communities still controlled vast areas of the globe and were only marginally affected by either governments or commercial business enterprises. Now, however, *commercialization* has become a global process that has destroyed or transformed virtually all previous cultural adaptations and has given humanity the power not only to bring about its own extinction as a species but also to speed the extinction of many other species and to alter basic biological and geological processes as well. This can be clearly seen in the pattern of "local" crises now occurring simultaneously throughout the world.

If the commercially driven global culture were to disappear overnight, it would leave an impoverished planet; in contrast, the extinction of humans during the Paleolithic era would have been of no more global significance than the passing of the woolly mammoth. The human impact of the present crisis is also far greater in scope than that of any previous crisis because far more people are now alive than at any time in the past. The 8 million people that may have populated the world by the end of the Paleolithic represent less than .001 percent of the 5.6 billion people living in 1994.

Crisis Levels

We are presently confronted with crises on the global, national, community, and household levels. Globally, the biosphere's capacity to absorb human insults is being seriously strained, and such critical world resources as clean water, fossil fuels, and biological diversity are rapidly shrinking. Individual national governments must meet these crises while at the same time confronting a multitude of domestic threats in the form of political instabilities and social and economic distress. Many countries are now hard pressed in their efforts merely to continue satisfying minimal human needs for food, shelter, health, and education and seem totally incapable of meeting rising demands for increased levels of material consumption. Individuals may temporarily ignore certain global and even national-level crises; but at the community and household levels, where daily needs must be met, we are now being confronted with health, family, and value crises of unprecedented frequency, scope, and complexity. Whatever level we consider, our cultural means of individual and collective survival seem to be falling behind in their ability to cope with crisis.

CRISIS INTENSITY

> Whether we have 10 years or more like 20 to 30, unless we systematically find
> new large-scale solutions, we are in the gravest danger of destroying our soci-
> ety, our world, and ourselves in any of a number of different ways well before
> the end of this century.
>
> (PLATT 1969)

In 1969 John Platt published an article in *Science* in which he estimated the
intensity or potential severity of various world problems in order to set priorities for scientific research and intervention. He organized these problems
into eight categories, ranging in severity from the threat of total annihilation
of humanity due to nuclear war to overstudied noncrisis problems such as
space exploration. He predicted that within twenty to fifty years the nuclear
war threat would either be solved or we would all be dead. Fortunately, the
Cold War ended in a peaceful standoff that could hardly have been predicted in 1969. We can now focus on the second-order crises of famine, ecological imbalance, development failures, local wars, and the rich-poor gap that
still carry the potential for great destruction and change. Platt correctly predicted that we would be forced to confront these crises within five to twenty
years. The third-order crises of poverty, pollution, and environmental degradation that would also bring "widespread, almost unbearable tension" within five to twenty years have also arrived on schedule. This crisis ranking
clearly puts in perspective seventh-ranked issues such as melting of the polar
ice caps and rising sea levels due to global warming. This potential crisis
would not arrive until the middle of the twenty-first century and is therefore
overshadowed by the immediacy and intensity of the social and political
crises related to economic development.

CRISIS AWARENESS AND RESPONSE

> There is a question in the air, more sensed than seen, like the invisible
> approach of a distant storm. . . . "Is there hope for man?" [The] question
> asks . . . whether we do not foresee in the human prospect a deterioration
> of things, even an impending catastrophe of fearful dimensions.
>
> (HEILBRONER 1974:13)

The emergence of the global market economy has intensified many preex-
isting problems and has touched off a variety of new crises. Qualitatively
unique social problems, international political problems, and now an environmental crisis have all suddenly materialized in rapid succession since the
Industrial Revolution began in the eighteenth century and have now widened

to include the entire globe. Cultures perceive and respond to crisis in many different ways, but in view of the pace and scope of the present "multiple crisis," our capacity to adjust is clearly in doubt. As industrial civilization has progressed into its crisis, many individuals and institutions have sounded the alarm, and the initial negative feedback mechanisms have been activated, but corrective response has been painfully inadequate.

Certainly the earliest and most bitter resisters of the global commercial culture have been the tribal peoples who have become forced participants, but they have not been alone or unsupported in their resistance. During the height of colonial expansion in the late nineteenth and early twentieth centuries, a very active group of British anti-imperialists (Porter 1968) condemned the entire colonial adventure that was then feeding the expanding global economy and called for reduced industrial output. These scattered protests, however, were easily swept aside.

The enormous social upheavals produced by the introduction of the factory system during the early phases of the Industrial Revolution in England were widely perceived as a crisis. These changes in the ownership and technology of production were designed to increase profits, but they proved profoundly disruptive of the social order and spawned an almost instant outpouring of social criticism, dire predictions, and outright resistance. On the eve of the Industrial Revolution, the Luddites, unemployed English textile workers who lost their jobs to industrial mechanization, attempted to halt the entire process by attacking the new machines directly, and by the mid-nineteenth century, Karl Marx and others predicted the collapse of at least one form of industrial civilization because of its "inherent contradictions." Many of these more obvious human costs of economic inequality were partially met with belated laws setting minimum wages, providing social welfare, prescribing work conditions, allowing workers to organize, and attempting to regulate corporate economic power. The belatedness of such efforts is apparent in the fact that in the United States there were no laws prohibiting child labor in mines and factories until after 1900.

At the level of international political organization (thanks to the new industrial tools of war and the new demands for resources) the growing potential for destructive military conflict met with equally slow response even though many individuals perceived the threats. Immediately after World War I, in which nearly 13 million soldiers were killed, there were tentative efforts to regulate international conflict, but it was not until 30 million people died during World War II that more effective international regulatory organizations were established.

Industrial society's impact on the environment has been a more subtle crisis, and its full potential for catastrophe has only recently become widely recognized. The general feeling that a rapidly evolving technology could overcome any environmental limitations seems to have blinded most scientists, economists, and government planners to the need to acknowledge the world's finite supply of resources until those limits became undeniably obvious. In the United States a group of scientists representing the American Association for the Advancement of Science petitioned Congress as early as 1873 for resource conservation measures. But the first forest reserve was not even established until 1891, nearly twenty years later (Gustafson et al. 1939:7); and it was not until Earth Day in 1970, almost a century later, that Americans generally began to acknowledge that industrial progress might not be fully compatible with nature.

So far there has been a general pattern in the responses to crises by modern nations. Once the factors that will lead to a crisis are set in motion, considerable time passes before anyone perceives the potential problem. There are further delays before the problem is widely perceived, and still further delays before corrective action is taken. For example, DDT, "discovered" in 1934, was being used as an insecticide by 1943, was killing birds by the late 1950s and fish by the early 1960s, and contaminating milk in 1963. Yet it was not even partially banned until 1972. In this case, nearly thirty years' lag time was required before a biologically disastrous technology was regulated, even though its harmful aspects had been apparent to many scientists for some two decades. Unfortunately, DDT is still being used in many countries, and the potential for damage remains. For a cultural type that seems to value changes so highly and has indeed achieved a very high rate of change, such a correspondingly slow capacity for adjustment to obviously detrimental changes seems incredibly maladaptive.

This poor response to crisis lends support to those who hold out gloomy prospects for human survival. Aside from religious movements that periodically have predicted the end of all things, only in recent decades have a significant percentage of the members of any culture had reason to seriously question the fate of humanity. This increasing doubt about the future is itself an important cultural fact that serves to highlight the gravity of the present crisis.

From a different perspective, a very powerful segment of the global culture looks enthusiastically toward the future because the end of the Cold War and the expanding information technology do open tremendous opportunities for capital growth. Trend forecasters John Naisbitt and Patricia Aburdene (1992), looking ahead to the millennium, exuberantly predict that almost everything will be better for everyone. In their view, thanks to new technology and the global market, there will be no limits to economic prosperity and no energy crisis. Instead there will be a renaissance in the arts, an exciting global life-style for all, and individuals will be liberated to develop their full potentials. Naisbitt (1994) even predicts that, paradoxically, a booming global economy will give small nations, small companies, and even individuals greater power. Historian Paul Kennedy finds this rosy view "breathtakingly naive in the light of this planet's demographic, environmental, and regional problems" (Kennedy 1993:53). He presents a contrasting view, arguing that large multinational corporations are actually more power-ful than individual nations because in a borderless world they will be able to shift their vast financial capital to wherever their profits are highest regard-less of the jobs lost or environments damaged in local communities. Furthermore, corporate ownership is highly dispersed and impersonal, lim-iting social responsibility and accountability, while free-market principles have no necessary connection with social justice and fairness.

ANTHROPOLOGY'S CONTRIBUTION

I hope to demonstrate that a clear understanding of the principles of anthro-pology illuminates the social processes of our times and may show us, if we are ready to listen to its teachings, what to do and what to avoid.

(BOAS 1928:11)

We have defined the general nature of the world crisis and suggested some of the possible dangers and difficulties inherent in the slow response that is occurring. Now we must argue that anthropology has something important to say to these issues.

The problems facing us are unmistakable but complex, and acceptable solutions are still neither obvious nor easily implemented. In recent years there has been an enormous outpouring of crisis-related literature, special conferences, and commissions. Specialists in many disciplines have attacked isolated problems. Unfortunately, however, overall results have been limited. Such apparent ineffectiveness despite intense activity is partly due to redun-dancy and extreme specialization in research efforts and to the complexity and interrelatedness of underlying causes. But it is perhaps mainly due to a lack of genuine overview on the part of the problem-solvers. It is time to divert at least some of our research energies away from the minutiae of diverse problems and to focus on their broader context. What has been miss-ing is perspective—a combination of detachment; a predilection for viewing the total picture in the widest spatial-temporal frame; and a clear recognition of the interrelatedness of social, cultural, biological, and psychological fac-tors. As an academic discipline, anthropology is uniquely qualified to offer just such an overview. An anthropological overview might not provide all the answers we seek, or even many easily acceptable solutions, but it can show us how we got where we are and suggest how we might get out.

In a sense, anthropology has been remarkably "preadapted" to serve as a sort of early-warning, equilibrium feedback function for cultures such as our own that are obviously slipping out of balance. From its first establishment as a professional discipline, anthropology has been defined by its holistic, cross-cultural, and evolutionary approaches. These methodological special-ties provide the very perspectives that now are most needed. Each of these viewpoints offers special advantages in the present crisis and deserves to be discussed individually.

The Holistic Approach of Anthropology

Anthropology calls itself the *study of humanity* and is clearly the broadest in scope and most generalizing of the disciplines. With a little organizational shuffle, virtually all other social sciences, the humanities, and portions of the physical sciences could easily be accommodated as subdisciplines of anthropology. Anthropologists ordinarily receive general training in—or are concerned with—the biological, cultural, social, linguistic, and psychological aspects of humans, but they may specialize in any of these subfields. Those researchers emphasizing the sociocultural areas must deal constantly with the interaction of economic, social, and ideological systems and must place these systems in relation to the natural environment. Only this kind of overview can hope to place the present problems in their full context.

The holistic approach leads naturally to the broad kinds of questions that we must ask if contemporary problems are to be adequately understood. For example, only an anthropologist might be expected to examine the psychobiological limits of our ability to adapt to a rapidly changing culture or to explore systematically the interrelationships between symbolic religious systems and a culture's adaptation to nature. This freedom to jump readily between subsystems and to follow research leads even across disciplinary barriers is a marvelously adaptive quality in a time when solutions must be found rapidly. In anthropology, the research problem is what determines one's subdisciplinary orientation. Specialist expertise and methodology are problem-solving tools, not ends in themselves. In many other disciplines the opposite situation seems to be too often true.

If it is true, as ecologist Barry Commoner (1971) persuasively argues, that overspecialization is one of the primary reasons for our lack of response to crisis, then any discipline that is willing to lower its disciplinary boundaries should offer special advantages. Interdisciplinary environmental science programs, in which the problem defines the specialties, are a hopeful move in the right direction. Anthropologists should fit comfortably into such programs.

The Cross-Cultural Approach

No approach to our present problems can hope to be successful if it restricts itself to a single culture or even to a single cultural type. We cannot be certain that the problems we see are unique to industrial civilization or to specific subtypes of industrial civilization. But more importantly, other cultures might well have successfully avoided certain problems that we now find insurmountable. Like biological diversity, cultural diversity is critical for the survival of the species. It is anthropology's job to compare cultures in order to understand how they work and to identify the most important differences.

Cross-cultural research also has certain other advantages. It requires a degree of objectivity and detachment that is often difficult to achieve when one deals with one's own culture. Relationships may stand out far more clearly in an exotic culture merely because they occur in an unfamiliar setting, and an outside observer may be more willing to draw conclusions that might conflict with comfortable patterns of thought. The fieldwork experience itself also encourages researchers to view their own culture through outsiders' eyes. There are, of course, limits to the insights that the cross-cultural perspective can provide. Even those anthropological interpretations that seem most objective are guided by the larger cultural and historical context from which anthropologists operate, as shown by our changing image of tribal culture.

The Evolutionary Approach

Biological and cultural evolution afford a remarkable time perspective on our present condition. Without such a viewpoint, we would lack any clear picture of our own origins, and it would be difficult to understand how we have changed or what it really means to be human. In its broadest sense, evolution implies change; and evolutionary change is what brought human beings as a species from the tribe, to the state, and finally to a global culture.

THE SIGNIFICANCE OF CULTURAL SCALE

The problem-solving advantages of anthropology's eclectic combination of holistic, cross-cultural, and evolutionary approaches emerge most clearly when they are used to sort cultures into three broad categories: small, large, and global. Small-scale tribal cultures constitute anthropology's traditional specialty. They represent humanity's way of life before the emergence of politically centralized, large-scale, urban civilizations and kingdoms some 5,000 years ago. Furthermore, small-scale cultures are humanity's only cultural system with an archaeologically demonstrated record of sustained adaptive success. They have existed since the dawn of humanity some 50,000 years ago, and they successfully satisfied basic human needs without the aid of cities or states and without high levels of energy consumption or elaborate technology. Politically autonomous small-scale cultures still occupied much of the world alongside ancient regional civilizations, until approximately 1800, when globally organized commercial cultures began to dominate the world. Perhaps anthropology's most striking and relevant generalization about small-scale cultures is that they are totally different from both our own global-scale culture and the large-scale ancient civilizations that preceded us.

We can certainly learn a great deal about the nature of contemporary human problems by carefully comparing our own situation with related aspects of small-scale cultures. Such a comparison will be one of this book's primary objectives. The secret of tribal success is almost certainly related to the absolute small scale of their populations and the relative simplicity of their technology, but the real key lies in the structure of the culture itself. In fact, small-scale cultures represent an almost total contrast in adaptive strategy and basic cultural design to our own unproven cultural experiment.

The Uniqueness of Small-Scale Cultures

Authentically primitive and maximally civilized traits are, I believe, as antithetical as it is possible for cultural attributes to become within the limits of an established human condition.

(DIAMOND 1968:110–11)

The concept of small-scale culture is a very useful problem-solving device, but it can be easily misunderstood and must be used cautiously. Because small-scale cultures were the first cultures appearing simultaneously with physically modern humans, human language, religion, and art, they can legitimately be considered "primitive" in the sense of "earliest," "original," or "basic." That is the sense in which anthropologist Stanley Diamond used the term in the above quote to stress the uniqueness of the cultural type in contrast to historically more recent cultures that are organized according to dramatically different cultural principles. Anthropologists have been reluctant to refer to any contemporary peoples as "primitive" because historically that label was misused by European colonialists to denigrate the original occupants of the territories they invaded as "backward" and "inferior." Such labels were used to justify the most outrageous human rights abuses against autonomous tribal peoples. However, calling attention to the historical priority of small-scale cultures can be a powerful means of demonstrating their human survival value and their genuine humanity.

The term *tribal* is used here to refer to politically and economically independent small-scale cultures, emphasizing their lack of centralized political authority, governments, and markets, and their correspondingly high levels of social equality. *Tribal* must also be used cautiously because for some it may have the negative connotations of the term *primitive*, but it highlights the community-level control of vital cultural and natural resources that may be a key organizational feature underlying the success of small-scale cultures. Contemporary descendants of conquered tribal societies often identify themselves as "indigenous peoples" to call attention to their attachment to the land and their cultural heritage.

Several remarkable contrasts are immediately apparent when the socioeconomic organizations of small-scale cultures are compared with large- and global-scale cultures. Autonomous tribal societies are quite small in scale, with densities that seldom exceed more than one person per square kilometer and maximum total populations of 500 to 1,000 people divided into self-sufficient, kinship-based bands or villages of twenty-five to a few hundred people. In comparison, preindustrial states and ancient empires were relatively large-scale societies containing hundreds of thousands and even millions of people, whose well-being depended on decisions made by ruling elites in often remote capital cities. Today the daily lives and future prospects of virtually all of the world's 5.6 billion people are shaped by the demands of a single global economic system based on perpetual capital accumulation, risk-taking, and great inequality. This contrast in scale of society undoubtedly contributes to the obvious differences in distribution of wealth, power, and opportunity between small-, large-, and global-scale cultures. Within small-scale cultures social status is normally a matter of gender, age, and personal qualities, and there is generally free access for all individuals and households to the natural resources, food, shelter, and basic services needed to reproduce themselves and their culture. The ancient empires were characterized by great individual differences in material wealth and political power based on rank and social class, but because they relied so heavily on human energy, the elites had a vested interest in meeting the minimal needs of all households. In the global-scale culture, safe drinking water and basic nutrition are not available to millions, and even in the United States many people are too impoverished to successfully raise a family. These conditions would be considered inhuman and incomprehensible by anyone from a small-scale culture and would have also seemed odd to the rulers of ancient civilizations. On the basis of these striking cultural differences, it might be assumed that many of our contemporary personal and social problems related to inequality, such as poverty, powerlessness, and alienation, are not characteristic of tribal cultures but may be intrinsic aspects of the global culture.

The extreme contrasts between tribal and global forms of production and distribution also have obvious implications for the differential impact of these two cultural systems on the environment. Most significant is the fact that tribal economies are locally self-sufficient, subsistence-based systems characterized by reciprocal exchanges and few cultural incentives for growth. The global market economy thrives on high levels of local specialization and interdependence in which local communities generally do not consume the products they produce and market exchanges occur with individual profit as the primary motive. The goods and services that sustain life have become commodities that are not freely available. In tribal systems production stops when everyone has goods and services sufficient for their needs. At the same time, because all production is locally controlled, people can respond immediately to detrimental impacts on their resources. The globally organized system requires continuous expansion of production and consumption and

shifts to new, totally different resources and territories in response to depletion or reduced profits.

Many anthropologists writing on cultural evolution (Morgan 1877;
White 1959; Redfield 1953; Service 1962) have emphasized the contrasts
between tribal cultures and civilization outlined here. They also have
stressed the *qualitative* transformation that has occurred with the development of civilization. It seems clear that, at least in their general configura-
tions, small- and global-scale cultures lie at opposite and incompatible poles.
Tribal cultures are so different that they need maximum autonomy if they are
to operate within the commercial economy and still retain their distinctive
cultural features. Successful competition in the global market economy may
require the surrender of important degrees of local self-reliance in order to
allow the profit system to operate freely. These changes open the door to
inequality of wealth and social stratification, as well as a chain reaction of further changes that can lead to the complete transformation of the original
tribal culture.

OUR TRIBAL SUPERIORS

French social critic Jean Jacques Rousseau (1712–1778) was one of the earliest modern observers to comment on the success of tribal cultures. In the
eighteenth century, at the very beginning of the Industrial Revolution, he
observed that the period of human history dominated by tribal cultures

> . . . must have been the happiest and most durable of epochs. The more we
> reflect on it, the more we shall find that this state was the least subject to revo-
> lutions, and altogether the very best man could experience . . . all subsequent
> advances have been apparently so many steps towards the perfection of the
> individual, but in reality towards the decrepitude of the species.
>
> (ROUSSEAU IN FAIRCHILD 1928:33)

Rousseau was responding to the excesses of the European aristocracy
and the impending social upheavals and revolutions of his time by imagining
a more egalitarian, less materialistic culture. Even though he had no firsthand experience with tribals, he nevertheless identified some valid points of
cultural contrast. Unfortunately, Rousseau's fanciful assessment of the pre-
state human condition presented a distorted "noble savage" image that
obscured the reality of tribal culture.

Drawing on the wealth of modern ethnographic material, a few widely
known anthropologists have unabashedly followed some aspects of
Rousseau's assessment of tribal cultures. Leslie A. White, for example, called

nonagricultural hunting societies "the most satisfying kind of social environment that man has ever lived in" and further elaborated:

> . . . [T]heir social systems . . . were unquestionably more congenial to the
> human primate's nature, and more compatible with his psychic needs and
> aspirations than any other of the cultures subsequent to the Agricultural
> Revolution, including our own society today.
>
> (WHITE 1959:277–278)

Numerous other writers have also praised tribal cultures for successfully satisfying basic human needs. The evidence for this apparent success of
tribal culture seems undeniable, especially when one considers the many
thousands of years they have endured, their generally slow and conservative
patterns of change, and the reluctance of surviving tribal peoples to abandon
their life-styles.

THE DANGEROUS SPIRIT OF ROUSSEAU

Anthropologists who acknowledge any particular admiration or respect for
small-scale cultures are likely to be accused of "Rousseauean romanticism."
In general, romanticism seems to rank alongside ethnocentrism as the weakness to be most avoided by scientific anthropologists, and apologies are in
order whenever tribal cultures are described in a favorable light. Edward
Sapir (1964:96–97), for example, tells us that a sensitive ethnologist who has
had firsthand field experience with a "primitive" society simply cannot help
but admire the "well-rounded life" that the average member of that society
leads. Even Ruth Benedict felt compelled to point out in her famous book
Patterns of Culture that she is not using "primitive" case materials with any
intention of "poeticizing the simpler peoples" and explicitly rejects as
"romantic Utopianism" the possibility that "primitives" have qualities that
we might profitably consider as alternatives to our own "maladies":

> But it is not in a return to ideals preserved for us by primitive peoples that our
> society will heal itself of its maladies. The romantic Utopianism that reaches
> out toward the simpler primitive, attractive as it sometimes may be, is as often,
> in ethnological study, a hindrance as a help.
>
> (BENEDICT 1959:31–32)

Even more recent writers who actually have pointed out some specific
advantages of small-scale culture are still apologizing. When Carleton S.
Coon (1971:10) praises hunting peoples for having lived harmoniously with
their environments, he hastens to add that he is not trying to follow Jean
Jacques Rousseau's tradition by drawing a "glowing picture of the noble savage"; instead, he is interested in basic questions such as our own survival. In

a similar manner, when physical anthropologist V. Neel suggested a number of important principles, derived from research among tribal Brazilian and Venezuelan Indians, that modern society might follow to improve the genetic quality of its population, he was careful to include the disclaimer: "These suggestions do not stem from any romanticism concerning the noble savage" (1970:820).

ROMANTICISM: WHY NOT?

The earliest accounts of South American Indians to reach Europeans often contained obvious romantic distortions. The first explorers quickly and correctly recognized the relative social equality of many Amazonian societies, the ease of subsistence, and the de-emphasis on wealth accumulation and property rights. They were especially impressed by the unselfconscious nudity and physical vitality of the people. However, the accuracy of these observations was easily ignored because they were embellished with outrageous claims that the Indians were "noble savages" living in an earthly paradise. For example, Pietro Martire d'Anghiera reported in 1500 that the Indians "naturally follow goodness" (Hemming 1978:15). Another early observer claimed that "in every house they all live together in harmony, with no dissension between them . . ." (Hemming 1978:15). One need not be an anthropologist to know that such perfection is simply fantasy, and that no people live together in total harmony. People who live together, whether in tribes or states, do quarrel and occasionally even kill each other. However, anthropologists who emphasize what might be considered "positive" elements of tribal cultures are not necessarily fantasizing about "noble savages" because there are real contrasts between cultures of different scales.

In a television interview (Charbonnier 1969:21–37) the famous French anthropologist Claude Levi-Strauss was asked to discuss the fundamental contrasts between tribal societies and civilization. He emphasized that tribal societies are like clocks in that they strive for stability, unanimity, and equality, whereas modern society could be compared to a steam engine because its hierarchical structure assumes a built-in disharmony and antagonism. The interviewer was amazed at this apparent violation of a familiar anthropological taboo, and incredulously said to the great man: "I seem to detect an echo of Rousseau's ideas in what you are saying."

Levi-Strauss responded simply: "Why not?"

This seems a fair question. Exploring the contrasts between small- and global-scale cultures is certainly a legitimate and even critical activity for anthropologists, whether or not it is considered romanticism. Actually, the term *romanticism* is somewhat misleading when applied to tribal culture. By definition, *romanticism* can mean a preoccupation with the picturesque and imaginary or unreal. Certainly, tribal cultures are often picturesque and even exotic when compared with our own, but they are real. Their exotic qualities have never been presented as a reason for not studying tribal cultures; and, in fact, studying such qualities has often been thought to be anthropology's principal reason for being. Of course, an overidentification with tribals resulting in erroneous data on exotic cultures could justifiably be labeled romanticism, but Rousseau himself has not often been accused of that. Instead, at least one authority observed that Rousseau "simply admires them [tribals] for qualities which they admittedly possess" (Fairchild 1928:133).

Overall, the validity of the primary organizational features we are attributing to tribals has never been seriously challenged by careful field research. What the "romanticist anthropologists" actually seem to be doing is critically investigating tribal cultures, finding them in many respects superior to our own, and expressing regrets that we have destroyed these cultures instead of learning from them. This kind of romanticism is clear in Coon's confession of admiration for tribal hunters: "I respect and admire them . . . they led full and satisfactory lives, and it will do us no harm to reflect on the advantages of some of their age-old ways of dealing with nature and with each other" (Coon 1971:xix).

But why should there be such concern over this apparently innocuous kind of romanticism? It is evident that the possibility that overinvolvement with tribals may bias ethnographic data is not the principal fear; rather, the real danger is that romanticism might threaten the position of applied anthropologists in the culture modification–economic development field. Even more serious is the danger that an anthropology overidentified with tribals will disappear with them.

In spite of their general reluctance to engage in "romanticism," it is fortunate that at least some anthropologists have explored these areas and reached some startling conclusions. For example, the work of Neel, the physical anthropologist referred to earlier, sheds interesting light on the problem of how well individual potential may be achieved in tribal society. After an eight-year interdisciplinary, team-conducted field study of some of the most autonomous Amazonian Indians, Neel concluded:

> It is a sobering thought that the relatively egalitarian structures of most primitive societies, plus the absence of large individual differences in material wealth, seem to ensure that, within the culturally imposed boundaries, each individual in primitive society leads a life (and enjoys reproductive success) more in accord with his innate capabilities than in our present democracy.
>
> (NEEL 1970:821)

At this point, it would be appropriate to examine some of the qualities that other "romanticist" anthropologists consider characteristic of tribal societies.

THE ORIGINAL AFFLUENT SOCIETY

In 1965, seventy-five anthropologists assembled in Chicago for the Wenner-Gren sponsored symposium on "Man the Hunter." They examined the latest research findings on the world's last remaining tribal foragers, or hunting and gathering peoples, who were expected to soon become extinct. The result (Lee and DeVore 1968) was a new description of life in these technologically simplest of ethnographically known societies, showing their existence to be stable, satisfying, and ecologically sound, and not at all "solitary, poore, nasty, brutish, and short," as Thomas Hobbes had proclaimed in *Leviathan* (Part 1, Chapter 13) in 1651. It was learned, for example, that even remnant hunters such as the Bushmen, who survived in extreme and marginal environments, were not eking out a precarious existence, constantly on the edge of famine, as was previously thought; instead, they devoted only a few hours a week to subsistence and suffered relatively little seasonal scarcity. When in control of their resources, tribal hunters seemed to enjoy good health and long lives, while they had the good sense to maintain their wants at levels that could be fully and continuously satisfied without jeopardizing their environment. Marshall Sahlins even suggested that this was, after all, the original "affluent society." Other researchers have since challenged some aspects of this interpretation, as will be discussed in later chapters, but the general conclusion that foragers enjoy many advantages over farmers seems to be valid.

Most significantly, when the discussions ended, the participants concluded that the hunting way of life, which had dominated perhaps 99 percent of humanity's cultural life span, had been "the most successful and persistent adaptation man has ever achieved" (Sahlins 1968). In comparison, newly arrived industrial civilization was in a precarious situation with the "exceedingly complex and unstable ecological conditions" it had created. At least one distinguished participant even felt that we should study why hunters were so successful, and that our civilization might actually learn something from them. These were remarkable conclusions from members of a profession that was vigorously disassociating itself from its long-exclusive identification with tribal peoples and that rigorously avoided any hint of romanticism whenever it studied these so-called preliterate or preindustrial peoples. Hard ethnographic facts were forcing anthropologists to reconsider Rousseau's position.

THE DESPICABLE SAVAGE

Although many anthropologists view small-scale cultures in a positive light, a minority have portrayed these cultures in emphatically negative, anti-noble savage terms. Hallpike (1979), for example, argues that tribal peoples are really mental children. He suggests that in developmental terms they resemble twelve-year-olds, incapable of formal logical thought. If this view were to be substantiated, it would certainly have important implications for our understanding of tribal culture; however, Hallpike has found little support among other anthropologists (see, for example, Shweder 1982). It seems that many of the apparent differences in the mental processes of tribal peoples are actually related to their preliterate cultures and tell us little about their real capabilities (Goody 1976).

A more extreme stance, which might be called "the Despicable Savage" view, is taken by psychological anthropologist Arthur Hippler, who states emphatically that tribal cultures are inferior to modern civilization. Hippler argues that many anthropologists simply prefer tribal cultures to civilization and choose to ignore the negative aspects of the former. He, of course, labels this Rousseauean romanticism, but goes beyond that to suggest that anyone who sees positive aspects of tribal cultures is actually suffering from a "pathological rebelliousness" against civilization (Hippler 1979a:510) or even an "irrational anthropological hatred of Euro-American . . . society" (Hippler 1979b:494). Hippler emphatically prefers civilization to the extent that he totally deprecates tribal cultures. In his view, ". . . there is no question that Euro-American culture is vastly superior . . . to any primitive society extant" (Hippler 1981:395). Tribal cultures are "transparently, clearly, patently less adequately organized expressions of human beliefs and actions . . ." (Hippler 1979a:510). Hippler feels that romantic anthropologists have systematically ignored the "often outrageous intrusions on individual capacities or crushing of human personality so common in primitive communities" (Hippler 1979ac:294). Hippler uses a long list of deprecatory terms to describe tribal cultures. For example, he finds them rigid and unattractive, incredibly repressive, inadequate, and personally destructive. He believes that they stunt child development and create terrified, emotionally and cognitively deficient adults.

Hippler's underlying theory (1977) is that tribal cultures do an inferior job of childrearing and thus create inferior adults. He presents his own analysis of traditional Eskimo and Australian aboriginal cultures as support for his argument. Anthropologists well acquainted with the peoples that Hippler describes have strongly rejected his interpretations (see, for example, Hamilton 1979, Berndt 1981, Reser 1981). Hippler's critics point out serious deficiencies in his fieldwork and his failure to adequately take into account the social problems created by detribalization and cultural change. No one would deny that cases of poor childrearing practices can be found in tribal societies, or in any society, but it is clear that Hippler's description is an inaccurate caricature. Furthermore, he draws a dubious connection between childrearing practices and adult culture.

Although I emphatically reject both the Despicable Savage approach and the Noble Savage fantasy, in the following chapters I will deliberately emphasize certain aspects of small-scale culture where they can highlight the problems that our own global-scale culture has created and point to solutions.

UNDERSTANDING GLOBAL-SCALE CULTURE

This theory of the global system, then, revolves around the perceived necessity for global capitalism to continually increase production and international trade, to guarantee the political conditions for this to occur uninterruptedly all over the world, and to create in people the need to want to consume all the products that are available, on a permanent basis.

(SKLAIR 1991:54)

The scale of the global culture and the significance of its unique cultural organization must be carefully considered before contemporary problems can be productively understood. The entire world is now driven by a dominant cultural process that can be called *commercialization*. This process makes perpetual capital accumulation the primary objective, producing great inequalities of wealth and power. In this system the economy is in a sense disembodied from the rest of the culture, symbolically becoming an autonomous entity whose growth is considered essential for human well-being. This reverses the cultural order in small-scale cultures, where the *sapienization* process dominates, and goods and services are produced to meet basic human needs while promoting long-term survival.

The world's 5.6 billion people are now combined into a single commercial network ultimately dependent on computerized financial transactions taking place in a few organized markets in the richest countries. Money; government and corporate bonds; shares in corporations; and contracts for the future sale of food, fiber, and other commodities change hands daily, and vast quantities of raw materials and manufactured goods move physically between markets as investors seek commercial profit. The purpose of all this activity is to keep the global "economy" growing as measured by the steady accumulation of financial capital and increases in GNP. The curious thing about all of this is that it is directed and controlled by relatively few people, the outcome need have no bearing on basic human needs, and the actual risks and rewards are very unevenly distributed. In reality, costs are systematically shifted downward to those least able to pay, while rewards flow disproportionately to the wealthiest and most influential corporations and individuals. Just as the earlier politicization process made the needs of governments more important than the interests of households and villages, the commercializa-

TABLE I.I

Transnational Agents in the Global System,
According to Leslie Sklair (1991)

SPHERES	PRIMARY AGENTS	TRANSNATIONAL PRACTICES (TNP)
Economic	Transnational Corporations (TNCs)	Commodities Production and Marketing Services Job Creation and Destruction
Political	Transnational Capitalist Class (TCC)	Political Support for Marketing and International Trade
Cultural-Ideological	Transnational Mass Media and Advertising	Consumerism

tion process now makes the needs of giant corporations and anonymous investors more important than either governments or communities. Indeed, it could be argued that governments now exist primarily to make the world safe for business enterprise. Individuals with no direct investments in the global economy are important only as consumers of commercial goods and services or as minimum-wage laborers.

Sociologist Leslie Sklair (1991) observes that it is no longer very helpful to focus on the activities of nation states because the primary agents in the world system are all *transnational:* 1) transnational corporations (TNCs); 2) the transnational capitalist class (TCC); and 3) the transnational mass media and advertising. Sklair identifies each of these agents with three analytical spheres of the global system: the economic, political, and cultural-ideological spheres, respectively. Each agent is functionally distinguished by its particular set of transnational practices (see Table 1.1). The economic sphere is dominated by the TNCs and the special institutions that support them such as the World Bank, the International Monetary Fund, the United Nations, and the various stock markets and commodity exchanges. The transnational capitalist class is composed of the corporate managers, politicians, and other elites that make the system work. Their nationality is irrelevant. Making the global system work requires maintaining dominant influence, or cultural hegemony, over billions of people. The concept of cultural hegemony was originally developed by the Italian Marxist Antonio Gramsci (1891–1937), who argued that the ruling elites define the dominant symbols and thoughts of a people. When the elites do this successfully people internalize the ideals of the culture and behave appropriately. In the global system the cultural hegemony function is most effectively carried out by the transnational mass media and advertising, which maintain consumerism as the dominant cultural value. Increasing consumption of commercial goods and services is presented as the cultural norm, the ultimate goal of life.

The absolute power of transnational corporations and the capitalist class is indicated by the astounding fact that the combined 1992 revenues and sales of just 750 of the world's largest companies represented 42 percent of the global GNP in 1991 (*Fortune* July 26, August 23, 1993, *World Development Report 1993*). A single giant company, General Motors, owned 312 other companies and employed 750,000 people in 36 countries. Its total 1993 sales were $132 billion, exceeding the gross domestic products of all but 18 of the wealthiest countries in the world.

While corporate stock ownership is widely dispersed, a surprisingly small group of interconnected people control these powerful TNCs as board members and chief executives. For example, the 1993–94 boards of directors of a sample of eleven of the largest *Fortune* 500 American companies yielded 137 people, who also helped control 155 other *Fortune* 500 companies. Collectively these companies controlled roughly half of the total assets or sales of the *Fortune* 500 in thirteen major sectors of the economy. These same individuals were also associated with many other companies, foundations, universities, commissions, government agencies, and civic organizations where they could promote their corporate interests. The top ten individuals were linked to thirty-seven companies whose combined assets represented 10 percent of the global GNP in 1991. In an exhaustive study of the American institutional elite in the early 1980s, Thomas R. Dye (1983) found that just 5,778 individuals "ran" the giant corporations, the federal government, the news media, and the primary cultural institutions in the country as a whole.

No analysis of contemporary problems and solutions would be complete without considering the cultural organization of wealth and power in the world, because our problems are cultural problems. They are not problems of human nature and they will not be solved by a narrow technological approach. Solving contemporary human problems will require a careful assessment of the way the world is culturally organized in relation to the full range of cultural possibilities. The following chapters will explore particular types of problems and solutions while devoting special attention to the role of 1) corporate business enterprises; 2) governments; and 3) local communities. An anthropological perspective suggests that solving human problems will require designing cultural systems that establish a more humane balance between the three cultural processes that shape our lives: 1) sapienization; 2) politicization; and 3) commercialization. This will permit small-, large-, and global-scale cultures to coexist in ways that will maximize human well-being.

Adaption, Culture Scale, and the Environmental Crisis

Nor are those cultures that we might consider higher in general evolutionary standing necessarily more perfectly adapted to their environments than lower. Many great civilizations have fallen in the last 2,000 years, even in the midst of material plenty, while the Eskimos tenaciously maintained themselves in an incomparably more difficult habitat. The race is not to the swift, nor the battle to the strong.

MARSHALL SAHLINS AND ELMAN R. SERVICE (EDS.),
Evolution and Culture, 1960

MANY GENERAL CONCLUSIONS OF direct relevance to our own environmental situation emerge from the cultural ecological data that anthropologists have compiled over the years. Perhaps the most important conclusion to be drawn is that small-scale cultures were more sustainably adapted to their environments than the present global culture. Although tribal peoples certainly did modify their environments and manage their resources, there was clearly a pattern in which long-term, relatively stable balances were established between human populations and natural communities. These balances were often disturbed for a variety of reasons, but even so, the contrast with the scale of disruption and the degree of instability characteristic of the present world where commercial interests are dominant is truly striking. If the scale of culture had never increased to large and global scales, it is likely that an environmental crisis of the magnitude we are now experiencing would never have arisen, except perhaps through some natural catastrophe. Small-scale cultures, whether foragers, herders, or farmers, are clearly more stable and better suited to long-run survival than any more "highly evolved" cultures. These facts challenge many once widely accepted interpretations of cultural evolution and adaptation, and raise important questions about our own ability to survive.

CULTURAL EVOLUTION AND ADAPTATION

Among the popular misconceptions regarding cultural evolution and adaptation is the view that evolutionary progress has meant greater security, greater freedom from environmental limitations, and greater efficiency of energy use. In many minds, higher levels of evolutionary development have also been equated with greater adaptive success. However, as anthropologist Roy Rappaport (1977) has pointed out, the increasingly hierarchical structures of more complex cultural systems tend to become maladaptive. Higher-level decision makers are likely to be inadequately aware of the local impacts of their actions. If theories of cultural evolution are to be harmonized with what is known about the obvious ability of small-scale cultures to avoid environmental catastrophes, then these theories and their interpretations must be examined more closely.

The principal pioneer of modern cultural evolutionary theory, Leslie A. White (1949), defined evolutionary progress largely in relation to per capita rates of energy utilization. A culture that consumed more energy per capita was simply more highly evolved. Other writers (Sahlins and Service 1960) elaborated on this theory, arguing that two kinds of cultural evolution were involved, *general* and *specific*. General evolution is concerned with levels of evolutionary progress, the more "advanced" forms that interested White. These higher forms are defined by energy consumption, organizational complexity, and the ability to exploit a wider range of environments and to replace cultures at "lower" levels. This kind of evolutionary development corresponds closely to the concept of cultural scale, such that small, large, and global scales could represent increasing levels of organizational complexity. Paradoxically, general evolutionary cultural progress of this sort may actually reduce security, diversity, and energy efficiency, and dramatically increase the likelihood of environmental crisis. Furthermore, it may increase the workload and reduce the life chances of individuals. Specific evolution means *adaptation to local environments*, and it is clear that cultures at lower levels of evolutionary progress, as defined above, may be far more efficient in energy input-output ratios, and far more stable and successfully adapted to their environments than more "advanced" cultures.

Many of these points were previously disregarded by anthropologists who were particularly impressed with the undeniable material accomplishments of industrial civilization, and who did not pay close attention to the differences between general and specific evolution. For example, in an attempt to describe general levels of cultural evolution using adaptation, Yehudi Cohen (1974:45–68) stated that at each stage of progress (he used hunting-gathering, cultivation, industrialism), people became better adapted for survival, more secure, freer from the environment, and more energy-efficient. In Cohen's view, cultural evolution has been achieved because people have sought to gain mastery over nature, and it has been inhibited in certain areas through ignorance of basic technologies. Other research on such critical evolutionary advances as food production and state organization suggests that the role of invention and discovery was greatly overemphasized by earlier theorists. It is more likely that such changes were gradually forced on reluctant people as a result of unintended demographic imbalances. In this sense, "mastery over nature" was not something eagerly sought by inventive minds; rather, people have been compelled to accept certain burdens and assume new adaptive risks by the grim need to readjust to altered circumstances.

Progress can indeed open more habitat types to exploitation by a given cultural type, but such progress is not escaping the limits of nature, and it may prove highly maladaptive. Cohen devotes considerable attention to the "freedom from environmental limitations" argument and reaches some surprisingly shortsighted conclusions that directly conflict with more realistic assessments of the adaptive shortcomings of industrial culture. He argues, for example, that increasing mastery over nature leads to an increasingly secure food supply, and points to supermarkets and the ability to eat fresh fruit out of season as great triumphs over nature. Strawberries at Christmastime are, in this regard, "perhaps one of man's greatest achievements . . . ." However, if viewed from a wider perspective, we have supermarkets and Christmas strawberries because they produce profits in the global economy. And they carry hidden cultural and environmental costs that must be examined if sustainability is the issue.

Many earlier writers confidently measured the "higher" adaptive success of industrial culture by its apparent reproductive success and by its ability to displace and destroy "lower, less effective" cultures. What such assessments overlook is the time factor. As Sahlins points out in the quotation introducing this chapter, real adaptive success can only be measured by survival—over the long run. If we insist on considering short-term reproductive success, or proliferation of people, an indication of adaptive achievement, then perhaps a new "law" of cultural evolution can be formulated: *Culture evolves as the global biomass becomes increasingly converted to the human sector.*

Certainly, a clear trend in cultural evolution to date has been toward a remarkable increase in the human sector of the global biomass (humans and domestic plants and animals) and a corresponding reduction in the earth's natural biomass. This reduction in the nonhuman sector is necessary because of the simple ecological fact that a fixed amount of solar energy fuels the planet's primary producers (green plants); consequently, there are absolute limits to how many consumers can exist. Biochemist and science fiction writer Isaac Asimov (1971) placed the actual limit of consumers at about 2 million million tons of biomass. As human consumers increase, natural consumers must decrease. The ultimate pinnacle of evolutionary achievement, then, should be the point when every gram of living material on earth has been transferred to the human sector and every natural "competitor" has been eliminated. In 1971 Asimov estimated that at the present rate we could reach such a point by A.D. 2436.

NATURE AND SCOPE OF THE ENVIRONMENTAL CRISIS

In its most basic sense, the environmental crisis is a deterioration of environmental quality with a corresponding reduction in carrying capacity due to human intervention in natural processes. At the present, given the existing global social order, we are clearly running up against basic limits to the earth's ability to supply the resources that we consume and to absorb our industrial by-products. Later chapters will treat the specific environmental problems of food, energy, population, and resources in more detail; but first, it may be useful to consider the general implications of our intervention in the biosphere.

The environmental crisis is not new. It has developed as general cultural evolution, by increasing the scale of culture, has given us greater ability to influence nature, increased population and per capita consumption rates, and altered distribution patterns. Tribal hunters have contributed to the creation of grasslands; pastoral nomads have overgrazed their lands; peasant farmers have caused deforestation and erosion. From archaeological evidence it is clear that tribal cultures and early civilizations at times faced their own local environmental crises as imbalances occurred, and were forced to abandon certain regions or drastically alter their cultures. However, the scope and quality of the changes that the global commercialization process has set in motion over the past 200 years make these earlier problems seem quite insignificant. We now have the potential for disrupting basic life support processes and may already be inadvertently reducing our own prospects for survival. The following examples should make this clear.

BIODIVERSITY AND THE DEATH OF THE TROPICAL RAIN FORESTS

In a 1973 article published in *Scientific American*, Paul W. Richards, then one of the world's leading authorities on tropical rain forests, very calmly and objectively, with only a slight trace of bitterness, made the following announcement:

> It appears likely that all of the world's tropical rain forests, with the exception of a few small, conserved relics, will be destroyed in the next 20 to 30 years. This destruction will inevitably have important consequences for life on the

earth, although the nature and magnitude of these consequences cannot be forseen with precision.

(RICHARDS 1973:66)

Tropical deforestation is an excellent example of the difficulties of understanding and responding to contemporary environmental issues. This is because tropical forests are biologically the richest ecosystems in the world. Destroying them can dramatically reduce biological diversity. Rain forest plants are a major source of pharmaceuticals, vegetable waxes and oils, and cosmetics, as well as hardwoods and edible fruits and nuts. Because of their high biomass, tropical rain forests are important reservoirs of global carbon, and deforestation contributes carbon dioxide to the atmosphere, enhancing the greenhouse effect and global warming. The loss of tropical rain forests also causes regional flooding, decreased rainfall, and degradation of soils, placing many communities at risk. These broad patterns are clear enough, but not everyone agrees on the urgency of these issues, the causes of deforestation, or what action should be taken, because different groups have very different interests in the forest and different degrees of influence with national policy makers.

It is risky for even well-informed scientists to attempt to draw public attention to potential environmental risks such as deforestation because the relationship between complex ecosystems and the global culture are extremely complex and unpredictable. Not all experts agree on details. Critics can easily brush aside warnings by citing different opinions or show-ing that specific predictions did not come true. Some writers have used the disagreement over specific rates of deforestation to argue that "environmen-talists" have exaggerated the problem in order to impose "sweeping curbs" on forest-related development. For example, in a prominent article in *U.S. News and World Report* on "The Doomsday Myths," Stephen Budiansky (1993) disputed widely cited claims that 40 million acres of tropical forest and 50,000 species were being lost annually because different authorities had challenged the research methodologies behind the estimates. Budiansky's cri-tique might lead the casual reader to conclude that tropical deforestation and biodiversity loss were "myths" and the earth was maybe not really in danger after all. In fact, a multitude of studies using a variety of methods leave little doubt about the global trend.

Michael Williams (1990) estimates that some 8 million square kilome-ters of forest have been cleared worldwide since 1650, while acknowledging a wide margin for uncertainty. During many centuries prior to that time only some 1.5 million had been cleared. He attributes modern deforestation to "the emergence of an integrated world economy from the late fifteenth cen-tury onward . . ." and estimates that the "developing world" has lost half of its forests since 1900. Actual rates and the specific causes of deforestation vary from country to country and from year to year, but from a long-term

perspective there can be little doubt that globally all forests, including tropical forests, are undergoing a drastic decline due to human intervention. This
is true even though reforestation means there may now actually be more
trees (small trees) in many regions than there were in the recent past. Simply
replanting trees does not automatically restore complex forest ecosystems.

Richards's prediction of the virtual disappearance of tropical forests by
1996–2006 was a general warning, not a precise projection, because strictly
speaking there can be no accurate projection of deforestation rates. Even
well-informed observers have disagreed widely on degrees of forest cover
and rates of deforestation because foresters have not always defined and measured forests in the same way and different rates may not be comparable. For
example, in 1992 the UN definition of forest included natural forest, planta-
tion, and woodlands with 20 percent cover of trees over seven meters tall. A
careful, country by country assessment of the status of the tropical forests in
1989 using remote sensing techniques such as air photos and satellite
imagery showed that approximately 60 percent of the world's original tropical forest cover was gone (Myers 1992). The average rate of destruction was
1.8 percent per year, suggesting only another 55 years or so until
Richardson's prediction would be fulfilled if the trend continued.

Scattered populations of tribal farmers, hunters, and fishermen have
lived successfully in Amazonia, the world's largest tropical rain forest, for
several thousands of years by relying on shifting cultivation (Lathrap 1970,
Meggers 1971, Moran 1993). Their adaptation rested on their ability to
maintain fallow periods of sufficient length to allow regrowth of the primary forest before replanting. Large-scale commercially driven permanent
farming or ranching systems have destroyed the forest, leaving rain-leached,
impoverished, rock-hard soils and degraded scrub thorn forests in their
place. Myers (1992) suggests that worldwide, *shifted* farmers account for
more tropical deforestation than all the commercial logging, ranching, and
other causes combined. Shifted farmers, as distinguished from indigenous
shifting cultivators, are the dispossessed rural poor who do not have the
political or economic power to control enough high quality farmland to support themselves, and are forced to open undeveloped forest lands. Thus,
while establishing forest reserves and curbing commercial logging will be
important ways to safeguard the forests, the cultural conditions that make it
impossible for rural people to make a living will need to be changed.

ECOCIDE SOVIET STYLE

When historians finally conduct an autopsy on the Soviet Union and Soviet
Communism, they may reach the verdict of death by ecocide. . . . No other
great industrial civilization so systematically and so long poisoned its land, air,

water and people. None so loudly proclaiming its efforts to improve public
health and protect nature so degraded both.

(FESHBACH & FRIENDLY, JR. 1992:1)

Both free-market capitalism and centrally planned socialist systems have created environmental problems. It is concentrated economic power and poorly regulated economic growth, regardless of political ideology, that can
damage the environment and undermine human health. The former Soviet
Union is a frightening, science fiction-like, worst-case scenario of the consequences of decades of misguided economic development. The 1986 explosion of the nuclear reactor at Chernobyl near the Ukrainian city of Kiev
spread radioactive fallout over the western Soviet Union, east and central
Europe, and as far north as Sweden. It was an environmental disaster that
could not be hidden from the world, nor from Soviet citizens. The smolder-
ing shell of the reactor inspired public demonstrations against decades of
failed environmental policies. Anti-pollution rallies turned into mass political rallies in which the individual Soviet republics pressed for full autonomy.
Even before the Soviet Union dissolved itself in 1991, Gorbachev's policy of
glasnost, or openness, began to lift the veil of secrecy that had covered the
almost unbelievable extent of military and industrial pollution in the country. While the full details can never be known because even secret official
records were often systematically falsified, it is now becoming clear that all
of the now independent states of the former Soviet Union face severe environmental crises.

Murray Feshbach, specialist on Soviet health, and environmental
reporter Alfred Friendly, Jr., (1992) chronicle some of the damage in their
book *Ecocide in the USSR*. In order to increase agricultural output, the Soviets
poured vast quantities of toxic chemicals on their farmland, while soil fertility actually declined, and foodstuffs were often badly contaminated. Deadly
pesticides were misapplied to crops by poorly trained workers in order to
meet government quotas. Dioxin, which is one of the most toxic synthetic
substances known and has been linked to cancer and birth defects, was used
on crops freely for more than twenty years. DDT continued to be used
secretly long after it was publicly banned. Poorly planned irrigation projects
led to erosion, flooding, and salinization. Raw chemical wastes from government owned industrial factories left three-fourths of the country's surface
waters dangerously polluted, while industrial smokestacks dumped pollutants
into the air at levels five times or more over minimum air quality standards
for 70 million people in 103 cities. The air in one city showed benzopyrene
levels nearly 600 times acceptable levels. The soil in many industrial centers
became so badly contaminated with zinc, lead, molybdenum, and chromium
that it was unsafe for children to play in their sandboxes.

One of the most visible Soviet ecological disasters was the drying up of
the Aral Sea, formerly the fourth largest lake in the world. Soviet agricultur-

al planners recklessly diverted most of the water from the two major rivers that fed the Aral Sea in order to irrigate newly opened monocrop cotton and rice fields in the Central Asian desert. Between 1960 and 1990 the area of Aral was reduced by 44 percent and converted into two small, forty-seven-foot lower saline lakes that left the fishing port of Muynak 40 miles inland from the retreating shoreline. Windstorms carried toxic dust and salt from the dried lake bed over the adjacent land to mix with the toxic agricultural chemicals. The local climate was disrupted, agricultural soils waterlogged, wells contaminated, and the regional economy devastated. Soviet geographer Arkady Levintanus (1991) called the Aral region "amongst the world ecological disasters of the twentieth century" and proposed an ambitious twenty-year restoration plan, but this had to be tabled during the political turmoil resulting from the collapse of the Union.

Perhaps the clearest measure of Soviet ecocide can be seen in its impact on human health. Even though Soviet statistics have been notoriously unreliable, it is now apparent that an unprecedented public health crisis is underway. While for a time the Soviet Union made enormous strides in improving living standards in the country, the government's emphasis on industrial development at all costs eventually poisoned the environment while simultaneously undermining the health care system. The result can be plainly seen in shocking rates of birth defects, malnutrition, cancer, respiratory problems, and infectious disease, leading to reduced life expectancy and elevated infant mortality rates. Nationwide in 1991 life expectancy for Russian men was just sixty-four years, and infant mortality in 1989 was 25 per 1000. In Uzbekistan under the impact of the Aral Sea disaster, infant mortality rates soared to 50 per 1000. Comparable rates in the United States were seventy-two years for American men and 9.8 per 1000 for infants. Officially only thirty-two people were killed by radiation from the Chernobyl disaster. The real figures will never be known, but the World Health Organization estimates that 4.9 million people were exposed to dangerous levels of radiation (Edwards 1994). The disaster led to the resettlement of 200,000 people, and 50,000 square miles were contaminated. Thousands continue to live in unsafe areas, and cases of radiation-related illnesses seem to be increasing.

The Soviet system proved exceptionally damaging because highly centralized controls and high levels of secrecy made it difficult for local communities to respond to environmental problems as they arose. The powerful central government imposed their own development program and then did not effectively enforce environmental safeguards. The diffuse nature of most pollution problems made it difficult if not impossible to link specific deaths to specific pollution problems, even when broad trends became clear as general statistics were published. The Soviet experience gives us a glimpse of what could happen anywhere, and demonstrates the obvious—uncontrolled industrial expansion is dangerous to health. The challenge for epidemiologists is how to establish safe levels for industrial pollutants, and for community development planners, how to reduce the need for dangerous contaminants.

ENVIRONMENTAL CRISIS AND CULTURAL CHANGE

Environmental crisis has been a factor in cultural change throughout human history and prehistory. However, the present environmental crisis is very different from any in the past, not only because of its scope but because it is being accelerated by cultural features that never existed in the past. In the broadest sense, an environmental crisis is any imbalance between a human population and its resource base that diminishes the ability of the natural environment to meet human demands. Such a crisis could be initiated naturally by a climatic fluctuation that caused a reduction in available resources. More likely, it could also be related to changes in cultural scale and the associated increases in population, as well as intensifications of technology and consumption rates.

The environmental changes associated with tribal cultures tend to unfold gradually and are much more likely to lead to new, relatively stable balances. In contrast, large- and global-scale cultures are associated with rapid, often catastrophic environmental crises that arise more and more frequently. Prehistoric Europe provides an example of gradual change introduced by tribal cultures.

Neolithic shifting cultivators began to move into Europe some 8,500 years ago from Southwest Asia, and gradually reached the limits of their subsistence adaptation within 4,000 years or so. Forest fallow periods were steadily shortened as population density increased and domestic grazing animals further inhibited the regeneration of forest. Eventually, permanent open country and heath lands appeared over large areas of what had been a vast expanse of virtually unbroken forest that hunting peoples had kept intact for tens of thousands of years (Clark 1952). As a result of this gradually unfolding environmental crisis, shifting cultivation eventually became all but impossible; the natural fertility of the forest soils was being exhausted; and a period of population movement, warfare, and dramatic culture change ensued. When conditions finally stabilized, it was at a higher population density on a different ecological basis and level of cultural complexity. Tribes were replaced by politically centralized chiefdoms and settlements became more permanent. The shift to large-scale culture is reflected archaeologically in megalithic burials and the use of metal.

Numerous examples of environmental crises and cultural changes in large-scale cultures can be cited. Detailed archaeological data document the collapse of a stratified chiefdom-level culture on Marajo Island at the mouth of the Amazon River just prior to the arrival of Europeans, apparently due to the vulnerability of intensive subsistence farming in the tropical rain forest. There is clear evidence that intensive agricultural practices in ancient Mesopotamia, where irrigation favored the gradual accumulation of salts in the soil, were also contributing factors in the fall of Sumerian civilization after 2000 B.C. (Jacobsen and Adams 1958), although climatic fluctuation may also have played a part. In the New World, it was long assumed that the collapse of lowland classic Mayan civilization in the ninth century A.D. may have been caused by increased demographic pressures on a limited resource base and that some kind of environmental crisis either occurred or was developing (Willey and Shimkin 1971, Culbert 1974). However, more recent archaeological research (Demarest 1993) and deciphered Mayan glyphs (Schele & Freidel 1990) suggest that chronic warfare between rival kings was a major factor in the collapse. It appears that the Mayan kings developed intensive agricultural systems that proved unsustainable during times of political conflict. Thus, large-scale cultures under the influence of the politicization process ultimately made it more difficult for people to maintain a viable balance with their environment.

Such collapses and transformations must have occurred many times, and would seem to be the inevitable fate of any expansive, disequilibrium culture. However, on the basis of present anthropological data, it can be stated that, in the absence of politicization, small-scale foragers and village farming peoples are unlikely to accelerate their population and consumption rates to the point that environmental deterioration and a reduced carrying capacity result. The social stratification, inequality, urbanization, and political centralization associated with large-scale cultures set in motion a system that is almost inherently unstable. Today the industrial production, expanding markets, and high rates of consumption characteristic of the global system make environmental disequilibrium almost a certainty. The key difference now, however, is that the disequilibrium culture is a global culture, and we are seeing a global environmental crisis unfolding. The predictable future transformation of the global-scale culture will, like the passing of the tropical rain forests, be a "major event in earth history."

GLOBAL DISEQUILIBRIUM: BEYOND "THE LIMITS TO GROWTH"

We can thus say with some confidence that, under the assumption of no major change in the present system, population and industrial growth will certainly stop within the next century, at the latest.

(MEADOWS 1972:126)

The basic behavior mode of the world system is exponential growth of population and capital, followed by collapse. . . . [T]his behavior mode occurs if we assume no change in the present system or if we assume any number of technological changes in the system.

(MEADOWS 1972:142)

In 1798, on the eve of the Industrial Revolution, English economist Thomas R. Malthus (1766–1834) warned of population's potential for exponential growth and pointed out that, if unchecked, population would outstrip the ability of a country or the world to produce food. He revised and refined his basic argument several times in the face of a barrage of criticism that held that there was no such tendency, or that the potential of the earth was virtually limitless. Many critics, particularly economists and social planners, argued that population growth was essential for industrial growth, and that together these would assure continued happiness and prosperity for humanity. This growth concept has certainly been a central theme in the world view of the global-scale culture, and perpetual expansion, whether in population or consumption, is in fact one of the distinguishing features of capitalist economic systems. Malthus was not alone in his pessimism over growth. Other early economists, including Adam Smith (1723–1790) and David Ricardo (1772–1823), also felt that continual economic growth would not be possible forever because of ultimate limits and inevitable diminishing returns from a dwindling resource base. Any stabilization of the industrial economic system was thought to be so far in the future that no one need worry about planning for it. Only in recent years have significant numbers of scientists begun to doubt that continual growth can be sustained by a finite planet long into the foreseeable future.

In 1864, American scholar and pioneer conservationist George P. Marsh (1801–1882) published a massive indictment of the deterioration of the natural environments of Europe and America that had already occurred because of human intervention. He boldly warned that a "shattered" earth and the extinction of the species might result from further human "crimes" against nature.

Over the next 100 years after these early warnings, the hazards of constant growth in a finite world were largely ignored thanks to the dramatic achievements of science and technology in increasing production. Few people seemed to worry that a sudden switch to nonrenewable new energy sources (coal and oil) and the imperialist expansion into Africa and Asia might only increase the disequilibrium and temporarily delay a stabilization while greatly raising the cost of readjustment and heightening the potential dangers.

In 1954, as the great effort to achieve global economic development gained momentum, the combined problems of population growth, industrial expansion, and the limitations of the world to support such developments were posed as serious threats to the future survival of humanity in a provocative book by Harrison Brown titled *The Challenge of Man's Future*. Brown suggested that the most likely outcome would be the irreversible collapse of industrial civilization due to its own instabilities and the destruction of its resource base through inadequately regulated exploitation. The only other likely outcome that Brown could imagine that would permit the limited survival of industrial civilization would be careful planning and rigid restriction of individual freedom by authoritarian governments. In effect, new mechanisms of social integration would need to evolve. Similar pessimism and warnings were expressed in 1974 by economist Robert L. Heilbroner, who a short time earlier was an optimistic champion of worldwide industrialization.

One of the most ambitious and authoritative attempts to examine the implications of the present instability of the global-scale culture is *The Limits to Growth* (Meadows et al.), published in 1972. This study was the result of some two years of research by a seventeen-member international team of experts working with a complex computer model of the global system devised by Jay Forrester of the Massachusetts Institute of Technology. Starting from certain basic assumptions about the interrelatedness of population, agricultural production, resource depletion, industrial production, and pollution, the team set out to estimate how these factors might interact to set limits on the future expansion of industrial civilization (see Figure 2.1). The results of this research were surprising to many people and distressing to everyone. No matter how the variables were manipulated (that is, by technological solutions, assuming twice as many natural resources, solving the problem of pollution, and so on), the system collapses before A.D. 2100 because of basic environmental limits. Figure 2.2 illustrates how a collapse might occur if present trends continue. Stabilizing population extends the system somewhat, but collapse still occurs because resources are exhausted. According to these projections, the only feasible solution for maintaining global-scale culture as a viable adaptation is to stabilize both population and industrial production as quickly as possible.

The Limits to Growth prompted severe criticism from technological optimists who argued that the long-run limits are still far in the future and undefinable (see especially Cole 1973). Others stressed that limiting growth would be immoral because it would hurt the poor (Walter 1981), or that given human ingenuity and the operation of market incentives, resources should really be considered infinite (Simon 1981). The world model was criticized as imprecise, too complex for wide understanding, and oversimplified. These critics suggested that it might be dangerous to attempt to bring economic growth to a halt, and those desiring stability were accused of being elitists who only wished to maintain the status quo in their favor.

In 1992, twenty years after *The Limits to Growth*, the original authors issued a sober restudy called *Beyond the Limits: Confronting Global Collapse, Envisioning a Sustainable Future* (Meadows, Meadows, and Randers 1992). The new work responds to the critics by stressing that sustainability, not fixing a doomsday date, is the issue. Yet the authors conclude that resource consumption and pollution has already exceeded sustainable rates in many countries. Their updated computer projections continue to show that global declines in per capita economic production will eventually occur unless we choose to design a world order that maximizes "sustainability, sufficiency, equity, and efficiency." It means we must plan ahead and decide what kind of future we want.

Assuming that the relationships between trends shown in the world model are valid, many anthropologists are re-evaluating their own position on the desirability of economic growth and the meaning of development. In the past anthropologists actively promoted economic growth throughout the world without always considering the real distribution of costs and benefits, or the long-term prospect of continued growth. It is becoming more apparent that development that emphasizes sustainability with social equity is a more desirable goal.

ENVIRONMENTAL COMMISSIONS: GLOBAL 2000 AND OUR COMMON FUTURE

The most knowledgeable professional analysts in the executive branch of the U.S. Government have reported to the President that, if public policies around the world continue unchanged through the end of the century, a number of serious world problems will become worse, not better . . . the world in 2000 will be more crowded, more polluted, less stable ecologically, and more vulnerable to disruption. . . . Serious stresses involving population, resources, and environment are clearly visible ahead . . . the world's people will be poorer. . . .

(BARNEY, THE GLOBAL 2000 REPORT TO THE PRESIDENT OF THE UNITED STATES, 1977, VOL. I:XVI, I)

In 1977 American President Jimmy Carter commissioned a special study of global trends in population, resources, and environment up to the year 2000

FIGURE 2.I   THE GLOBAL SYSTEM

The entire world model is represented on the following pages by a flow diagram in formal System Dynamics notation. Levels, or physical quantities that can be measured directly, are indicated by rectangles; rates that influence those levels, by values; and auxiliary variables that influence the rate equations, by circles. Time delays are indicated by sections within rectangles. Real flows of people, goods, money, etc. are shown by solid arrows; and causal relationships, by broken arrows. Clouds represent sources or sinks that are not important to the model behavior. (Donella H. Meadows et al., *The Limits to Growth* (New York: Universe Books, 1972), 102–3.)

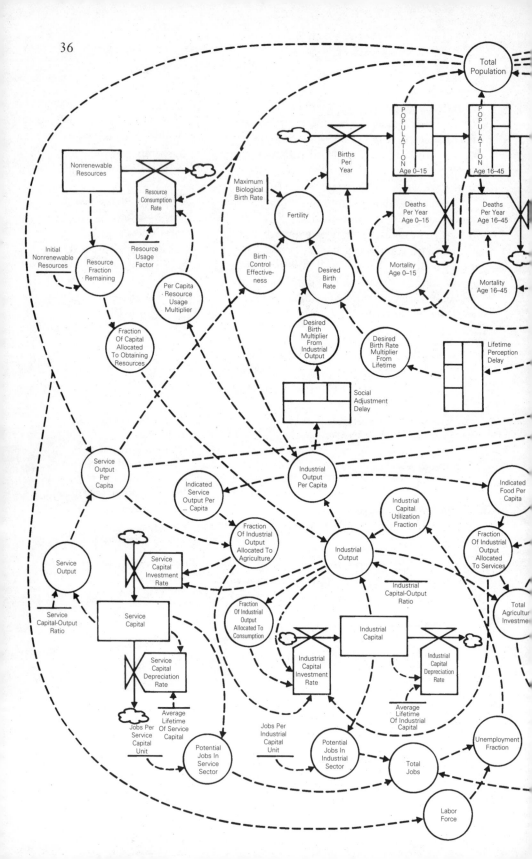

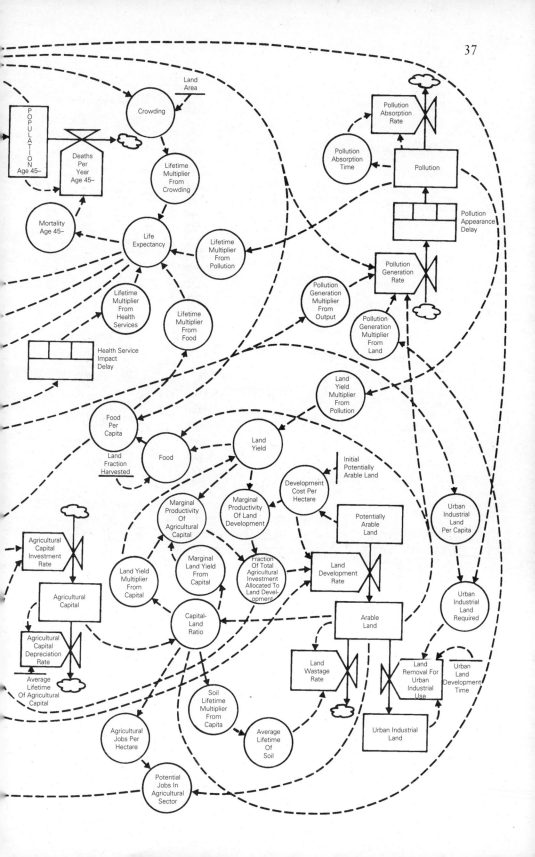

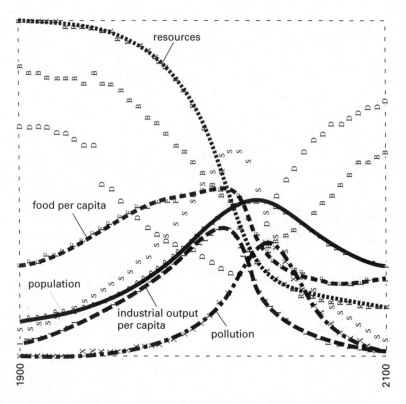

FIGURE 2.2   WORLD MODEL, STANDARD RUN

The "standard" world model run assumes no major change in the physical, economic, or social relationships that have historically governed the development of the world system. All variables plotted here follow historical values from 1900 to 1970. Food, industrial output, and population grow exponentially until the rapidly diminishing resource base forces a slowdown in industrial growth. Because of natural delays in the system, both population and pollution continue to increase for some time after the peak of industrialization. Population growth is finally halted by a rise in the death rate due to decreased food and medical services. B=crude birthrate (births per 1,000 persons per year). D=crude death rate (deaths per 1,000 persons per year). S=services per capita (dollar equivalent per person per year). (Donella H. Meadows et al., *The Limits to Growth* (New York: Universe Books, 1972), 124.)

to facilitate long-range planning by U. S. government agencies. *The Global 2000 Report to the President of the United States* was over two years in preparation and ultimately involved a budget of nearly $1 million, thirteen government agencies, and scores of advisors and researchers. In general this study was similar to *The Limits to Growth* in its attempt to project the future outcome of present trends at a global level. However, *Global 2000* was much more cautious than *The Limits to Growth* in that some of the subsections of the study, such as food production, did not always take into account losses caused by activities in other sections, such as industrial pollution. Furthermore, the *Global 2000* study looked only to the year 2000, whereas *The Limits to Growth* looked much further ahead. The *Global 2000* study was also quite conservative; it assumed continued technological progress, no major political upheavals, and a continuation of the existing world political system. In view of all of these conservative elements, it is significant that the conclusions of *Global 2000* still contained ominous warnings of serious problems in the near future, as indicated in the summary quote cited above. The Carter Commission did not predict a catastrophic collapse of the world system, but it correctly warned of population increases, serious water shortages, major deforestation, deterioration of agricultural lands, and increased desertification, together with more poverty, human suffering, and international tension. What it missed, of course, was the end of the Cold War.

The issues raised by these studies, and the increasingly visible evidence of worldwide environmental deterioration, had finally become so undeniable that by 1983 the United Nations General Assembly passed a resolution setting up a World Commission on Environment and Development (WCED). Fears over the state of the environment were officially recognized as a legitimate problem by the highest levels of the global culture. The UN Commission, which became known as the Brundtland Commission, after its Chairman, Norwegian Prime Minister Gro Harlem Brundtland, issued its landmark report in 1987. It acknowledged that environmental deterioration and human impoverishment were indeed a threat to the future of humanity. The Commission cautiously recommended that development should be sustainable. This was not a very remarkable conclusion given the overwhelming evidence already accumulated, but from a global perspective it was perhaps the highest level commission to reach such a conclusion and it understandably commanded international attention. The Brundtland Commission's principal contribution was to redefine development in reference to sustainability and basic human needs, rather than strictly in regard to increasing GNP. The Commission gave priority to the needs of the world's poor and defined sustainable development as "development that meets the needs of the present without compromising the ability of future generations to meet their own needs" (WCED 1987:43).

The UN responded surprisingly quickly following the Brundtland Commission's report. In 1989 the General Assembly called for a major world conference, the United Nations Conference on Environment and Development (UNCED), "to devise strategies to halt and reverse the effects of environmental degradation in the context of increased national and international efforts to promote sustainable and environmentally sound development in all countries." The British government responded quickly with a white paper environmental strategy of its own, *This Common Inheritance*, issued in 1990 (United Kingdom, Dept. of the Environment). UNCED met in Rio de Janeiro in June 1992 and adopted Agenda 21 as its formal action plan to deal with environmental issues into the twenty-first century. The conservative consensus that these commissions and conferences reached was that further economic growth would be needed to reduce environmental deterioration and poverty. World leaders were not yet ready to imagine that major changes in the structure of the global economy might be needed to achieve sustainability.

At this point it will be useful to examine some of the explanations that have been offered for our present environmental difficulties before moving to the perspectives that can be gained from small-scale cultures.

"ROOTS" OF THE ENVIRONMENTAL CRISIS

The basic causes of the environmental crisis are best understood as an imbalance between pressures on the environment and the environment's ability to meet them. Resources are being consumed at a rate greater than they are being produced by natural biological or geological processes, and wastes are being created that disrupt natural cycles. This imbalance may conveniently be considered a problem of per capita *overconsumption* in order to emphasize that more is involved than an absolute increase in population. *Overconsumption* may be defined as consumption in a given area that exceeds the rates at which natural resources are produced by natural processes to such an extent that the long-run stability of the culture involved is threatened. Every culture certainly has the potential for overconsumption, and this potential could be realized by a simple increase in population over the carrying capacity of a given region. However, this overconsumption seldom occurs in small-scale cultures because negative feedback systems are activated to reduce population or because cultural mechanisms to promote better distribution are used. Unusual increases in per capita consumption rates could also initiate overconsumption; but again such an outcome is normally prevented by negative feedback mechanisms. Unfortunately, the global commercial culture has short-circuited the normal cultural feedback mechanisms that prevent overconsumption in at least four critical ways:

1. Dependence on nonrenewable resources
2. Dependence on imports
3. Urbanization
4. Institutionalized inequality

Perhaps the most critical turning point in the development of the global culture was its shift away from renewable resources to overwhelming dependence on stored fossil fuels, which have become substitutes for both solar energy and natural products such as fibers. These resources have been "banked" in the earth over millions of years, and in fact represent stored solar energy; yet they are now being used to temporarily support a tremendous overgrowth of consumption far beyond what could ever be supported by local renewable resources. The danger in this case is that by the time these stored resources have become significantly depleted we may well have "overshot" our renewable resource base to such an extent that collapse will be assured. A culture relying largely on local renewable resources would feel an impending shortage much sooner and could make corrective adjustments, either by intensifying its productive technology or, more wisely, by reducing its population or consumption, or both.

A second critical way in which the global system has temporarily escaped an inevitable balancing with resource limitations has been through its enormous reliance on large-scale global trade. Intercultural trade or exchanges of resources are perhaps cultural universals, following the economic principle of "comparative advantage," according to which different regions exchange items that each produces most efficiently. Prior to the development of large- and global-scale cultures, trade was often limited to ritual items, or a narrow range of raw materials such as salt, obsidian, and ochre, that spread widely along decentralized reciprocal exchange networks. Often the primary purpose of trade was maintaining friendly relations and encouraging intermarriage between groups that might otherwise be hostile. Commercial trade involving highly concentrated economic power allows resources extracted from poor areas to be wastefully consumed in rich territories at otherwise unsustainable rates. Reliance on imported resources to support otherwise unsupportable growth and consumption is an obvious source of instability and carries the same danger of overshoot and collapse as does reliance on stored nonrenewable resources.

Urbanization creates a similar problem because urban populations must be supported by internal "imports" from rural areas. The urban consumers are far removed from their resources and are unlikely to become immediately aware of impending shortages or of any other environmental impact of their consumption patterns.

Institutionalized inequality is normally defined by differential consumption patterns and serves to promote overconsumption while diverting much of its adverse impact onto "lower" classes who must first pay the real costs. Prices in the global market thus do not always accurately reflect the true costs of commercial products. This inequality diverts and delays the mechanisms that would otherwise maintain consumption within environmental limits.

In addition to overconsumption, the global culture has greatly increased the probability that it will cause environmental crises by disrupting natural cycles and simplifying ecosystems on a vast scale. Natural cycles have been disrupted by the introduction of new synthetic materials, such as plastics and organochlorine pesticides, which have been used to support overconsumption by replacing degraded natural systems but which cannot be readily broken down by nature into their constituent parts for reuse. Waste, or pollution, is a cultural product that does not exist in nature because all natural materials are continuously recycled. Furthermore, commercially generated "natural" organic wastes such as sewage and feedlot wastes have been created and concentrated in ways that have blocked their effective recycling and degrade ecosystems. In this regard we have consistently violated what ecologist Barry Commoner (1971) has called the basic laws of ecology. Simplification of ecosystems is best exemplified by the industrial factory farm that attempts to remove all but one or two "desirable" species. This process greatly lowers the biological productivity and stability of an ecosystem and can only be maintained at enormous cost in imported energy and by increased use of pesticides and synthetic fertilizers, which in turn deplete nonrenewable resources and disrupt natural cycles.

Thus, our present environmental crisis is the direct result of overconsumption, disruption of natural cycles, and simplification of ecosystems. Since all cultures seem to have the potential for degrading their environments by such means, it remains to be explained why large-scale cultures— and the global-scale culture in particular—have been much greater culprits in this regard than small-scale cultures. Many writers point out a single basic cause, such as misuse of technology, overpopulation, or misplaced values, and emphasize it almost to the exclusion of other factors. Their arguments run as follows: If we can simply develop better technology, achieve zero population growth, or invent a new value system, our environmental problems will be over. The population and technology arguments will be examined later, but for now the values argument may profitably be examined.

IDEOLOGICAL ROOTS

Much of the discussion of the need for a value change stems from an article published by historian Lynn White, Jr., in 1967 (see also Anderson 1969). The author points out that religion promotes certain attitudes toward nature that are in turn reflected in ecological processes. Christianity is held responsible for our present crisis because in Genesis God gave man dominion over nature, thereby initiating our victorious battle with nature. On the other hand, it is argued that tribal animism, which makes man part of nature, prevents such a battle and avoids the crisis. This viewpoint has much to recommend it, and it does emphasize important differences between tribal religions and Christianity; however, it confuses *association* with *causation* and may divert attention from the more fundamental changes that are needed. Anthropologists, especially those with a cultural-materialist perspective, generally see religion in a support role, helping to maintain socioeconomic systems rather than directly causing them. From this perspective, religious ideologies reflect economic adaptations and are more likely to change with them rather than vice versa. White concludes: "Since the roots of our trouble are so largely religious, the remedy must also be essentially religious . . . ." This approach might be going at the problem backwards. More direct results might be achieved through a socioeconomic reorganization, and then religious ideology would swing in line. However, it also seems clear that real socioeconomic change may require the direct support of religious ideology in order to mobilize human action. The rulers of ancient civilizations certainly made effective use of religion as they carried out the politicization process.

HERDERS, SELF-INTEREST, AND TRAGIC COMMONS

In his influencial article "The Tragedy of the Unmanaged Commons: Population and the Disguises of Providence," biologist Garrett Hardin (1968) saw the environmental crisis as a failure to define maximum good. For Hardin, the crisis was the inevitable outgrowth of individuals seeking their own self-interest in combination with a failure of appeals to conscience and social responsibility. This implied a repudition of Adam Smith's belief that an "invisible hand" operated in the market economy such that self-seeking individuals ". . . without intending it, without knowing it, advance the interests of society . . ." (Smith [1759] 1976:304). Hardin called for mutually agreed on coercive restraints to maintain population and pollution within safe limits and suggested that these problems, strictly speaking, had no technical solutions. Like Lynn White, Jr., he felt that a change in values was required, but added the important additional qualification that political regulations must be strengthened.

It is clearly not possible to optimize both population and consumption, because limiting consumption will allow a larger population, and vice versa. Cultures must, in effect, define "maximum good" and then adjust population levels in conformity with the ability of specific environments to supply that "good" on a sustainable basis. Hardin correctly saw the solution of this problem, either implicitly or explicitly, as critical to the stability and survival of any cultural group. But initially, at least, he seemed not to recognize that the problem had already been solved by tribal cultures without direct physical coercion. Regarding maximum good, Hardin asked, "Has any cultural group solved this practical problem at the present time, even on an intuitive level? One simple fact proves that none has: there is no prosperous population in the world today that has, and has had for some time, a growth rate of zero" (Hardin 1968).

This, of course, overlooks the fact, discussed in Chapter 1, that small-scale cultures have maintained their stability by defining maximum good at easily satisfied levels, and in their own terms have achieved both "affluence" and environmental balance. At the same time, they have done so without the coercive restraints that Hardin felt would be needed to control the dangers of the pursuit of self-interest. Hardin (1991) later observed that "shame" rather than physical coercion could operate to inhibit destructive overuse of resources in small-scale, face-to-face communities of 150 people or less. The absence of commercial incentives for overproduction are perhaps even more critical. Under the right cultural conditions there need be no inherent conflict between individual self-interest and the interests of society as a whole. Based on his survey of small, domestically organized farming systems thoughout the world, cultural ecologist Robert McC. Netting (1993:322) observes, "Communities of smallholders have the demonstrated capacity for cooperative management of environmental resources without the untrammeled individual competition that brings on a 'tragedy of the commons.'"

The example Hardin used to illustrate destructive self-interest in the exploitation of a "commons" or public resource was misleading because it failed to consider anthropological data from small-scale cultures. Hardin assumed that a traditional herding society was kept in balance with its resources only because of warfare, poaching, and disease, which prevented individual herders from expanding their herds. Hardin supposed that when these controls are eliminated individual herdsmen would continue to add extra animals to their own herds even beyond the point at which environmental damage would result from overgrazing because they would receive full advantage for each additional animal, whereas the costs of overgrazing would be shared by all herders. In his view each herdsman was thus caught in a conflict between social responsibility and personal self-interest, and only coercive force would make it obviously in his best interest to refrain from expanding his herd.

Anthropological research has shown that small-scale subsistence herding societies operating outside of the market economy represent quite a different situation (see also McCay & Acheson 1987). There is seldom any conflict between individual self-interest and social responsibility. Where self-sufficient individual households or small household groups must depend on herd animals for their primary subsistence, maximum herd size is determined by the number of animals a given herder can safely handle, quality of pasture, and daily grazing requirements of the animals, in addition to sociopolitical considerations such as the size of local kin groups and the vulnerability of herds to raiders. A large herd of large animals in an area of poor pastures would quickly become impractical, because the herd would need to move so rapidly to get enough to eat that productivity would decline (Spooner 1973).

The successful adaptation of herding societies is clearly illustrated by the traditional herders of Southwest Asia and the Middle East. Nomadic pastoralism emerged in these regions as a means of exploiting the vast steppe areas that were created by climatic changes beginning some 10,000 years ago. Given the particular mix of poor rainfall, poor soil, and rugged topography, these regions are unsuitable for any form of permanent agriculture but can support herds of grazing animals such as sheep and goats. Using ground surveys together with satellite pictures researchers (Casimir, Winter, and Glatzer 1980) collected basic ecological data on herders during a two-year study conducted in Afghanistan before the civil strife that followed Soviet intervention in 1980. Their research showed convincingly that traditional herders do not necessarily overgraze their pastures under normal climatic conditions. The researchers measured the biological productivity of all major plant communities in the region and calculated the food requirements of the animals. They found that, during the study, the herders were using only 23–32 percent of the available sustained yield forage production of the natural pastures.

Other researchers have used dynamic mathematical models to explore the relationship between soil moisture, grass and shrub biomass, and grazing pressure in the semiarid savannas of South and East Africa (Walker et al. 1981). Their work suggests that traditional cattle herders maintained a very resilient balance between grassland and shrubs because their grazing system was "irregular and opportunistic" and the human population remained relatively low. Under these conditions the natural pastures tolerated even intense grazing because it was only periodic. Herd productivity was also relatively low, but perfectly adequate for domestic needs in a nonmarket subsistence economy. Animals that appear to be unproductive and of poor quality by commercial standards may actually be well suited to poor grazing and frequent drought (Coughenour et al. 1985, Western & Finch 1986). Traditional herders thus actually favored the growth of a wide variety of grass types, and these wild pastures became more productive. However, settled peasant farmers and commercial ranchers replaced many of the tribesmen after 1900, when the colonial period began, and introduced a much less variable grazing system that has proven less stable. The result is that now there is often serious overgrazing, leading to reduction in the water-absorbing capacity of the topsoil and a replacement of grass by less productive woody shrubs. Overall, there is often a striking reduction in the ability of the natural pastures to support grazing animals.

On marginal grazing lands in many parts of the world, overgrazing is often encouraged when outside energy sources are introduced, making it possible to concentrate animals by drilling wells and hauling feed, and when animals are raised for the market rather than for direct subsistence. Many such developments have been promoted by governments interested in increasing the productivity of pastoral nomads. These developments have often included settlement schemes. Unfortunately, the result has often been serious overgrazing as traditional negative feedback mechanisms have been subverted. Only then does self-interest come into conflict with social responsibility.

PLEISTOCENE EXTINCTIONS

Some observers have maintained, in spite of overwhelming evidence to the contrary, that tribal cultures have no special advantages in their relationships to the environment in comparison with the global-scale commercial culture. Friedman (1979:262), for example, in his zeal to purge anthropology of "romanticist" tendencies, asserted that "social systems have never been adaptive." Terry Rambo (1985) argued that forest clearing by the small-scale Semang shifting cultivators of Malaysia modified the local climate and introduced particulate matter and carbon dioxide into the atmosphere. He described the Semang as "primitive pollutors" that demonstrated ". . . the essential functional similarity of the environmental interactions of primitive and civilized societies" (1985:78). Geoscience researcher Paul S. Martin (1967, 1984) maintains that within the last 15,000 years tribal hunters overhunted and destroyed hundreds of species, especially large mammals. He concludes:

> The thought that prehistoric hunters . . . exterminated far more large animals than has modern man with modern weapons and advanced technology is certainly provocative and perhaps even deeply disturbing.

> (MARTIN 1967:115)

This view of early hunting cultures quickly found its way into introductory anthropology texts. For example, Marvin Harris stressed the "basic insecurity" of hunting and gathering cultures and called their potential for overhunting a "basic weakness" that could "easily result in the extinction of the natural biota." Echoing Martin, he specifically charged that the "unprecedented efficiency" of upper Paleolithic technology contributed to the ecological catastrophe of the extinction of Pleistocene megafauna (Harris 1975:186).

The "Pleistocene overkill" or "blitzkrieg" argument is certainly dramatic and, if it could be substantiated, would clearly temper our view of small-scale cultures and their relationships to the environment. The implications of this problem are certainly serious enough to merit careful examination. The undisputed facts are briefly as follows: Throughout the world during the late Pleistocene period, some 200 genera rather suddenly disappeared. These extinctions involved many large animals, such as the mastodon and mammoth, giant birds, giant kangaroos, and other "mega" forms. These animals were not replaced by related species. Although the chronology of these extinctions is not precise, early human populations were colonizing new portions of the globe and improving their hunting technologies during roughly the same time period.

When Martin first presented his argument, it was based largely on circumstantial evidence and the absence of equally plausible counter-evidence. More recent research has both challenged some of Martin's basic assumptions and in some cases made his argument stronger. The overkill hypothesis is strengthened by the apparent correspondence of New World extinctions with the arrival of humans (Martin 1984), yet numerous Pleistocene megafauna survived in Africa, where humans originated. In Australia, climate change now appears to be a stronger cause of megafauna extinctions than overhunting (Horton 1984).

In some cases extinctions actually preceded the arrival of humans with advanced hunting technologies, and they involved more than merely big game species (Webster 1981). There is now also more evidence that vegetation changes related to climate change were important factors contributing to the extinctions of the late Pleistocene. Furthermore, anthropological interpretations of small-scale hunting cultures suggest that overkill to the point of exterminating major prey species is theoretically very unlikely (Lee and DeVore 1968, Hayden 1981b, Webster 1981). In the first place, hunters rarely relied exclusively on a single prey species, and often the bulk of their diet was based on plant foods. Furthermore, hunting systems stressed predictability and energetic efficiency. Any subsistence system based on deliberately hunting key prey species to extinction would have been extremely unreliable, wasteful of time and energy, and disastrous in the long run. This is, of course, not to say that tribal hunters never wasted game animals, because even though there was often a strong ethic against wasteful overhunting, certainly in many cases full utilization of game killed was impossible or impractical. It is also now generally appreciated that tribal hunters maintained low population densities and low growth rates. The general pattern was to maintain long-term balances with their resource base.

Impressive evidence for such long-term balances is represented by the archaeological record left by middle and late Stone Age peoples in southern Africa, covering a time span from the recent past to over 130,000 years ago. B. P. Richard Klein (1979, 1981, 1984) made a careful study of the age and sex distribution of the game animals taken by Stone Age hunters, based on an analysis of the bones left in their camps. He discovered that the pattern of human predation on large, dangerous game animals such as buffalo closely resembled that of natural predators such as lions. Human hunters took only the very young or very old individuals. He concluded that "the age distribution of buffalo in the archaeological kill samples is what one might expect if the Stone Age hunters were to enjoy a lasting, stable relationship with prey populations of buffalo" (Klein 1979:158). Furthermore, he found no evidence of a decline in the buffalo population, even though they were hunted for tens of thousands of years. Klein found that even species of docile or small antelope, such as the eland and steenbok, which were easily driven or trapped, showed no evidence of any significant decline in numbers, even though they were utilized relatively intensively. Extinctions of game animals did occur during the period of human occupation, however, and Klein raised the possibility that improved hunting technology may have been a factor in some of these cases.

It is important to keep the issue of Pleistocene extinctions in perspective. Even if it can be demonstrated that tribal hunters did play a significant, albeit indirect, role in these extinctions, these losses are quite trivial when compared with the scale of extinctions underway today. According to W. V. Reid (1992) of the World Resources Institute, 60 bird and mammal species have disappeared worldwide between 1900 and 1950. At that rate, the 1,556 birds and mammals in the United States could disappear within 13 years and the world's 13,000 species could be totally exterminated within just 127 years. Few would dispute the human role in contemporary extinctions. Habitat destruction is probably the most important cause of extinction, although direct overkill has also been a factor.

SMALL-SCALE CULTURES AND THE ENVIRONMENT

The narrow range of environments that individual small-scale cultures exploit is one of the most striking features of their adaptation when compared with the global-scale culture. Distinguished ecologist and conservationist Raymond Dasmann (1976) highlighted this contrast when he drew a distinction between "Ecosystem" and "Biosphere" peoples. Dasmann's definition stressed the fact that Ecosystem peoples, or people living in small-scale cultures, depend on the resources supplied by local ecosystems and know immediately if their exploitation patterns are damaging. Biosphere peoples extract resources from throughout the globe and may not even be aware of, or immediately affected by, the local destruction of ecosystems that they might cause. If too wide a range is exploited, a culture might escape the ecological constraints of a given local environment, become unresponsive to natural equilibrium mechanisms, and thus ignore its own detrimental impact on that environment. Industrial nations are dependent on resources from throughout the world and can bring overwhelming forces to bear on particular local environments; in the short run, however, they remain immune to whatever damage they may cause. For example, at the present time the Amazon rain forest ecosystem is being systematically destroyed by remote forces ultimately deriving from the industrial capitals of the world, while the tribal cultures occupying the area remain dependent on their local environments and can respond immediately to detrimental changes within them (Meggers 1971). Roy Rappaport (1971) makes the same point using a New Guinea example. Recognizing this critical contrast does not mean that self-sufficient indigenous peoples are "ecologically noble" (Redford 1991, Alvord 1993). They need not be intentional conservationists, but they do demonstrate some obvious advantages of locally managed cultural systems that respond to local needs.

Environmental modifications occurring as a result of the intervention of small-scale cultures in general appear to be much more gradual and more akin to "natural" environmental processes than the modifications caused by the commercially driven global culture, which are often extremely rapid and qualitatively unusual. Commercial manufacturing processes often introduce completely new environmental pollutants that may have the potential to disrupt natural biochemical processes. At the same time, ecosystems modified by the demands of the global culture tend to become much simpler, less efficient, and more unstable than those affected by small-scale cultures. Such differences sometimes result directly from contrasting subsistence systems. For example, the ecological advantages of traditional root crop shifting cultivation over intensive monocrop systems in tropical areas have frequently been noted (Geertz 1963, Rappaport 1971). In their crop diversity and organization, the small garden plots of shifting cultivators structurally resemble the rain forest ecosystem, and thereby utilize solar energy with great efficiency and minimize the hazards of pests and disease. Netting (1993) notes that labor intensive smallholder production systems, even when they are highly intensive and combine market and subsistence production, are likely to be more productive per unit of land, more energy efficient, more sustainable, and more conserving of nonrenewable resources than large-scale, capital intensive, fully commercial agricultural systems. These points are discussed more fully in Chapter 4.

The massive, government financed development programs of the twentieth century largely ignored the human advantages of small-scale production systems. Development planners arrogantly dismissed domestically organized systems as "primitive," "pretechnological" cultures, assuming they had little knowledge of their environment and no "control" over it. Yet the data provided by researchers in the field of cultural ecology indicate that small-scale cultures actually possess deep and highly practical knowledge of their environments, based on intimate experience accumulated over countless generations. For example, Nelson (1969) reported that Inuit-speaking Eskimo peoples of north Alaska who hunt on sea ice employ an elaborate vocabulary with dozens of special terms to describe the thickness or age of ice, conditions related to ice movement, and ice topography. Native peoples in interior Canada, who must travel over frozen lakes and rivers, distinguish thirteen categories of ice according to eight dimensions. Their labels distinguish whether the ice is solid, melting, or cracked, details of water under the ice and on its surface, ice texture, thickness, clarity, color, and stages of cracks (Basso 1972). Tribal knowledge of the complex and varied tropical rain forest environment is equally impressive. The Hanunoo of Mindoro Island in the Philippines are tribal peoples practicing shifting cultivation. Conklin (1954) found that they distinguish 10 basic soil types and 30 subtypes, 450 animal types, and more than 1,600 plants, including some 400 types not recognized by botanists. They cultivate 430 plant varieties. In the Brazilian Amazon rain forest, Carneiro (1978) found that the Kuikuru Indians could name at least 187 different tree species. They identified every specimen he tested them on, including tiny seedlings and dead leaves plucked from the forest floor.

The notion that small-scale cultures have no control over their environment is based on a misunderstanding of what constitutes control. If "control" is understood to mean a stable and predictable exploitation of the environment, then tribal cultures might well exercise greater real environmental control. The basic difference here seems to be that whereas the global culture prides itself on its apparent ability to defy nature and struggles constantly to subdue it to its own ends, small-scale cultures are designed to work within the natural limits of their environments. In this regard, long centuries of success would suggest that the tribal approach to control is far more knowledgeable.

FIRE AND TRIBAL RESOURCE MANAGEMENT

I have stressed that before they were engulfed by the global culture, tribal cultures tended to maintain balances with the natural environment. It is also important to emphasize again that tribals were not living in some passive "state of nature." They were not surrounded by an undisturbed wilderness. There is abundant evidence to show that tribal peoples deliberately managed local ecosystems, often on a large scale, to increase "natural" biological productivity for human benefit. Perhaps the most striking example of such resource management is the use of selective burning by hunting and gathering peoples to deliberately create and maintain "game parks." Although the earliest European explorers often recorded that tribal peoples regularly burned vast areas of forest, brushland, and savanna, the significance of these practices was largely overlooked. Today, foresters and range management scientists generally recognize that carefully controlled, frequent burning can dramatically increase ecosystem productivity. For example, as Mellars (1976) shows, burning in forests can improve soil fertility, favor the growth of herbaceous plants, promote vigorous growth of trees and shrubs by "pruning," and induce germination of fire-dependent species. Such burning increases both the quantity and the nutritional quality of the forage available to game animals. This elevates the game-carrying capacity three to seven fold, and means that there will be more animals that are healthier and that reproduce faster. Hunting game is also facilitated because it is easier to move through the forest and the game is easier to see. Furthermore, frequent burning reduces the accumulation of combustible material and makes natural fires less destructive.

Anthropologist Henry Lewis (1982) investigated the use of fire by indigenous peoples in northern Alberta, Canada. He found that they clearly understood the ecological effects of burning and carefully timed their burning to speed the growth of forage in the early spring. This was also the time when fire was most easily controlled, because prairie soils were still frozen and snow was still on the ground in the forest. Native Americans deliberately burned the grassland to increase the populations of bison, elk, and deer and to control their movements. They were also interested in increasing the production of wild berries, reducing noxious insects, and creating supplies of dry firewood. They burned lake shorelines to improve nesting and feeding habitats for waterfowl and to increase the food supply for muskrats. Within the forest they used fire to create and maintain small prairies, and to extend the microenvironments along streamsides that were favored by moose.

There are documented examples of similar uses of fire by indigenous peoples in many other parts of the world, including Australia (Gould 1971, Hallam 1975, Lewis 1982). The Kakadu National Park in the far north of Australia's Northern Territory uses burning by traditional aboriginal landowners as a regular land management regime. In all these cases, the timing and frequency of burning are critical factors, and the success of the technique depends on a detailed knowledge of a wide range of environmental variables. This type of resource management resembles agriculture in some respects, but selective burning involves much less human manipulation of natural systems and does not require nonrenewable energy.

ECONOMICS OF SMALL-SCALE CULTURES

Given the critical role that economics must play in any culture, some of the most important contrasts between small- and global-scale cultures should be expected here. This is a complex problem because small-scale cultures include autonomous tribals existing in a world without governments, as well as relatively self-sufficient rural communities where householders may pay taxes or tribute and are often involved with the market economy. Such communities may also exist at widely different population densities, in different environments, and with different subsistence technologies. They may also differ in the extent to which resources are controlled by households or communally, and in degrees of wealth inequality between households. What they have in common is their emphasis on local self-sufficiency and community sustainablity, domestic level management, and absence of community level class divisions. These systems can all be disrupted by the intervention of governments or external commercial forces.

Unfortunately, attempts by earlier anthropologists to describe tribal economic systems as if they merely represented simplified capitalist market economies resulted in misunderstanding of the economic patterns of small-scale cultures. In the older anthropological literature it is not uncommon to find such inappropriate terms as *investment* and *interest* applied to tribal ceremonial exchanges, a bow and arrow called *capital*, and a shell necklace labeled *money*. At least one major economic anthropology textbook (Herskovits 1952) attempted to follow classical economic analysis throughout, assuming that tribal systems displayed capitalist economic institutions, if only in a blurred and generalized fashion. This viewpoint has been called the "formalist approach." Shed of some of the language of capitalist economics, it stresses that people everywhere are driven by self-interest and ever expanding wants, and always seek to maximize ends and minimize means (see especially Dowling 1979). Unfortunately, such interpretations have obscured both the significant accomplishments and the unique qualities of tribal economic systems.

In the mid-eighteenth century Karl Marx identified some of the important contrasts between tribal and market economies when he coined the terms *use value* and *exchange value* (Caulfield 1981). According to Marx, tribal, or what he called primitive, communal economies were based on use value because people produced for their own use. In capitalist economies, people produced not primarily for their own use, but rather for sale or exchange, and land, labor, and money are all for sale. Of course, goods are both used and exchanged in both types of economies. However, in a tribal, or use value, economy, producers are directly involved in production decision making and are immediately concerned with both the environmental and social consequences of production. Economic anthropologists who emphasize these contrasting features of tribal and market economies identify themselves as "substantivists," as opposed to "formalists." The substantivist view of tribal economic systems is well represented in the works of Dalton (1961, 1965) and Sahlins (1972). The substantivist economic distinctions proposed by Eric Wolf (1982) between cultures in which production is shaped respectively by kinship relationships, tribute extraction, or capitalist social classes modes of production correspond broadly to the small-scale, large-scale, global-scale scheme used in this book. These distinctions draw attention to the dual impact on the domestic economy (small-scale cultures) of surplus extraction by the state (large-scale cultures), as well as the tendency of capitalist systems (global-scale culture) to alienate rural peoples from their subsistence bases to convert them into a wage dependent labor force. Certainly the most significant contrast between small-scale cultures and both large- and global-scale cultures hinges on the relative importance of markets and domestic, kinship-based social formations. A small-scale economy is represented as an ideal type, existing without governments or markets, by Dalton's definition of a tribal economy:

> In marketless communities, land and labour are not transacted by purchase and sale but are allocated as expressions of kinship right or tribal affiliation. There are no formal market-place sites where indigenously produced items are bought and sold. These are subsistence economies in the sense that livelihood does not depend on production for sale. The transactional modes to allocate resources and labour as well as produced items and services are reciprocity and redistribution.
>
> (DALTON 1965:51)

A substantivist perspective does not deny economic rationality to peoples operating outside of market economies. All peoples probably economize with their time and energy, as optimal foraging research has shown (Winterhalder & Smith 1981).

Other substantivist writers such as Redfield (1947) have emphasized the relative technological simplicity of tribal economies, the fact that there is a minimal division of labor, or that everyone has equal access to the means of production, and that tribal societies are basically economically self-sufficient. Radin (1971) argued that tribal economies are distinguished most remarkably by their emphasis on a concept of an "irreducible minimum." According to Radin, tribal economies operate on the principle that "every human being has the inalienable right to an irreducible minimum, consisting of adequate food, shelter and clothing" (1971:106). In other words, tribal economies are designed to satisfy basic human needs, in sharp contrast to large-scale systems in which tribute supports an elite class, or in the global system, in which commercial profit furthers capital accumulation.

Whereas tribal economies are often correctly described as cashless, subsistence based, and simple in technology, these obvious contrasts alone do not explain their achievements. Equally important are the built-in limits to economic growth that characterize tribal cultures, and the fact that they explicitly recognize their dependency on the natural environment. In this respect, one of the key concepts in tribal economics is *limited good*, described by George Foster (1969:83) as the assumption that "*all* desired things in life . . . exist in finite and unexpandable quantities." Tribals make this principle central to their economic system, while market economies operate on the diametrically opposed principle of *unlimited good*, which assumes that "with each passing generation people on average will have more of the good things of life." Within a tribal economy several specific attributes, such as wealth-leveling devices, absolute property ceilings, fixed wants (Henry 1963), and the complementarity of production and needs, all center on the principle of limited good and contribute directly toward the maintenance of a basically stable, no-growth economy.

In a tribal society, wants are not considered open to infinite expansion, and the economy is designed to fill existing wants by producing exactly what is culturally recognized as a need. Conspicuous wealth inequalities may be considered direct threats to the stability of a tribal community, and individual overacquisitiveness may be countered with public censure, expulsion, or charges of witchcraft. At the same time, individuals may obtain prestige through generosity, and the redistribution or destruction of excess goods is accomplished through kinship and ceremonial obligations, feasting, and gambling. In contrast, the global market economy operates on the assumption that wants must be continually expanded. Specific mechanisms, such as advertising agencies, are employed to increase wants, and with individual acquisitiveness and increased consumption comes greater prestige.

Formalist anthropologists seem to minimize the significance of growth-curbing mechanisms in tribal economies, and instead represent as cultural universals the unlimited acquisitiveness characteristic of our economic system and the parallel inability to satisfy all of society's wants:

> We have seen that the scarcity of goods in the face of the wants of a given people at a given time is a universal fact of human experience; that no economy has been discovered wherein enough goods are produced in enough variety to satisfy all the wants of all the members of any society.
>
> (HERSKOVITS 1952:17)

Cultural devices to curb wants in tribal societies are also sometimes attributed to unavoidable circumstances, such as the fact that any accumulation of unessential goods would merely be an undesirable and impossible burden for nomadic peoples. This explanation may be valid in some cases, but it does not apply to villagers, to whom limits on property accumulation are also important. To explain their culturally imposed limits on economic growth, such villagers often simply state that property must not be allowed to threaten their basically egalitarian social systems. This is a significant point, for tribally organized economic systems, with their careful limits on material wealth, do in fact occur within relatively egalitarian social systems. In contrast, fundamentally nonegalitarian societies are characteristic of market systems. Clearly, if we want to understand the stability of tribal economies, we must look to other explanations.

Some ethnocentric economic development writers have suggested that the only reason tribal societies curb their wants is because their technologies cannot fill them, the implication being that more productive techniques would free people's innate capacity for unlimited wants: "[People] in every culture harbor unexpressed wishes to have more in order to be more. Once it becomes evident to them that it is possible to desire more, they will, by and large, want more" (Goulet 1971:76).

Indeed, at various times anthropologists have dramatically overemphasized the supposed technological deficiencies of tribal economies (see, for example, Herskovits 1952:16, Levin and Potapov 1964:488-499, Nash 1966:22, Dalton 1971:27). Tribal systems have been described as if they were barely able to meet subsistence needs, and it has been assumed that tribal peoples faced a daily threat of starvation that forced them to devote virtually all their waking moments to the food quest. This traditional view remained almost unchallenged until careful studies of productivity and time-energy expenditure in tribal societies revealed that even the most technologically simple peoples were able to satisfy all their subsistence requirements with relatively little effort. Much of this data was reviewed by Sahlins (1972). It has been shown, in fact, that many of these societies could have produced far more food if they had been so inclined; instead, they preferred to spend their time at other activities, such as socializing and leisure. It was discovered that hunters such as the Bushmen (Lee 1968) and certain Australian Aborigines (McCarthy and McArthur 1960), who were thought to be among those groups closest to the starvation level, put in on the average no more than a twenty-hour workweek getting food. Other researchers (Carneiro 1960, Rappaport 1971) have shown that shifting cultivation systems offer a reliable subsistence base that may actually be more efficient than the "factory farm" techniques replacing them.

On the basis of this kind of evidence, it can now be assumed that tribals did not deliberately curb their wants and operate stable economies merely because they were incapable of either producing or desiring more or because circumstances automatically prevented the accumulation of goods. Rather, it would appear that such systems survived and proliferated because of their greater long-run adaptive value.

NATURE IN TRIBAL IDEOLOGY

Numerous anthropologists have emphasized the fundamental contrasts in values, religion, and world view between tribal and industrial cultures in relation to the natural environment (see, for example, Gutkind 1956, Spoehr 1956). The most remarkable general difference is that tribal ideological systems often express humanity's dependence on nature and tend to place nature in a revered, sacred category. As Lynn White, Jr., and others have noted, the notion of a constant struggle to conquer nature, which is so characteristic of the global culture, in which it may be supported by biblical injunction, is notably absent in tribal cultures. Indeed, tribals generally consider themselves part of nature in the sense that they may name themselves after animals, impute souls to plants and animals, acknowledge ritual kinship with certain species, conduct rituals designed to help propagate particularly valued species, and offer ritual apologies when animals must be killed. Animals also abound in tribal origin myths; and, at death, one's soul is often believed to be transformed into an animal. Careful research has shown that many of these seemingly irrational beliefs may actually contribute directly to the stability of tribal cultures by contributing to the regulation of both population size and levels of resource consumption. Population growth, for example, is curbed by beliefs calling for sexual abstinence, abortion, infanticide, and ritual warfare, and various taboos control the exploitation of specific food resources. McDonald (1977) has shown that in Amazonia special taboos restricting the consumption of specific game animals by certain categories of people are most often applied to the animals that would be most vulnerable to overhunting. In highland New Guinea, it has been argued that ceremonial cycles help maintain a balance between the human population, pig herds, and the natural environment (see Chapter 6, Rappaport 1968). Other writers (Bartlett 1956) have pointed out that sacred groves in many parts of the world have maintained forest remnants and reduced soil erosion, while under Christian influence the forests have been chopped down, with unfortunate results. It is significant that tribal belief systems often disintegrate under the impact of the commercial culture, and are replaced by other beliefs that accelerate environmental disequilibrium.

THE DESANA EQUILIBRIUM MODEL

The case of the Desana Indians of the Colombian Amazon provides a specific example of the unique characteristics of tribal ideological systems contributing toward a balance with the resource base. It also shows how this balance may be disturbed by the impact of the global scale culture. The Desana are a tribal society of some 1,000 hunters and manioc farmers living in the Vaupes region of Colombia. Colombian anthropologist Gerardo Reichel-Dolmatoff (1971:219) argues that Desana culture "has formulated a series of very strict norms to assure the maintenance of a biotic equilibrium." However, there is no empirical evidence that the Desana system actually works in the way he proposes.

Perhaps the most intriguing aspect of Desana culture is that its norms appear to be explicitly based on such fundamental ecological principles as the energy cycle and the interdependence of life forms. The Desana assume that the fertility of both humans and animals is dependent on the same finite circuit of recycling solar energy, and they recognize that uncontrolled human population growth would unbalance the entire energy system through overhunting. Various cultural mechanisms are employed to prevent disequilibrium, including contraceptive herbs, used to support the stated norm of no more than two to three children per family, and a variety of sexual taboos and specific ritual observances that limit the frequency of hunting. The availability of game animals is believed to be under the control of a supernatural being, the "keeper of game," who can restrict supply or cause illness if the norms regulating hunting and sexual activity are not observed. The shaman plays a key role, mediating between the demands of society for meat and the limited resources available. In order to carry out this duty, he communicates with the "keeper of game" by using hallucinogenic drugs and attempts to gain his favor while keeping the hunters informed of his demands.

The entire Desana culture is supported by its creation myth and is constantly reinforced by daily ritual activities, periodic ceremonies, and, more importantly, its obvious success. The system is designed to operate indefinitely into the future, and archaeological evidence shows that the Amazon tropical forest cultural adaptation, which the Desana represent, has already existed for at least 4,000 years (Lathrap 1970). However, Christian missionaries could replace Desana beliefs with a global religion, and settlers seek a share of Desana resources.

It would be inappropriate to say that Amazonian peoples were self-conscious conservationists, even though they have done demonstrably better at keeping their ecosystems intact than the commercial system that is now transforming the Amazon. Empirical field studies of indigenous hunters in the Peruvian Amazon showed that although some hunters observed religious taboos against killing deer, overall they appeared to maximize short-term harvest rates of prey species with no apparent concern for possible long-term impacts (Alvard 1993). Such hunting patterns are predicted by optimal foraging theories and need not conflict with long-term resource equilibrium as long as human densities and overall hunting pressure remain low. Under such conditions the conservation effect could be considered epiphenomenal (Hunn 1982).

PACIFIC ISLAND CHIEFDOMS AND THE ENVIRONMENT

To conclude this chapter, here is a description by anthropologist George Peter Murdock of the condition of the high tropical islands of the Pacific after centuries of undisturbed occupation by Polynesian chiefdoms:

> There was no destruction of forests by reckless lumbering with resultant reduction in water retention. There was no wholesale replacement of natural cover by cultivated crops such as occurs with modern sugar or copra plantations or intensive rice cultivation. There was no pollution of streams or coastal waters by sewage or chemical plants; no flooding of valleys by artificial lakes

constructed for irrigation or hydroelectric power; no ruining of land surfaces through strip mining or slag piles; no massive earth removal for roads or air strips. There was no extensive soil erosion initiated by careless plowing or by overgrazing. The indigenous pig does not compare with the goat or the sheep as a conservationist's nightmare.

(MURDOCK 1963)

This picture is generally correct, but it must be moderated. The economic systems of most Pacific islanders were political economies with varying degrees of tribute collection and centrally controlled redistribution. These systems were severely constrained by the small size of most islands. When Murdock wrote, there had been relatively little archaeological research to verify his generalization. It is now known that Polynesian chiefdoms actually had a rather large environmental impact on their island homes, including deforestation, erosion, and overfishing in some cases, but this impact was qualitatively different from the unsustainable impact of the global commercial economy. For example, archaeological research has shown that after 3,000 years of continuous human occupation, the natural ecosystem on the tiny Polynesian island of Tikopia was virtually replaced by a human managed system of permanent gardens and domesticated forests that proved both sustainable and self-sufficient (Kirch & Yen 1982).

Natural Resources and the Culture of Consumption

*The biosphere with industrial man suddenly added is like a
balanced aquarium into which large animals are introduced.
Consumption temporarily exceeds production, the balance is
upset, the products of respiration accumulate, and the fuels for
consumption become scarcer and scarcer until production is
sufficiently accelerated and respiration is balanced. In some
experimental systems balance is achieved only after the large
consumers which originally started the imbalance are dead.
Will this happen to man?*

HOWARD T. ODUM
Environment, Power, and Society

IN THE PREVIOUS CHAPTER two specific aspects of the environmental crisis—resource depletion and pollution—were related to overconsumption. The present chapter will further explore the problem of overconsumption, because it appears to be the critical defining feature of the global culture in contrast with small-scale cultures, and because it is the feature that contributes most to the present instability of the contemporary world. Here we shall be concerned specifically with how globally organized commercially driven systems extract and utilize energy and other natural resources in comparison with patterns typical of small-scale cultures, and how these patterns relate to the environmental crisis.

ENERGY AND CULTURE: BASIC CONSIDERATIONS

It becomes the primary function of culture, therefore, to harness and control energy so that it may be put to work in man's service. . . . The functioning of culture as a whole therefore rests upon and is determined by the amount of energy harnessed and by the way in which it is put to work.

(WHITE 1949:367–68)

Culture evolves as the amount of energy harnessed per capita per year is increased, or as the efficiency of the instrumental means of putting the energy to work is increased.

(WHITE 1949:368–69)

Anthropologist Leslie A. White elaborated a simplistic but important theory of the evolution of culture based largely on energy utilization. In White's view, the earliest small-scale cultures necessarily remained at a very low level of evolutionary complexity as long as they relied on their own human energy and minimal use of wind, water, and fire. The additional control of solar energy through domesticated plants and animals released vast amounts of energy and made possible higher levels of social complexity, greater productivity per unit of area, and greater population density. These developments culminated with the appearance of state organization.

Since White first published this evolutionary scheme in 1949, other researchers have shown that his theory was quite misleading. In fact, prior to the use of fossil fuel energy sources, per capita energy use did not increase significantly—humans remained the basic source of mechanical energy. The real difference was that domestication supported higher population densities and larger total populations, and thus larger total energy was available for building cultural complexity (Sahlins 1972:5–6). That increased complexity can arise without domestication, or with only minimal use of domesticates, is demonstrated by the emergence of complex chiefdoms along the desert coast of Peru 4,000 years ago based on the exploitation of rich marine resources rather than cultivated food crops (Mosely 1975, Quilter & Stocker 1983).

White felt that the full potential for cultural evolutionary advance on the basis of agriculture alone was realized before the Christian era, and that further advance into industrial civilization was only made possible by the *fuel revolution*, his term for the utilization of fossil fuels. With the discovery of nuclear energy, White felt, culture was poised on the verge of a major new energy revolution that could lead to even higher levels of evolutionary progress. Brazilian anthropologist Darcy Ribeiro (1968) confidently applied the term *thermonuclear revolution* to this new era, but neither White nor Ribeiro considered the full cost of nuclear energy.

It is certainly reasonable and useful to describe general evolutionary progress in terms of energy utilization; but if we are concerned with the environmental crisis and with achieving a successful and sustainable cultural adaptation, it will be more useful to compare cultures according to the rate at which nonrenewable resources are being depleted. The global energy resources that are most significant for human use can be divided into three categories: 1) solar radiation; 2) fossil fuels; and 3) nuclear energy. Solar radiation can be considered a steady "income" energy source that is renewed daily or annually, and is converted by green plants, or through the movement of water and wind, into other usable forms of energy. Solar energy may also be concentrated and converted directly to heat for human use. Only a very small, relatively constant quantity of energy can ever be provided by this source, and because of the Second Law of Thermodynamics, the amount of energy available for use is constantly reduced at each conversion.

Fossil fuels supply solar energy that was trapped by green plants and stored in the earth through incomplete oxidation over the past 600 million years. The process of fossil fuel formation is still underway but at a rate too slow in relation to human needs for this energy source to be considered anything other than nonrenewable. Any use of this stored energy is a withdrawal from a steadily dwindling stock.

Nuclear energy can be released from its storage within the atomic structure; but the most easily utilized radioactive fuels are in limited supply, and all controlled releases of nuclear energy require enormous additional inputs from other energy sources to be safely maintained, to deal with the waste heat, and to warehouse the dangerous radioactive by-products for millennia. Nuclear energy also has serious limitations because it must be converted into heat and electrical energy before it can be widely used, and thus it seems an unlikely replacement for all present uses of fossil fuels.

Cultures can be divided into "high-energy cultures" and "low-energy cultures" in regard to energy use. These categories have immediate implications for both evolutionary "progress" and adaptive success. The quantitative differences between high- and low-energy cultures can be seen easily in reference to per capita levels of energy consumption. It has been estimated that prior to the fuel revolution no state-organized cultures utilized more than 26,000 kilocalories per capita daily, whereas small-scale tribal cultures, whether foragers or farmers, utilized between 5,000 and 12,000 kilocalories per capita daily (see Figure 3.1). These cultures could all be considered low-energy cultures, especially because these rates are not much above the 2,000 kilocalories of food energy needed for daily per capita human nutrition. In contrast, early industrial commercial cultures utilizing fossil fuels consumed approximately 70,000 kilocalories per capita daily, and by 1970 Americans had elevated that rate to 230,000 (Cook 1971). Contrary to projections for continued growth in American energy consumption, by 1991 the per capita rate appeared to have leveled off at 1970 levels. However, global rates continued to rise, increasing 25 percent between 1971 and 1992. Given that global population also increased, the total human demand on the world's energy resources continued to expand. However, the actual distribution of consumption reflects global inequities in wealth. Per capita energy consumption rates in high-income countries in 1991 averaged fifteen times the rates of low-income countries (World Bank 1994:170–171, Table 5).

Given the apparently immutable laws of thermodynamics and the physical limitations of the global energy budget, any culture that taps renewable solar energy sources must necessarily remain a low-energy culture relative to those drawing on stored, depletable sources. Theoretically, low-energy cultures could exist another 5 billion years until the sun burns out, whereas high-energy cultures must be transformed to low-energy cultures when their depleted energy stores are burned up. Or, their growth may be halted by the adverse impacts of the waste heat they unavoidably produce through energy conversion. High-energy cultures thus have limited life spans that can easily be predicted for comparison with the 5-billion-year life expectancy of low-energy cultures.

Estimates for the depletion of fossil fuels vary slightly, depending on accepted rates of utilization and the estimates of total reserves, but the general magnitude of the figures is clear. Global production of petroleum seems to be following the total life cycle projected by geologist Hubert King in 1969. His conservative estimates predicted that global production would peak at approximately 25 billion barrels a year around 1995 and would decline rapidly thereafter. The actual 1991 annual production was 24 billion barrels, almost precisely what King had predicted, while existing reserves in 1992 were estimated at 989 billion barrels (*World Almanac* 1994). At the 1991 production rate all known reserves would be gone by the year 2032. This date is somewhat earlier than the 2053 oil depletion date projected by the *Global 2000* presidential commission in 1980. Based on 1976 production rates, this study also showed natural gas depleted within 170 years and coal in 212 years (Barney 1980, vol. 2:189–93). The number of proven fossil fuel reserves will certainly increase as these fuels become more costly and more expensive recovery techniques become feasible. We should also stress that all these projections are based on differing assumptions concerning future economic conditions, population growth, and how "known reserves" are calculated. However, in spite of all the unknowns, the overall magnitude of the resource depletion problem suggests that consumption patterns that have characterized the second half of the twentieth century will not continue indefinitely.

If we assume that oil and natural gas are indeed depleted as quickly as the *Global 2000* study predicted, then a switch to full reliance on coal would greatly accelerate its depletion. The most optimistic estimates would show oil depletion by late in the twenty-first century and coal depletion within 500 or 600 years, but dramatic technological fixes would probably be required before that. High-grade uranium ores needed to support our present nuclear fission technology will be in very short supply, and a switch to vastly more costly and unproven systems such as "breeder" and fusion reactors will be urgently needed if a high-energy culture is to be sustained indefinitely.

63

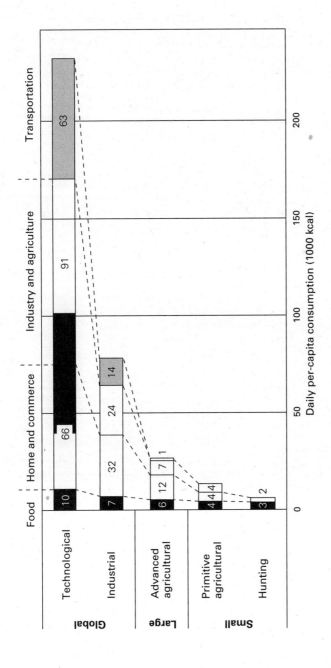

FIGURE 3.I

Daily consumption of energy per capita by culture-scale level. Cultures identified by Earl Cook as "hunting" and "primitive agricultural" are equivalent to foraging and shifting cultivation. ("The Flow of Energy in an Industrial Society," by Earl Cook. *Scientific American* 224(3):136. Copyright © by Scientific American, Inc. All rights reserved.)

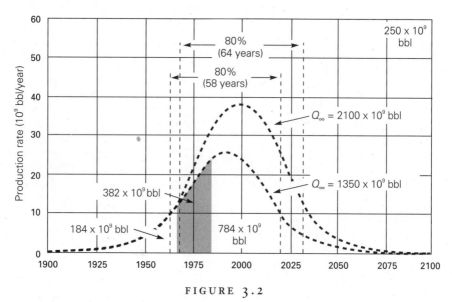

FIGURE 3.2

Petroleum is perhaps global culture's most vital nonrenewable resource, yet its total availability is strictly limited as this chart of complete cycles of world crude-oil production demonstrates. (Hubert 1969:196.)

Even if this transition is successfully achieved, continued progress appears unlikely because even at the present rate fossil fuel combustion may adversely impact global climate. After 10,000 years of stability, atmospheric carbon dioxide has already increased 25 percent since the Industrial Revolution began. This increased carbon dioxide traps heat like a greenhouse, contributing to global warming. The UN sponsored Intergovernmental Panel on Climate Change (IPCC) estimated that the greenhouse effect could cause global mean temperature to rise by 3 degrees centigrade (5.4 degrees Fahrenheit) over the next century (IPCC 1991:xxv). Within 200 years, a mere 5 percent annual increase in world energy production would produce waste heat equal to that received from the sun, and all life on earth would cease (Luten 1974). Long before such a Sun Day could possibly arrive, however, the polar ice caps would melt, flooding most of the world's urban centers, and enormous adverse changes in world vegetation would occur.

Thus, a continually expanding high-energy culture will be self-terminating, and its maximum life expectancy can be no more than a few hundred years. Furthermore, it is doubtful that relatively high levels of energy utilization can be stabilized at safely sustainable levels with nuclear technology, because of its known and unknown risks, and because of the uncertainty that unstable high-energy cultures will evolve the social mechanisms needed to achieve such a transition. Ultimately, of course, the Law of the Minimum, discovered by nineteenth-century German chemist Justus von Liebig, could eventually slow the growth of global culture. More than energy alone is necessary to sustain a high-energy culture, because if that energy is used to produce what Leslie A. White called "human need-serving goods and services," other raw materials must also be consumed. Liebig's law states that an organism's growth and survival will be limited by the essential material that is present in the lowest quantity. The dramatic figures in *The Limits to Growth* (Meadows et al. 1972) predicting that certain minerals were approaching imminent exhaustion, such as copper in 48 years and aluminum within 55 years, were misleading. Mineral depletion dates are subject to many uncertainties; however, the U.S. Geological Survey's generous calculations of "Ultimate Recoverable Resources," based on mineral abundance on the earth's crust, show a 340-year supply for copper, but only 162 years for lead (Nordhaus 1974:33). Mineral depletion will be a strong economic incentive for conservation and recycling.

Any culture defined by perpetual growth in either consumption or population is certain to be self-limiting. Although it is not possible to precisely estimate the life expectancy of the global culture, it can confidently be stated that it will not exceed the 50,000-year record of small-scale Australian aboriginal culture, or the 3,500-year span of large-scale ancient Mesopotamian civilization.

THE CULTURE OF CONSUMPTION DEFINED

The global culture has developed into something totally unique in the evolution of culture—*a culture of consumption* (Bodley 1975:4-5). The culture's major economic, social, and ideological systems are geared to nonsustainable levels of resource consumption and to continual, ever-higher elevation of those levels on a per capita basis. This is *overconsumption*, not only in terms of reduced cultural viability, but also in a strictly biological sense, as ecologist Howard Odum explained:

> In the industrial system with man living off a fuel, he manages all his affairs
> with industrial machinery, all parts of which are metabolically consumers. . . .
> The system of man has consumption in excess of production. The products of
> respiration—carbon dioxide, metabolic water, and mineralized inorganic
> wastes—are discharged in rates in excess of their incorporation into organic
> matter by photosynthesis. If the industrialized urban system were enclosed in a
> chamber with only the air above it at the time, it would quickly exhaust its oxy-
> gen, be stifled with waste, and destroy itself since it does not have the recycling
> pattern of the agrarian system.

(ODUM 1971:17)

Odum estimated that on a global scale "human industries add about a 5 percent excess of consumption over production." Overconsumption also produces a phenomenal quantity of garbage that can be a gold mine for archaeologists, both today and in the future (Rathje & Murphy 1992), but clogged landfills also suggest waste and system imbalance.

Growth through increased consumption is so much a part of our present economy that most economists find it difficult to imagine any other state, even though perpetual growth is only possible in an infinite environment. Some writers (Boulding 1966) have characterized the present economy of growth as a "frontier" or "cowboy" economy, meaning that it is the type of economic system that might be appropriate to a particular period of expansion into a new environment, but it becomes inappropriate when that historical period has passed and further expansion threatens to become destructive. A more descriptive term might be simply *consumption economy;* the important point is that such a system is defined by a continual increase in "throughput," that is, production and consumption measured by gross national product (GNP). There is little consideration given to the unintended by-products of the process. Waste, depletion, pollution, and various indirect social costs or "externalities" do not immediately detract from the gross national product and may actually be a positive aspect of it. For example, accidents and diseases caused by the production and consumption process contribute to economic growth because further output of goods and services must deal with them. Adverse side effects of growth will be certain to make growth self-limiting in the long run; but because of the investment process, a consumption economy is focused only on the immediate future and disregards impacts even twenty-five to fifty years into the future.

Perpetual economic growth is firmly entrenched in the culture of consumption and has become the way to both produce and sustain a grossly stratified, nonegalitarian social system. Disruptive dissatisfaction among the lowest classes due to poverty and unemployment can be prevented without the wealthy sacrificing their positions if the total volume of wealth can be steadily increased, or if people can believe that they have the possibility of improving their material condition. In this way the poor gradually become "wealthy," or nurture hope of doing so, while their relative position remains constant or declines. The same principle operates between countries at the global level. "Poor" nations might be prevented from warring against rich nations if the possibility of certain minimal levels of economic growth can be maintained.

Sociologist Leslie Sklair (1991:42) calls the culture-ideology of consumerism "the fuel that powers the motor of global capitalism." In his view the global system is driven by a powerful, commercially generated ideology that convinces people that perpetual economic growth will benefit everyone. Social science theorist Immanuel Wallerstein (1990) calls this the "myth of the rising standard of living," because it masks the realities of poverty and the unequal economic relationships between rich and poor countries, as well as the physical impossibility of perpetual expansion in consumption. As discussed in Chapter 1, Leslie Sklair (1991) identifies "consumerism," as promoted by the transnational mass media and advertising, as the dominant element in the ideology of the global system. He states:

> The cultural-ideological project of global capitalism is to persuade people to consume above their own perceived needs in order to perpetuate the accumulation of capital for private profit, in other words, to ensure that the global capitalist system goes on forever.

> (SKLAIR 1991:41)

Sklair notes that this "project" works best where peoples' prospects for self-sufficiency in basic needs such as food and shelter are reduced at the same time they are exposed to mass-media advertising. Stuart Ewen (1976), in his social history of advertising in the United States during the 1920s, argues that in the same way that clocks shaped people for factory work, advertising was needed to make people predictable consumers of factory made commercial products. Creating an American consumer culture also helped deflect social movements seeking greater social equality and more government regulation of commerce. In Sklair's view, the advertising "project" seeks to make consumption of commercial products the center of people's lives. As he observes:

> The culture-ideology of consumerism proclaims, literally, that the meaning of life is to be found in the things that we possess. To consume, therefore, is to be fully alive, and to remain fully alive we must continuously consume.

> (SKLAIR 1991:41)

The transnational corporations and the transnational elite that own and manage them will certainly prosper as formerly self-sufficient peoples become wage earners and consumers of commercial products, but the outcome for those marginalized in the process is less promising. Higher "standards of living" or improved "quality of life" may be illusory when they are measured by ever-increasing per capita consumption of energy, rising GNP, or national income averages. This illusory quality of the consumer culture is shown by other measures such as the Physical Quality of Life Index (PQLI) developed by Morris (1979). This index averages national-level data on infant mortality rates, life expectancy at age one, and literacy rates into a single index value. The PQLI is considered a simple, comprehensive, and relatively nonethnocentric measure of overall quality of life, at least for literate national societies. The PQLI demonstrates that there is no absolute relationship between quality of life and GNP. In the 1970s there were nations with low GNP that had high life-quality indices, such as Sri Lanka, Cuba, and Western Samoa, and nations with high GNP and low life quality, such as Libya and Saudi Arabia. Cross-national surveys (Mazur & Rosa 1974) suggest that only up to a certain point do increases in energy use correspond with rises in commonly accepted measures of quality of life in industrial countries, such as health care, education, and "cultural" activities. Very high energy levels may be part of evolutionary progress as Leslie White defined it, but they make little contribution to improving the quality of life. There are even indications that very high energy consumption rates are related to such negative qualities as high suicide and divorce rates, but the causal relationships have not been fully explored.

It is also widely believed that the ever-increasing output of household appliances has meant a steady reduction in housework and an increase in leisure time. Consumer appliances thus become principle indicators of a high standard of living. Anthropological research among foragers and shifting cultivators, however, has shown that they work far less at household tasks, and indeed at all subsistence pursuits, than any modern populations (Johnson 1975, 1985, McCarathy & McArthur 1960). Aboriginal Australian women, for example, were found to spend an average of approximately twenty hours per week collecting and preparing food (McCarthy & McArthur 1960), whereas women in rural America in the 1920s, without the benefit of labor-saving appliances, devoted approximately fifty-two hours a week to their housework (Vanek 1974). Some fifty years later, contrary to all expectations, urban women who were not employed outside of the home were putting in fifty-five hours a week at their housework, in spite of all their new "labor-saving" dishwashers, washing machines, vacuum cleaners, and electric mixers. This increase in work time shows how illusory the idea of an increased standard of living may be when judged according to the consumption culture's traditionally accepted measures. Some of this increased workload may be due to the need to spend more time on such consumption-related tasks as shopping and caring for an increased volume of clothing.

The relationship between a culture of consumption and the natural environment can be seen more clearly through the examination of specific examples. The following sections will deal primarily with the United States in order to illustrate specific principles that may be valid for all consumption cultures and that show how serious environmental crises may be precipitated by overconsumption.

RESOURCE CONSUMPTION IN AMERICA

The United States is without question the leading example of a culture of consumption. Shortly after World War II, it had become the world's major consumer of nonrenewable resources on both an absolute and a per capita basis. Estimates vary widely, but it appears that by 1970, although their population contributed only about 6 percent of the world's total annual production, Americans consumed some 40 percent of the world's total annual production, and 35 percent of the world's energy (Cook 1971). By 1992, after two decades of worldwide economic growth, the United States, with less than 5 percent of the world's population, managed to slightly increase its per capita energy consumption and remained a major global consumer, accounting for 25 percent of the world's commercial energy (World Bank 1994). Its consumption of 7,662 kilograms of petroleum per person annually was as much as China, Japan, Germany, the United Kingdom, and France combined. In comparison, China virtually reversed the figures, with 20 percent of the world's population consuming 8 percent of the commercial energy. The historic pattern of American consumption illustrates important trends that may be generally characteristic of consumption cultures.

High and rapidly increasing rates of American energy consumption were made possible by a switch from primary dependence on theoretically renewable "income" sources, such as fuel wood, to nonrenewable "capital stock" resources such as coal. In 1850, approximately 90 percent of America's energy was derived from fuel wood; but, by 1890, over 50 percent was supplied by coal. By 1960, nearly 70 percent came from oil and natural gas, and optimists hoped that in the near future nuclear energy would replace depleted fossil fuels (Landsberg 1964). In a mere 100 years Americans tripled their per capita use of energy and multiplied their total use thirty times. They have already made two major shifts in their basic energy sources and face shortages and further adjustments in the foreseeable future. Much of this increased use has carried an enormous environmental cost due to air pollution from burning the fuels, and from disturbances caused by drilling and mining operations and accidents such as oil spills. As more easily exploited energy resources have become depleted, higher extraction costs have forced the United States to rely heavily on imported energy. By 1992 nearly one-fourth of American energy was imported. Oil and natural gas were still predominant, accounting for 65 percent of consumption, with coal approximately 30 percent and nuclear 8 percent (*World Almanac* 1994).

Certainly, one critical question to ask is how a culture of consumption responds to the impact of its own consumption on what must be an ever-dwindling resource base. Small-scale cultures, as noted earlier, tend to respond quickly to adverse impacts on their resource base because they are immediately dependent on local resources. However, global-scale commercial cultures lack this instant responsiveness because of their complexity and specialization. They are especially vulnerable to overgrowth and collapse because of their rapid expansion. More importantly, they lack substitute response mechanisms and the market system seems to thrive on resource depletion. Governments have occasionally stockpiled certain critical resources as strategic military reserves; but, in general, present political institutions prefer to let market forces detect potential shortfalls. Some of the special commissions that have occasionally examined the problem are examined below.

TAKING STOCK

> Our nation, looking toward a future of continuing economic progress, is well-advised to take stock of its natural resources. Industry can expand only so far as raw materials are available.
>
> (DEWHURST 1955:754)

After World War II, in 1949, the United Nations brought together in New York over 700 scientists from over 50 nations to exchange information on world problems of conservation and resource utilization. In assessing the world mineral situation, H. L. Keenleyside, Canada's deputy minister of mines and resources, noted that between 1900 and 1949 more world mineral resources had been consumed than during all of humanity's previous existence. He felt that there were as yet no critical mineral shortages developing, but recognized future limitations:

> Thus it is quite clear that the combination of an increasing population and rising standards of living will place a strain on our metal resources which will almost certainly in the end prove beyond the capacity of man and nature to supply.
>
> (KEENLEYSIDE 1950:38)

To postpone the inevitable, Keenleyside recommended increased exploration for minerals, improved extraction and processing technology, conservation, and substitution. Given increasing demands, his warning was clear: "[Unless] there is a fundamental change in the economic fabric of human society we will ultimately be faced with the exhaustion of many of our mineral resources."

In the United States, no comprehensive inventory of natural resources was ever undertaken until 1908. There were early moves toward conservation, but little concern that serious problems might arise. A major study published in 1947, titled *America's Needs and Resources* (Dewhurst 1947), attempted to project national requirements for resources for 1960. It reported that no real resource exhaustion was likely within twenty years, although high-grade zinc, lead, and bauxite ores might be exhausted by that time and soil shortages might occur somewhat later. The report recognized that domestic mineral resources would ultimately be depleted; but it was felt that, given free access to foreign resources, an "expanding American economy" could be supported for "many decades" to come. Supporting an ever-expanding American culture of consumption has major implications for global resources. This, of course, is one of the reasons why global "free trade" is such an important part of the political ideology of the American elite.

Eight years later, the *America's Needs and Resources* study was updated with the publication of a new edition (Dewhurst 1955) that displayed a greater appreciation for the incredible consumption rates that Americans were developing. But this awareness was more than overshadowed by an even greater confidence in the country's ability to solve any problem. The study noted that by 1950 Americans were consuming some eighteen tons of raw materials per capita and that the United States consumed as much of many important minerals as the rest of the world combined. In spite of these staggering facts, the authors of the report were certain that there would be no insurmountable problems that would limit further growth:

> Despite man's seemingly devastating exploitation, he has merely scratched a small segment of this gigantic ball of resources on which he lives. Our power to use the materials in nature is growing rather than diminishing, through favorable technology and economic organization.

(DEWHURST 1955:754–755)

While in 1955 we may have been only scratching the surface of the globe's resources, the suddenly increased extent of this scratching was put in perspective in President Truman's *Resources for Freedom* study (United States, President's Materials Policy Commission 1952). This study pointed out that American consumption of most minerals and fuels since 1914 exceeded total world consumption from the dawn of human existence up to 1914. Furthermore, other projections show how quickly this minor scratching could have a serious impact on a finite earth. In 1956 geochemist Harrison Brown calculated that a world population of 30 billion (which will be reached by 2094 if the 1991 world population of 5.4 billion continues to grow at 1.7 percent per year), with nuclear breeder technology and the ability to extract all needed mineral resources directly from ordinary rock and seawater, would literally eat up the continents. The crust of the earth would be skimmed off at the rate of 3.3 millimeters a year, or over 3 meters every 1,000 years. Of course this scenario ignored conservation and recycling.

In 1963 a third major assessment of American resources was published by Resources for the Future (RFF). The 1,000-page report, titled *Resources in America's Future* (Landsberg et al. 1963), attempted to project supply and demand for natural resources up to the year 2000. The authors of the study recognized the general difficulty of any such projections but felt they were essential for decision making. They recommended that such studies be conducted or updated by a government agency every five years, perhaps through computer simulation techniques. This study, like earlier assessments, could foresee no immediate critical general shortages. Although the authors felt that some specific problems might arise, they assumed that any problems would be solvable. New technology, world trade, and careful utilization would maintain continued high consumption rates. On the basis of careful projections, which considered the interrelatedness of population, technology, and "demand" levels and assumed continued imports and no major wars or economic depressions, the RFF report concluded that by the year 2000 the United States would triple its annual consumption of energy, metals, and timber. According to the major summary of the RFF report by Landsberg:

> Neither a long view of the past, nor current trends, nor our most careful estimates of future possibilities suggest any general running out of resources in this country during the remainder of this century. The possibilities of using lower grades of raw material, of substituting plentiful materials for scarce ones, of getting more use out of given amounts, of importing things from other countries, and of making multiple use of land and water resources seem to be sufficient guarantee against across-the-board shortage.
>
> (LANDSBERG 1964:13)

This optimistic view was quite in agreement with earlier studies on this point: "On the whole, it seems clear that we shall not be hampered in meeting future needs by a shortage of raw materials" (Dewhurst 1955:939).

The RFF projections accurately predicted the continued technological advances, greater efficiency, and continued substitution of synthetics for natural materials that occurred in subsequent decades. Without constant technological "advance," it is clear that the culture of consumption would rapidly be faced with what the RFF report called "inconvenient and perhaps critical material limitations." For example, it was estimated that 64 percent of the fibers consumed by the year 2000 would be synthetics drawn largely from fossil fuel stocks. The report noted that by 1952 Western softwood forests were already being cut at over their replacement rate and warned that unless we wished to be extremely optimistic we could expect a continued depletion of Western forests. This prediction also seems to have been accurate. A 1992 inventory by the Forest Service showed that large diameter softwoods have steadily decreased in the West since 1952, such that, "For the first time in history, the United States does not have a large reserve of high quality softwood saw timber available for harvest" (Powell et al. 1993:20). The 1992 Forest Service study suggests that Eastern hardwood forests and imports should make up for the decline in Western forests. By the 1990s the value of American forest product imports had roughly tripled 1960 levels and American forestry planners acknowledged that American consumption patterns were having a global impact (Brooks 1993). As the discussion on tropical deforestation in Chapter 2 showed, the world's forests will probably not sustain the perpetual increase in harvests that commercial uses demand.

Eastern hardwoods will replace Western softwoods and tropical hardwoods may in turn replace the Eastern softwoods. Plastics will replace tropical trees.

It is difficult to escape the conclusion that the consumption culture is fighting a losing battle to support a rising level of consumption that must ultimately be insupportable. At any given moment some important material subsystem of the culture appears about to exhaust a particular resource and is forced to intensify its technology or move on to another resource to keep the system functioning a little longer through any means short of reduced consumption.

Shortly after publication of the RFF study, the National Academy of Sciences conducted its own two-year study, which took a much broader approach to the resources and consumption question. This work, *Resources and Man*, was published in 1969. It was concerned with the entire globe and looked beyond the year 2000. The outlook was far more sober and raised serious questions about the long-term viability of an ever-expanding industrial culture. It recognized that supplies of nonrenewable resources such as oil and coal were finite and in the near future might need to be replaced by nuclear technology. Some authors even felt that there were serious possibilities that certain critical mineral shortages might arise before 2000. The report was clear on one point—even given technological breakthroughs, continued expansion in consumption rates cannot be supported indefinitely. The report held out the hope that if population and consumption could be stabilized at reasonable levels, industrial society could last for centuries or millennia.

The National Academy of Sciences 1975 report *Mineral Resources and the Environment* (National Research Council 1975) carried the most pessimistic warning of all: "Man faces the prospect of a series of shocks of varying severity as shortages occur in one material after another, with the first real shortages perhaps only a matter of a few years away. . . ." Echoing King's (1969) projections, this report suggests that world oil supplies may be gone within fifty years and, for the first time ever, calls for a massive conservation program and an actual reduction in consumption:

> Because of the limits to natural resources as well as to means of alleviating these limits, it is recommended that the federal government proclaim and deliberately pursue a national policy of conservation of material, energy and environmental resources, informing the public and the private sectors fully about the needs and techniques for reducing energy consumption, the development of substitute materials, increasing the durability and maintainability of products, and reclamation and recycling.

According to these findings, the world's leading culture of consumption went from just scratching the surface of its own resources to the "bottom of the barrel" in a mere twenty years and was forced into increasing dependency on foreign resources.

THE ECONOMICS OF RESOURCE DEPLETION

Sooner or later, the market price will get high enough to choke off the demand entirely. At that moment production falls to zero . . . the last ton produced will also be the last ton in the ground. The resource will be exhausted at the instant it has priced itself out of the market. The Age of Oil or Zinc or Whatever It Is will have come to an end.

(SOLOW 1974:3)

The culture of consumption has clearly developed within the framework of an economic system that advances systematically from one resource to another, supported by theoretical assumptions that deny that "real" scarcity or limits to further growth can exist. We already have seen how industrialized centers in the global culture moved rapidly through several alternative energy sources as they became depleted or inadequate. This process occurs with different grades of ore and virtually every other depletable resource from whales to timber and represents the predictable operation of market principles in combination with continuing technological advances.

To orthodox economists, the simple solution to the obvious incompatibility between an ever-expanding economy and a finite world is to "redefine" *resource*. The whaling industry in the 1940s (Payne 1968), provides an example. Blue whales were being exterminated, then fin whales were declared a replacement resource, then Sei whales, and then sperm whales. When the whales are exhausted the whaling industry can convert itself into a krill-catching industry. Krill are an Antarctic shrimp eaten by whales. Indeed, by 1984, krill were labeled an "untapped bounty" and their commercial exploitation was already underway (Nicklin 1984).

A theoretical charter for such a process of self-perpetuating depletion and never-ending technical progress was clearly spelled out by economists Harold Barnett and Chandler Morse in their influential study *Scarcity and Growth: The Economics of Resource Availability*, published in 1963 for the Resources for the Future Corporation. The primary objective of this study was to disprove the notion of classical economists such as Thomas R. Malthus (1766–1834), David Ricardo (1772–1823), and John Stuart Mill (1773–1836) that resource scarcity would ultimately halt economic growth, leading to a stationary economy. Such an outcome, according to Barnett and Morse, would only be possible in a world without technological progress, and is therefore quite unrealistic. What Barnett and Morse were saying, of course, was that progress will end when progress ends, but they could not conceive of such a contingency: "The notion of an absolute limit to natural resource availability is untenable when the definition of resources changes drastically and unpredictably over time" (Barnett & Morse 1963:7).

In other words, today trees and whales, tomorrow plastic and granite. According to these enthusiastic consumption economists, depletion of resources will make way for economic alternatives of equal or even superior qualities and at reduced cost. Using language that contemporary eco-feminists would eagerly deconstruct, Barnett and Morse argued that industrial technology was virtually "turning the tables on nature, making her subservient to man." Whatever resource scarcity may exist is always relative, never absolute, and substitution always solves it. Resource limits cannot be defined in economic terms, so their argument went, and therefore must not exist. Attempting to conserve resources in the present might actually reduce the "heritage" of future generations because it could preclude future technological advances. Economist Julian Simon (1981) continued this anti-conservation argument, urging that the market price of resources should be the sole measure of their status. He maintained that trends in prices suggested that "... future generations will be faced by no greater economic scarcity than we are, but instead will have just as large or larger supplies of resources to tap, despite our present use of them" (Simon 1981:149).

SUSTAINABLE DEVELOPMENT FOR THE COMMON GOOD

Barnett and Morse and Simon represent the super-optimistic economic view that sustains the culture of consumption. The process of relative scarcity and substitution they describe typifies the operation of the consumption economy thus far, but there is no solid evidence that it will be able to continue to grow in this way indefinitely into the future, or that it would even be desirable for it to do so. Less orthodox economic theorists Herman E. Daly and John B. Cobb (1989) argue that a weakness of such perpetual growth economic models is that they externalize, and thus disregard, the physical/biological realities that real human communities depend upon. They note that money is an abstract symbol and suggest that it is "money fetishism" to believe that "if money balances can grow forever at compound interest, then so can real GNP, and so can pigs and cars . . ." (1989:37). The assumptions of Barnett and Morse were based largely on trends in the mining industry between 1870 and 1957 and ignored clear cases of increased costs and diminishing returns. By 1987, as discussed in Chapter 2, the mounting evidence of poverty, environmental deterioration, and resource depletion had become so undeniable at the global level that the UN-sponsored Brundtland Commission called for redirecting global economic goals toward sustainability. Unfortunately, some policy makers still seemed to deny the reality of limits to growth. For example, the 1993 study *World Without End* (Pearce & Warford 1993), commissioned by the World Bank, argued that simply correcting "economic distortions" would make growth sustainable. It must be stressed that while development may indeed become sustainable, growth, by definition, cannot be sustained indefinitely.

The real problem in replacing the consumption culture is how best to conceptualize genuinely sustainable development, because sustainability will require a major change in the global economic order. Herman E. Daly and John B. Cobb (1989) point the way in their book *For the Common Good: Redirecting the Economy toward Community, the Environment, and a Sustainable Future*. Development for Daly and Cobb (1991:70–71) refers to an increase in *Hicksonian Income* (HI), as defined by Nobel-prize-winning British economist Sir John R. Hicks (1904–1981). Hicksonian Income is the amount that can be consumed over a given period without impoverishment, and is calculated as GNP – Production Costs – Depletion of Natural Capital. HI is "a practical guide to avoid impoverishment by overconsumption" (Daly & Cobb 1989:84). An increase in HI would be sustainable by definition, and would not require the continuous quantitative economic expansion implied in the usual meaning of economic growth. For example, development could be achieved by simply reducing the costs of pollution control, or by improving conservation of resources. This HI concept of development recognizes that GNP by itself is a poor measure of the economic welfare of households and communities. In addition, this concept forces planners to take into account ecological carrying capacity. The HI approach also highlights the problem of global trading systems permitting one region of the world to draw down the natural capital of another region, thereby extending what would otherwise be unsustainable consumption at someone else's expense.

Embracing sustainable development also means rejecting orthodox economic models that assume an insatiable individual human desire for commodities as the primary human motivation. Daly and Cobb (1989:87) note that aggressive advertising would be unnecessary if human acquisitiveness were truly insatiable and always satisfied within the marketplace. They point out that relative well-being within a society may be more important than absolute levels of economic wealth. Arguing in favor of local self-reliance, they cite Thomas M. Power (1988), who suggests that the real economic base of a community includes, in addition to commodities:

> . . . all those things that make it an attractive place to live, work, or to do business. This means the economic base includes the quality of the natural environment, the richness of the local culture, the security and stability of the community, the quality of the public services and the public works infrastructure, and the quality of the workforce. None of these things are produced by the commercial economy or produced for export.
>
> (POWER 1988:127)

Shifting the focus of economic activity away from perpetually acquisitive individuals to the long-term needs of communities and households for meaningful employment, security of access to resources, and the noncommercial

things that make life worthwhile certainly does not mean that market systems must be abandoned. They simply need to be reshaped. The following
case studies are offered as further examples of the cost of a business as usual
culture of consumption.

THE CONSUMPTION CULTURE'S
ENVIRONMENTAL COST: WESTERN COAL

Any culture that continues to accelerate consumption in a fixed environment
will eventually be forced into making trade-offs between environmental
quality and a continuation of its consumption pattern. By 1992 it was obvious that the fossil fuel base of America's consumption culture was seriously
threatened—50 percent of its petroleum resources were being imported. By
the early 1970s, when petroleum imports stood at approximately 25 percent,
and it was recognized that nuclear energy would be more costly and haz-
ardous than supposed, the government readied a plan to strip the coal
reserves of the Western states. The objective was to meet the projected needs
of the country for ever-expanding energy consumption. In reality, actual
energy consumption did not rise as rapidly as projected, but it nevertheless
did continue to increase. Under the new federal coal-leasing program, vast
areas of the West, which had remained in almost pristine condition after supporting Native American cultures for perhaps 20,000 years, were slated to be
strip mined on a massive scale to perpetuate the culture of consumption for
a few more decades.

The 1974 Draft Environmental Impact Statement (U.S. Department of
the Interior) dealing with the coal-leasing program and written by the
Bureau of Land Management made the rationale for the stripping clear and
concisely summarized the costs. The entire procedure is a remarkable example of the extremes to which overconsumption can drive a culture. The fundamental assumption underlying the proposed stripping program was simply
that economic growth could not be sustained without it: "We assume the first
principal demand pressure for coal development will be from the physical
and economic inability of the United States to obtain sufficient oil supplies
to meet the demand generated by normal growth rates of the national economy" (Part 1:8).

"Normal growth rates" meant that by the year 2000 the population was
expected to have increased by less than 50 percent, but total energy consumption would double (see Figure 3.3). If we were having difficulties meeting our energy requirements in 1974, it should be no surprise that if total
consumption more than doubled by the year 2000, it would be at an enormous cost.

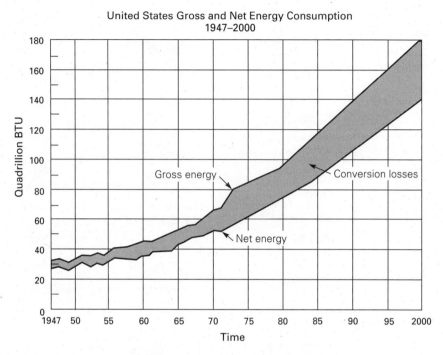

FIGURE 3.3   UNITED STATES
ENERGY CONSUMPTION

Gross energy=total amount of energy produced for the economy. Net
energy does not include loss caused by converting the primary source
to the secondary form, as for example in oil refining. (United States
Department of the Interior, Bureau of Land Management, *Draft
Environmental Impact Statement: Proposed Federal Coal Leasing Program*
(Washington, D.C.: U.S. Government Printing Office, 1974), 1: pt. 1: 26.

   Strip mining coal involves removing all the overlying surface material,
placing it to one side, and extracting the coal. Federal regulations require
"rehabilitation" of the site, but this term must be broadly interpreted. The
impact statement carefully understated the immediate effects of surface
mines in the following terms: "The operation completely eliminates existing
vegetation, disrupts soil structure, alters current land uses, and to some
extent changes the general topography of the area" (U.S. Department of the
Interior, BLM 1974, pt. 3:33).
   The report made it clear that surface drainage patterns may be disrupted; water sources might be eliminated; streams may be silted in and contaminated with toxic materials; big game wintering grounds and migration
routes and wildlife habitat in general would be destroyed; archaeological sites

would be destroyed; geological features and scenic resources would be destroyed or "disrupted;" and miles of impassable "high walls" might be left. Where underground mining takes place, surface collapses might occur. Contamination by radioactive fly ash would occur in the vicinity of the coal-fired electric plants. Local communities would be disrupted by a temporary influx of outsiders. A variety of other detrimental impacts can be predicted. In summary, the "grand scale of the operation impacts significantly on the environment."

In 1978 President Carter confirmed in a speech to Congress that a major expansion in American coal production would indeed be pursued as a way of coping with the "energy crisis" and the country's increasing dependence on foreign oil. He asked for an increase in coal production by more than two-thirds by 1985. The bulk of the targeted coal reserves in the West were, of course, on Native American lands, and as the new energy development programs were implemented, there was widespread protest by impacted Native American communities angered over the potential destruction of their grazing land, the pollution, and the loss of critical irrigation water (Anthropology Resource Center 1978).

"Restoration" of stripped areas was expected to require from twenty to thirty years, but the impact statement was concerned only with the period before 1985. "More lengthy projections" were considered "impractical." The statement glibly notes, however, that "man cannot immediately restore natural biotic communities." Experience with strip mining in Appalachia indicates that the worst erosion and pollution problems may occur up to twenty-five years after mining; in some cases, spoil piles were still eroding sixty-five years after the coal was extracted. Some researchers estimate that 800 to 3,000 years may be needed before toxic wastes will leach away (Spaulding & Ogden 1968). We know for certain that the leased areas will never be the same again, but the total cost is incalculable. What is most important for the culture of consumption is that the coal will be destroyed as well. It will again be time to look for another energy source to carry us to the next crisis.

CONSUMPTION CULTURE VERSUS TRIBAL CULTURE: BOUGAINVILLE COPPER

Overconsumption by the industrial nations not only destroys the physical environment, but it has also been the primary cause of the almost total destruction of tribal cultures over the past 200 years. Throughout the world, tribal cultures and their environments have been devastated as the resources they controlled have become necessary components of industrial growth. This subject has been dealt with at length elsewhere (Bodley 1988, 1990); but here a single example will serve to illustrate how the consumption culture's need for a critical mineral resource can totally overwhelm small-scale cultures thousands of miles away.

Copper was used in ancient Mesopotamia more than 7,000 years ago, and it continues to be a primary industrial raw material. In the early 1970s the industrialized nations were consuming it in such enormous quantities that the world's known supplies of copper ore would have been exhausted within twenty to fifty years (Meadows et al. 1972, Table 4). Nearly 60 percent of the world's annual copper production at that time was being consumed by three of the most highly industrialized nations—the United States, Japan, and the Soviet Union. By itself, the United States consumed 33 percent of the world's total production—substantially more than it was producing. In 1968 Americans were consuming the equivalent of 15 pounds of copper per person per year, much of it in the form of copper electrical wiring. Even though copper ore was becoming more difficult to find and the quality of the ore was steadily decreasing and production costs were steadily rising, there was little effort to limit consumption (Lovering 1968). Instead, high-grade copper ore was being exploited for the short-run benefit of the richest industrial nations—wherever in the world it could be found and regardless of the impact on local populations and their environments. Copper will, of course, never be totally exhausted, because, as with most minerals, a tiny percentage of copper is present throughout the earth's crust. The problem is the cost of extracting it. Ore grade is critical. A ton of copper can be produced by processing just 3 tons of rich ore, but poor grade ore would require processing 200 or more tons to produce 1 ton of copper and the process would burn up vast quantities of fossil fuels and leave mountains of spoil (Meadows, Meadows, and Randers 1992:84–85).

In 1963 the Australian administration of what was then the Trust Territory of New Guinea gave an Australian mining corporation, Conzinc Riotinto Australia, Ltd., permission to prospect for minerals in the center of Bougainville Island in an area occupied by subsistence-farming tribal peoples. Major deposits of copper that proved to be among the richest in the world were discovered, and soon a project described as "perhaps one of the most ambitious mining ventures ever undertaken" (Mining Magazine 1971) was underway. When production began in 1972, some $400 million had been invested, and a company-owned town of 3,000 people had been established at the mine site, which was connected by a pipeline and a sixteen-mile highway to a specially constructed public port town for 8,000 people built on the coast.

The environment posed seemingly insurmountable problems for the engineers because of the island's rugged topography, loose soil, and heavy rainfall. Constant slumping made road building in the area "a major engineering achievement" requiring constant relocation and the excavation of some 13 million cubic yards of material. When conventional underground mining techniques proved economically unfeasible, the company burned off the tropical forest cover and resorted to open-pit stripping techniques on an immense scale. The problem of disposing of the enormous quantity of tailings had not been solved when production was begun, and there was no discussion of the environmental impact of the project or possible plans for restoration of the region.

Whereas the physical environment posed a serious enough problem for the successful development of the mine, the company encountered "social barriers" that were even more difficult to overcome. From the time prospecting began, there were serious difficulties in securing the approval and goodwill of the indigenous people. As one report euphemistically explained, "The company encountered many difficulties in establishing its presence satisfactorily" (Ryan 1972). In the first place, under the existing tribal system of land tenure, no one had the right to transfer land to outsiders, and many people were very reluctant to accept any form of compensation or rent for the use of their land because they rightly feared they might thereby lose it completely (Dakeyne 1967). Not surprisingly, the company had a difficult time explaining to the indigenous people why it was necessary for them to move aside so that their homesites and gardens could be totally destroyed. In compensation, the Australian administration negotiated an agreement with the company in which the local people were to receive a rent of $2 an acre for their land, which they were to provide to meet the "reasonable needs" of the company. In exchange for their traditional homes, which were destroyed, the people were to receive "durable" buildings. Royalties would accrue to the administration to be used for the further "progress" of all the people in the territory, and various other inducements were offered to secure their cooperation, including employment opportunities, provision for resettlement, and opportunities to buy shares in the company.

The company reportedly (Ryan 1972) attempted to minimize the "inevitable" disturbances to the local people and, apparently making good use of applied anthropology, brought "experience, sound personnel and community management and enlightened policies" to bear on the problem of satisfactorily establishing its presence. Plans called for the integration of the people into the company's operation, and they were to feel that they would have some choice: "Policy seeks social integration which gives a local person some option on how fast he wants to go along this course." It is not clear what option was open to those who chose not to approve the "integration" course, but there certainly seemed no way for the people to resist the $400-million operation effectively. This lack of real choice was apparent when, during the company's negotiations for tribal land, the company refused to halt construction because it considered the expense involved in any work stoppage unacceptable. The people merely had to make the best of an unfortunate situation.

United Nations visiting missions to the area in 1968 and 1971 (United Nations, Trusteeship Council) found many local people disturbed over their treatment by the company and reported that violent disputes had occurred. However, the district police and the Australian administration sided with the company and violent resistance did not seem to be a viable option. The UN mission acknowledged that "mistakes" had been made, but felt that the islanders were being presented with a unique opportunity to raise their living standards. From the company's view, the whole problem was due to the natives' strong emotional ties to their land, and the natives' misunderstanding and "difficulty in comprehending the project" due to their having been "quite sheltered from contact with a western-type industrial society." The local people realized perfectly well what was happening to them, but they had few alternatives. Anthropologist Douglas Oliver summarized the native viewpoint in 1973:

> Most of them however appear to have become resigned more or less disconsolately to what they regard as another example of the white men's cupidity, deceit and irresistible power.

> (OLIVER 1973:162)

Bougainville Island was incorporated into Papua New Guinea when it became an independent country in 1975, and the Bougainville copper mines soon became one of the mainstays of the new economy, providing some 17 percent of the government's income and 40 percent of the country's exports. A separatist native rebel movement on Bougainville sought independence from Papua New Guinea and forced the mines to close in 1989.

Perhaps the most critical anthropological question is: What cultural forces drive the present consumption patterns of the consumption culture? We can say that overconsumption is not an innate human trait; it is culturally determined. It is also clear that high rates of consumption, or a lack of cultural limits on consumption, relate to social stratification within a culture; but there were many highly stratified, large-scale, ancient civilizations that set limits to consumption. In those cases wealth was concentrated primarily in support of the political system. Perpetual wealth accumulation and increasing consumption are intrinsic to a global-scale culture that concentrates the greatest power in commercial organizations. First and foremost, this system disproportionately serves the personal interests of the global elite who control the great multinational corporations and financial institutions. This is not a mysterious, decentralized, amorphous system. Control functions and the distribution of costs and benefits can be identified. Because food is such a key human need, the following two chapters will further explore the problem of overconsumption, the distribution of costs and benefits, and control functions in the global system by focusing on food systems in small- and global-scale cultures.

World Hunger and the Evolution of Food Systems

[The] power of obtaining an additional quantity of food from the earth by proper management and in a certain time has the most remote relation imaginable to the power of keeping pace with an unrestricted increase of population.

THOMAS R. MALTHUS,
An Essay on the Principle of Population

As long as food is something bought and sold in a society with great income differences, the degree of hunger tells us nothing about the density of the population.

FRANCES MOORE LAPPÉ AND JOSEPH COLLINS,
Food First: Beyond the Myth of Scarcity

FOOD SYSTEMS ARE CULTURAL mechanisms for meeting basic human nutritional needs. Every food system must confront two general problems if it is to continue to perform satisfactorily: (1) it must avoid long-term depletion of the natural resource base; and (2) it must equitably distribute essential nutrients to people. The existence of widespread hunger in the modern world indicates that many food systems are not performing adequately, but concerned observers have not always agreed on either the causes or the best treatment of the problem. Since the Paleolithic, production techniques have steadily intensified as human populations have increased. Yet it also seems clear, as British economist Thomas R. Malthus observed, that population always has the potential of increasing more rapidly than production. It also seems likely that chronic hunger is rooted in the structural aspects of society, particularly inequalities of wealth and power, in cultures that make food a commercial commodity.

THE MALTHUSIAN DILEMMA

The power of the earth to produce subsistence is certainly not unlimited, but it is strictly speaking indefinite; that is, its limits are not defined, and the time will probably never arrive when we shall be able to say that no further labour or ingenuity of man could make further additions to it. But the power of obtaining an additional quantity of food from the earth by proper management and in a certain time has the most remote relation imaginable to the power of keeping pace with an unrestricted increase of population.

(MALTHUS 1895:110)

Malthus was certainly the most influential early writer to raise the fundamental question of the relationship between population growth and food production. Writing in 1798, he argued that, if unchecked, human population has the natural capacity to expand at a geometrical, or exponential, rate, while over the long run, food production could only be expected to increase at an arithmetical, or linear, rate. The capacity for population growth is largely an empirical question and Malthus had data to support the view that a doubling every 25 years was possible. Reliable data on food production through time were unfortunately not available, but Malthus merely assumed that there were in fact ultimate limits and that whatever those limits were, food production could not long be expected to keep pace with a doubling population. He felt that as population began to press on the subsistence base "misery," in the form of poverty, would tend to reduce population growth, while greater efforts would be made to increase production through opening new land and improving agricultural methods until eventually a balance would be restored. Malthus was convinced that these principles were self-evident laws of nature.

In many respects cultural evolution has been based on efforts to avoid hunger by maintaining a secure subsistence base while minimizing the pain of regulating population. Diminishing returns are experienced in the intensification of food production systems. This is the Malthusian dilemma, and in a general sense Malthus was quite right. Small-scale cultures can often be reasonably viewed in these terms; but in a global-scale culture dominated by commercial interests and characterized by great inequality it would be a mistake to base assistance policies on the assumption that Malthusian limits are being exceeded. Unfortuately, many of the international assistance programs developed in the second half of the twentieth century assumed that world hunger was caused solely by overpopulation and inadequate production. Hungry people were assumed to be ignorant and technologically backward. It now seems obvious that hunger is also caused by poverty and landlessness, which in turn can encourage population growth. Hunger can be reduced by changes in social and economic policies to better provide people with the resources to feed themselves. Hunger is not a characteristic of small-scale cultures because they made the equitable satisfaction of the most basic human needs their primary objective.

To illustrate the operation of his "laws," Malthus projected population and food production trends for Britain and the world and correctly showed how quickly an exponentially growing population would surpass a linearly expanding food production system. Many of his critics misunderstood him on this point. He did not make specific predictions for future demographic patterns, but merely tried to show how unchecked population growth would compare with what he felt were optimistic projections for increases in food production assuming the operation of diminishing returns. Malthus certainly did not anticipate the enormous population expansion that has in fact occurred, yet this development has actually mirrored very closely the models of unregulated growth that he constructed. Figures 4.1 and 4.2 graph the population and food production curves for the world and for Britain that Malthus projected on the basis of his theoretical maximum population growth (doubling every 25 years) and simple linear growth in food production. His starting point of 1 billion people for the world is precisely the world estimate for 1800–1850 presently accepted by many demographers; however, at that time the world population was doubling only every 172 years. By 1950 the doubling time had dropped to just over 80 years and population growth began to rise dramatically. The *Global 2000* (Barney 1980, vol. 2:231) projection of an average doubling time of approximately 39 years from 1975 to the year 2000 (based on an average annual rate of 1.8 percent) appears to have been fairly accurate, at least to 1991, and approaches Malthus's "unrestricted" rate of population increase. By 1991 the actual rate of global population increase was actually 1.7 percent, down somewhat from a 1991 peak of 2.1 percent (Meadows, Meadows, and Randers 1992:23–24).

Thanks to dramatic technological advances, great expenditures of fossil fuel energy, and expansion into marginal agricultural lands, it appears that from 1950 to 1984, global food production stayed ahead of the unprecedented expansion of population. Since then food production seems to be faltering as both absolute and per capita yields level off, or even decline (Brown 1994). This does not mean that absolute global food production limits are being reached because there is still enormous elasticity in subsistence choices and food allocation systems. Nevertheless, as will be explored below, hunger has become a serious global problem, making it appear that human "misery" could act as a "natural" check on population growth just as Malthus predicted. In a general sense the statistics on hunger suggest that the world is now experiencing a "Malthusian crisis," but it must be emphasized that it is largely a cultural, not a natural, problem, because many cultural choices remain that would not violate the physical limits to the expansion of subsis-

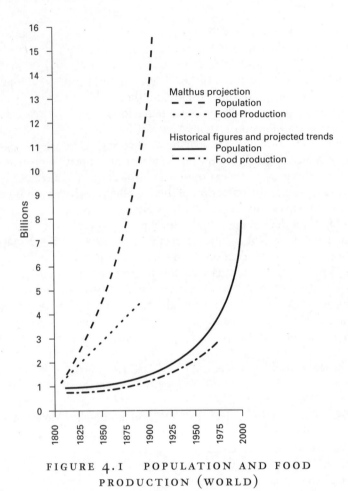

FIGURE 4.1   POPULATION AND FOOD
PRODUCTION (WORLD)

The gap between world population and food production is based on the
estimate of 50 million hungry made by the editors of *Time* (Nov. 11, 1974,
"The World Food Crisis," 66–80) and data from Malthus, 1895.

tence. Social inequality within and between nations and the specific ways in
which the global food system is commercially organized can significantly
accelerate the appearance of Malthusian symptoms.

Britain has followed the predicted Malthusian pattern quite closely.
However, viewing the trend only in these terms masks the enormous internal inequality and poverty of the country, and seems to justify the colonialist
expansion that helped maintain the system. Since 1798 the apparent gap
between domestic food production and population growth has widened very
much as might be expected given basic Malthusian assumptions, although

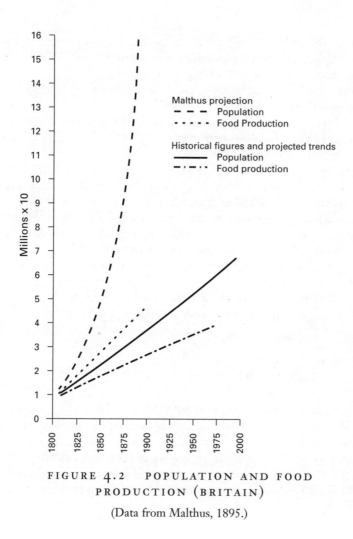

FIGURE 4.2   POPULATION AND FOOD
PRODUCTION (BRITAIN)

(Data from Malthus, 1895.)

both have grown much slower than Malthus predicted. In 1970 Britain was
only producing about two-thirds of its basic requirements in grain and meat,
and made up the deficiency through imports (Cooke 1970). This gap was
about what Malthus expected after 50 years of exponential population
growth in Britain. He suggested that food production in England might keep
pace with the first doubling of population during the first 25 years by opening up more land and offering "great encouragements" to agriculture, but he
was certain that domestic production would be unable to cope with the second doubling. The second doubling of population actually occurred shortly
after 1900, some 50 years later than in the Malthusian model, but food

production still did not keep up with it. In fact, while total acreage has varied only slightly through time, British wheat production per acre required 150 years to achieve its first doubling.

Significant advances beyond the first doubling were only possible through enormous applications of chemical fertilizers and the use of new high-yield varieties. Per-acre wheat production actually doubled again between 1948 and 1980, but both per acre yields and the area of cropland dropped between 1984 and 1988, and total production declined a surprising 21.5 percent in the United Kingdom as a whole (Great Britain 1982:253, Great Britain, Ministry of Agriculture 1990). Fortunately, the population of Britain was nearly stabilized at approximately 55 million by 1968, although it could reach 58 million by the end of the century. Even with the increases in domestic food production up to 1980, Britain produced only 60 percent of its total food supplies at that time according to official estimates (Great Britain 1982:253). If Britain were to support the 100 million people that technological optimists foresaw as a realistic possibility in the late 1960s (Cooke 1970), this could only be accomplished under vastly different cultural conditions, and with an even larger reliance on food imports.

THE EVOLUTION OF FOOD SYSTEMS

In a sense, the Malthusian dilemma—the need to balance the power of population with the power of food production—is the most basic adaptive problem that any culture must successfully solve if it is long to survive. Anthropologists have devoted a large share of their research effort to examining subsistence systems in various cultures, and archaeologists have focused much of their research on the evolution of food-producing systems. The major findings in both fields have contributed to a better understanding of today's food systems.

Much of the early theoretical literature on the evolution of food systems was cluttered by a consistent tendency to view each change in subsistence as a hard-won major improvement that was only achieved through some brilliant invention. Furthermore, "advances" in food production have traditionally been considered prerequisites for increases in population and other forms of evolutionary progress. These views apparently reflect the popular tendency to view all problems as simple technological issues and to underrate the intelligence of peoples in small-scale cultures. More recent approaches to food systems have been more balanced. At least three different interpretations of the causal factors underlying changes in subsistence technologies have been proposed.

The first approach, the *Population Pressure Model*, argues that increases in population mean that more food must be produced per unit of space (see, for example, Boserup 1965). This model reverses the earlier view that new inventions allowed population to increase. The issue involves a number of complex arguments and will be examined more fully in later sections. A second approach, the *Optimization Model,* assumes that people are striving for the most energy-efficient production techniques that will satisfy basic nutritional needs (see Winterhalder & Smith 1981, Johnson & Behrens 1982). This interpretation meshes well with the Population Pressure Model and allows one to predict what new techniques might be adopted if efficiency declines as population increases. However, efficiency analyses are usually based on average production rates and might not adequately consider long-term fluctuation in resource availability or environmental variables. Finally, the *Risk Minimizing, Subsistence Security Model* (Gould 1981, Hayden 1981a) argues that people are always most concerned with the long-run security of subsistence. This argument is not a revival of the earlier view that tribal peoples are always on the brink of starvation; instead it calls attention to the diverse measures these peoples have applied to maintain long-term subsistence reliability. Certainly all these factors—population stress, energy efficiency, and overall security—have in varying degrees shaped the food systems of tribal societies for tens of thousands of years. Large-scale cultures, with their built-in incentives to increase food production to support political elites and non-food producing specialists, along with the commercially driven economic structures of the global system, have distorted and displaced these adaptive processes such that today famine and malnutrition are commonplace and food systems are very fragile.

Anthropologist Brian Hayden (1981a) has presented an overview of subsistence strategies from the first appearance of hominids to the beginnings of farming following the Subsistence Security approach. Throughout, it appears that people have consistently sought to maintain maximum subsistence security and stability at the lowest possible cost in subsistence effort or population regulation. This involves difficult decisions and people probably leaned toward security in spite of the cost. A successfully balanced food system can be disturbed by either natural decline in the resource base (caused perhaps by climatic changes) or by a relative increase in the human population. Regulating population involves personal and psychological as well as social costs, as we will discuss later, but it certainly contributes to subsistence security. Increased subsistence effort and regional exchange backup networks also mean greater security.

According to Hayden (1981a), during the Lower Paleolithic early hominids were probably only able to scavenge and opportunistically capture a few species of small animals. As both organizational and physical abilities increased during the Middle Paleolithic, archaic *Homo sapiens* and Neanderthal subsistence diversified to include larger herbivores. Because a wider range of food sources became available, subsistence presumably became more reliable. During the Upper Paleolithic, beginning perhaps

50,000 years ago, physically modern humans developed highly effective hunting techniques and tools, including spear-throwers and finely made stone projectile points. During this period, virtually all game animals, including carnivores, were possible prey. This wide inventory of food resources would have helped minimize the stress caused by the large-scale climatic and vegetational fluctuations that occurred throughout the Pleistocene.

Further increases in subsistence reliability during the Mesolithic beginning about 14,000 years ago, involved significant use of small, rapidly reproducing, short-lived species (that biologists have called "r-species"), such as insects, fish, shellfish, and grasses, which were available in relative abundance but required special techniques to harvest and process efficiently. Thus, during this time grinding tools, nets, hooks, baskets, the bow and arrow, and hunting dogs, all came into common use in many parts of the world. These new production and processing methods certainly expanded the available range of food and would have provided a greater cushion against resource shortages, but they also involved greater effort and reduced energetic efficiency. Wild grass seeds, for example, may be very abundant seasonally, but they are not easy to harvest in quantity, and then they must be threshed, winnowed, milled, and cooked before they can be consumed. It seems unlikely that people would have included grass seeds in their diets unless they significantly increased subsistence security.

Even the most reliable local system of food production might still be vulnerable to unpredictable environmental factors such as periodic drought, so tribal peoples evolved mechanisms for maintaining permanent home territories while encouraging use of their resources by outsiders. Kinship ties and ritual practices provided opportunities for widespread sharing of resources, thereby providing an extra margin of security.

It appears that during the Mesolithic, people began to culturally manipulate their food resources by such methods as selective burning, as discussed earlier, but also by replanting roots, scattering seeds, and diverting water to increase wild plant productivity. Campbell (1965) discusses some of these practices by Australian aboriginal foragers. The productivity of game would be further increased by selectively killing certain age or sex categories, removing competing predators, holding and breeding captives, etc., as discussed by Hecker (1982). The result of these practices may ultimately have been "domestication" as it is usually conceived.

Ironically, although the drive to maintain subsistence security may have ultimately resulted in domestication, it is not totally clear that settled farm life was an obvious improvement over nomadic or seminomadic foraging. However, it may be that, for whatever reason, given greater population density farming necessarily becomes more reliable, even though reducing population density and returning to hunting and gathering would be more reliable yet. Foragers generally have a convenient cushion against food shortages because their subsistence depends on collecting food from a diverse range of species drawn from complex and stable natural or only partially modified ecosystems. Hunters can easily switch and choose among a variety of wild foods in the event that specific food sources fail, and if local conditions become very bad they may temporarily join kin in more favorable areas. Farmers, however, must rely on a few domestic species grown in artificial, highly simplified, and relatively unstable ecosystems. Such systems are quite vulnerable to many kinds of disruptions. When crop failures occur, famine is almost certain to follow if people do not have access to alternative resources, or if elites remove storable surpluses. Even regular seasonal scarcity, such as that preceding harvest, may be more exaggerated among farmers. For example, Richard Lee (1979:294–302) found no significant weight loss for the Kung Bushmen during the severest season of the year, whereas West African farmers showed losses of 6 percent of body weight before harvest.

Clear testimony to the greater overall security of foraging adaptations is also afforded by the cases on record of farming peoples joining neighboring foragers in order to weather out droughts (Woodburn 1968a, Colson 1979) and by the common tendency of foragers to reject farming until it is absolutely forced upon them. There are also cases of farmers who became foragers when the right conditions presented themselves. This is, of course, not to argue that occasional hungry times never occurred before farming. We know that people sometimes have starved in the harsh and often unpredictible conditions of the Arctic, yet it seems that hunger is less frequent and less devastating for foragers.

Not only is farming less secure than food collecting; it often involves longer, more monotonous work and a loss of independence and mobility. In some cases, it has even meant a switch to nutritionally inferior foods. Some anthropologists also point to demographic evidence of a decline in life expectancy for some populations after domestication, as well as a significant increase in women's domestic work loads (Harris & Ross 1987:41–43, 49–50). Given so many disadvantages, it seems remarkable that people ever bothered with domestication. Indeed, the explanation of domestication has been one of the longest running theoretical debates in anthropology.

It has become increasingly apparent that domestication was not a sudden or unique technological discovery. At best, it was a long process of transformation that occurred independently in perhaps five or more major areas of the world. Theories that stress the "invention" aspect of the process are quite misleading, because there is no reason to believe that peoples with the accumulated knowledge of many thousands of years of plant collecting would not realize that plants grew from seeds and cuttings. There are also many examples of food collectors who lived next to, or maintained trade contacts with, food producers for centuries and were well acquainted with the basics of farm life but apparently had no desire to emulate it. Australian Aborigines, for example, maintained contacts with New Guinean village people who raised pigs and planted gardens, but they did not themselves take up farming.

The most reasonable explanations of the domestication process are those that assume some kind of disequilibrium between population and food production in specific areas that demanded greater productivity per square mile. This issue is examined in the following cases.

The transition from foraging to farming in Mesoamerica was investigated archaeologically by Richard S. MacNeish, who conducted excavations in the Tehuacan Valley of central Mexico beginning in 1961. After several years of research on some 454 sites, MacNeish (1971) was able to construct a detailed cultural history of the period from 10,000 B.C. to A.D 1520. His work reveals a gradual shift in the organization of subsistence over the first 3,000 years, from small nomadic foraging bands that were heavily dependent on big game hunting to more careful scheduling of subsistence activities and a greater dependence on wild plant foods as gradual climatic changes brought environmental modifications that reduced the reliability of game supplies. It appears that these changes set in motion another gradual process of sedentarization, increased concentration of population, and increasing dependence on plant food. By approximately 4,000 B.C., 14 percent of subsistence was derived from cultivated plants. By about 1000 B.C., the role of domesticates had increased to 40 percent of subsistence.

A very similar picture of the origin of domestication has emerged for the levant region of the Middle East. In that area somewhat prior to 20,000 B.C. and up to about 10,000 B.C. a gradual process of subsistence intensification began. This process represented a shift away from reliance on large game to a "broad spectrum" of wild foods (Flannery 1969), including wild cereal grasses and small invertebrates. The subsistence shift occurred together with the adoption of sedentary village life. Kent Flannery argued that this change was a consequence of local population disequilibriums in game-poor areas caused in turn by population overflow from more game-rich zones. However, it is not clear what caused the initial overpopulation in the better hunting areas. Other investigators have argued that improved climatic conditions may have accelerated the process by encouraging semipermanent villagers to move toward domestication in order to keep an increasingly large community together year around (Moore 1983). Sedentary village life might have encouraged further population growth by disrupting prior checks on fertility and may have led to increasing pressure on marginal areas, where full domestication and farming eventually became a necessity. Incipient cultivation may have been underway as early as 9,000 B.C., just at the end of the last glacial period, while recognizable domesticated wheat and barley appear by 8,000 B.C. Apparently, seasonal foraging was not abandoned completely in the Middle East until after 6,000 B.C. By then individual villages may have contained several thousand people and were probably causing local environmental deterioration. Domestication was a complex process that required many intervening variables, such as peculiarities of climate and soil, together with suitable wild plants and animals.

The early dry-farming technique in the Middle East provided a relatively insecure subsistence system because total harvests of wheat might fluctu-
ate widely depending on weather conditions. Some of the domesticates even
displaced wild foods of higher protein and caloric content. The only clear
advantage of farming over hunting was that it supported a much denser population. There is also some evidence to suggest that although the total labor
input per unit of land was higher for early farming than for foraging, the
average yield for each unit of farm labor may have been higher. Thus an initial "victory" was scored in the struggle to keep food production in line with
an expanding population; but, as we shall see, the total costs were high. One
immediate, undoubtedly unexpected side effect of the change, at least in the
Middle East, was that cultivated grains quickly displaced the wild legumes
and grasses that were greatly valued as wild foods but could not compete successfully with the domesticates. These desirable wild plants were replaced by
relatively useless weeds such as ryegrass, and a major alteration of the native
flora ensued. Early cultivators almost literally burned their bridges behind
them and thus made a return to wild plant gathering very unlikely. It is, of
course, probable that the entire process took place so gradually over so many
generations that no one realized the full implications.

Some researchers have suggested that early moves toward domestication
in tropical areas occurred within a framework of careful ecosystem manipulation in which mixed communities of desirable food plants replaced less useful species in what became small domestic garden plots in the immediate
vicinity of households (Harris 1972, Lathrap 1977). Such a process of domestication might have occurred in a few specific zones of high biological productivity and seasonal variation in resource availability in connection with
sedentarization. Fixed plot horticulture was readily suited to sedentary living
because the rich organic wastes that tended to accumulate about house sites
provided an ideal environment and such gardens could be easily tended and
protected from competitors. As population density increased, it became necessary to increase productivity by opening larger gardens further from the
house, but these new gardens had to be periodically moved because of the
invasion of weeds, decline of soil fertility, and a variety of other reasons. The
result was a new form of cultivation, commonly called swidden, slash-and-
burn, or shifting cultivation, which proved to be a highly productive, very
adaptive subsistence strategy. In this system a garden site is cleared in the forest with the aid of fire or axes; the slashings are burned, providing a dressing
of fertile ashes and debris; and a garden is maintained for a year or two. A
new garden is then opened elsewhere, and the old plot is allowed to return
to forest. Such a pattern can greatly elevate the carrying capacity of a region
over what could be supported by foraging; and as long as the fallow periods
allow regrowth of the forest the system can be quite stable.

Two distinct forms of shifting cultivation apparently evolved separately,
each with quite different implications for ecological stability and cultural

evolution. In the more humid zones, swidden systems based on vegetative reproduction of root crops such as yams and manioc developed, whereas in the drier zones the emphasis was on seed crops such as corn, beans, rice, and millet.

Root-crop gardens are characterized by greater species diversity and the plants are usually arranged in a mixed pattern of overlapping layers resembling the structure of the unmodified tropical rain forest (Beckerman 1983). The result is the creation of a fairly stable ecosystem and a dense leafy canopy that maximizes incoming solar radiation for photosynthesis and minimizes potential erosion and leaching of nutrients from heavy rainfall. At the same time the crops utilized make only light demands on the soil. The primary disadvantage of this system is that the typical crops are usually poor sources of protein, meaning heavy reliance on wild fish and game.

Seed-crop gardens, in contrast, are not as diverse, do not form a protective canopy, and make greater demands on the soil. Thus they are more vulnerable to soil erosion, depletion of nutrients, fluctuation in weather, and invasion of weeds and insects. These problems are compensated for by the tendency of seed crops to be much richer in protein, thus opening a wider range of habitats because there is less need to depend on animal protein. As a result of some of these differences, cultures relying on seed-crop swidden cultivation tend to expand more readily into new environments and have even replaced more stable root-crop cultivators in several cases.

The transformation from food-*collecting* hunting and gathering or foraging systems to food-*producing* cultivating systems was without question an enormously significant event in the evolution of culture. If viewed as an expansion of the subsistence base in response to population pressure, it represents the failure of the cultural checks on population growth that must have been inherent features of most foragers. From the perspective of successful foragers, food production would not have been particularly attractive and it is therefore difficult to explain why it would ever have been adopted. It was a major evolutionary advance, however, in that it was related to increased population density, which also meant new forms of social organization and higher levels of integration. It must be emphasized that this assessment of the process is a reversal of the older interpretation, which held that food production was "discovered" and then population grew. It is also quite likely, as we shall see, that the state itself had a hand in promoting further population growth and technological "advance."

Food production has been widely acclaimed as a dramatic new source of energy and a labor-saving device that increased leisure and left people free to build culture. This does not seem to have been the case. Even with domesticated plants and animals, people still remained the basic source of mechanical energy until the dawn of the machine age. What actually happened in the domestication transformation was that more people worked longer, more regular hours than ever before to produce more food in a smaller area.

TABLE 4.1

Labor, Dependency Ratio, and Population Density in
Hunting and Shifting-Cultivation Cultures

SUBSISTENCE	CULTURE	HOURS OF LABOR PER WORKER ANNUALLY	WORKERS PER 100 PERSONS	POPULATION DENSITY PER KM^2
Hunting	Bushmen[a]	805	61	0.25
Cultivating	Tsembaga[b]	820	70	25.00

Sources: (a) Data from Lee 1969, (b) Rappaport 1971.

Because agricultural labor is seasonal, intensive, and monotonous, and because it requires a major reorganization of time budgets, any increases in productive efficiency may not have been dramatic enough to encourage foragers to adopt it as a means of increasing their leisure, except under certain ecological conditions. For example, some (Bailey et al. 1989) have argued that the scarcity of wild carbohydrates in tropical rain forests would make it difficult for foragers to exist without gardens or aquatic resources. Root-crop gardening is also highly productive, enabling the Machigenga, in the upper Amazon, to produce 90 percent of their diet by weight with an expenditure of half of their total subsistence effort (Johnson & Behrens 1982). The other 10 percent of their diet is derived from foraging, which provides most of their protein from fish and game. The contrast in costs and benefits between foraging and farming is shown in Table 4.1, which compares the San Bushman foragers and the Tsembaga shifting cultivators and pig-raisers of New Guinea. The Bushmen are hunter-gatherers in the harsh Kalahari desert of southern Africa, yet they work somewhat fewer hours per worker and are able to maintain a smaller percentage of their population in the work force than the cultivators. The Tsembaga, who work harder to maintain their gardens and domesticated animals in a more hospitable environment, are able to support a population 100 times denser than that of the San. The Tsembaga can also maintain larger local communities in year around settlements, while the San must move periodically throughout the year to maintain access to food and water.

THE DOMESTIC MODE OF FOOD PRODUCTION

In addition to the obvious technological differences, food production in small-scale cultures, whether foragers or farmers, differs in other very important respects from the food systems found in state or global cultures. Many of these critical differences were outlined in an important study by Marshall Sahlins, entitled *Stone Age Economics* (1972, especially Chapters 2 and 3). According to Sahlins, when food production is primarily for local, household, or village domestic consumption, as in all tribal cultures, actual production tends to be far below the maximum that might be sustained, given the potential limitations of technology, labor force, and resources. The result of the *underproduction* is that the danger of a tribal culture ever exceeding the carrying capacity of its environment at a given technological level is greatly reduced, as is the likelihood of environmental deterioration and famine. On the other hand, as political development occurs and the scale of culture increases food production must accelerate. And so does the possibility of over-shooting carrying capacities and the attendant famine and environmental deterioration.

Underproduction is an important concept, but it must be approached with caution. It does present an obvious contrast with the *overconsumption* of industrial cultures; but before the existence of underproduction can be established with certainty, some estimate of potential production or carrying capacity, like Hicksonian income in market economies, must be arrived at. The concept of carrying capacity must also be used cautiously, because it is at best an extremely crude device for discussing the relationships among population, technology, and resource base. In theory, all these are in relative balance in tribal societies over the long run because even slight imbalances over 1,000 years would almost certainly force a system change. However, it must be stressed that any balance is always relative and can be disrupted frequently and easily. The balance is also difficult to demonstrate empirically because, as Hayden (1975) points out, it might be impossible to realistically calculate the food production potential of any particular environment for a given tribal group, especially when cyclical fluctuations in resource availability are involved. Remember also that we are always dealing with a continuum of subtle changes in technology, any of which could amount to intensification and increases in subsistence output. Even resource deterioration caused by exceeding the carrying capacity for a given technology is not always easy to measure. It would certainly be ideal, as Hayden suggests, to measure increases in sickness and death related to resource shortages, but such data are rarely available for tribal societies. In spite of its theoretical limitations, the concept of carrying capacity will still be employed here as a rough impressionistic measure of the practical limits of particular subsistence systems.

Many estimates of potential carrying capacity are available for specific shifting cultivators. These are derived from simple calculations of the amount of land needed to feed an individual per year, the length of time a garden is cropped, and the length of the fallow period. For example, Robert Carneiro (1960) found that the Kuikuru in Brazil were at a population density of only 7 percent of the calories that could be produced by shifting cultivation in their immediate locality, although the real limiting factor was the more limited, but difficult to measure, availability of fish and game. Sahlins presents data from nine other traditional cultures practicing shifting cultivation in Africa, Asia, and New Guinea showing that actual population densities range from as low as 8 percent of the carrying capacity to an average of 50 percent. In only one culture in the sample did local areas appear to reach the full carrying capacity. Another study (Brown & Brookfield 1963) of twelve Chimbu subgroups in New Guinea found them ranging from 22 to 97 percent of maximum sustainable densities and averaging just 64 percent of capacity.

Precise figures on carrying capacity for hunter-foragers are difficult to calculate, but J. B. Birdsell (1971) has suggested that Australian Aborigines maintained themselves at an "optimum" carrying capacity that was 10 to 20 percent below "maximum" capacity. Other researchers have frequently commented that foragers seem generally not to be exploiting their food resources to the maximum potential. Similar observations have been made for tribal pastoralists. The problem here, of course, is that it is difficult for a field researcher at one point in time to estimate the extent of long-term fluctuation in the availability of resources. Cultures that do not store food must necessarily be restricted to the population that can be supported in the worst year.

Another approach to underproduction, which avoids the problem of carrying capacity, is simply to assess the labor potential of a given culture and evaluate how hard the population is working at food production (Sahlin 1972). There is actually very wide cross-cultural variation in the length of average working life span, the division of labor by gender, and seasonal labor. The outputs of individual households also vary within a given culture. For example, young adults may often be only marginally involved in food production and tribal cultures often retire adults far sooner than may be the case in large- or global-scale cultures. Young San Bushman males may be twenty-five years of age before they are actively involved in subsistence activities and older men may retire by age sixty. In tribal cultures generally labor tends to be irregular and intermittent. Particular tasks are easily and frequently postponed for what might seem to most trivial excuses—because of the weather, for a nap, for visiting, for feasting, or for no reason at all. Among farming peoples, and in some cases even among hunters, there can be seasonal slack periods with virtually no hunting or farming. There are also wide tolerances of individual variation in work load; some persons do far more than their "share" while others consistently loaf. Even the concept of "work" as opposed to "play" or "leisure" may not be an important distinction in all cultures. There seems little doubt that most tribal peoples could easily produce a "surplus" of food above their own immediate subsistence needs if they merely worked a little harder, put in a few more hours a week, or slightly reshuffled their labor force. The limitation on production, then, is not an inadequate technology or a scarcity of natural resources. It is the presence of a built-in cultural limit; or, phrased negatively, there is a cultural lack of incentive to raise production in tribal cultures in which production is essentially for domestic use.

It is a striking and well-verified fact that some households in tribal cultures at times do not actually produce enough to feed themselves and must depend on the overproduction of other households to provide their needs. This variation in household productivity may result from normal stages in the domestic cycles when households may be more vulnerable or from chance variation in dependency ratios. It may also be caused by random variation in success at hunting or farming, misfortune, or simply some households choosing not to work as hard as others.

Sahlins argues that what makes "Stone Age" or tribal economies unique in comparison with "more advanced" economies is that in tribal economies the basic production unit, and therefore the dominant institution, is the household. This creates a qualitatively very remarkable kind of economy, one whose operation can only be understood on its own terms. Most importantly, within this domestic mode of production lies a major key to the adaptive success of tribal subsistence systems.

The domestic mode of production is created by marriage and a minimal division of labor by gender, a simple technology that is available to all and in which each household can perform all the technological functions itself. Individual households in a tribal culture are not economically fully autonomous, but the critical point is that the objective of production is domestic use, the satisfaction of the most basic human needs such as nutrition. Food production goals are thus set by the individual food-consuming household. When the specific need—daily in the case of foragers, or annually in the case of garden planting—is met, then labor ceases. The system is not designed to produce a surplus above domestic needs. In a commercial market economy, production is for exchange, for cash, for profit. There is no culturally recognized limit to production, because the need for wealth is infinitely expandable. The distinctive features of food production in the global culture will be discussed in detail in Chapter 5, but here it may be noted that the contrasts between the domestic mode of production in a small-scale culture and the capitalist mode of production are so great that much of the economic behavior of tribal peoples in contacts with market-oriented outsiders has been considered quite irrational. What has been interpreted as laziness or ignorance on the part of tribals is actually the operation of a very unique and very adaptive system of food production.

Equilibrium mechanisms within small-scale cultures helping to maintain production at a low level relative to the maximum potential include the operation of "Chayanov's Rule." This basic labor principle was originally formulated by A. V. Chayanov (1966) in a 1925 study of Russian peasants who had limited access to the market. Chayanov noted that in larger households in which there were more workers each worker worked less than did the average worker in smaller households. Sahlins rephrases the rule as follows: "Intensity of labor in a system of domestic production for use varies inversely with the relative working capacity of the producing unit" (Sahlins 1972:91).

Thus the potentially most productive households automatically tend to slack off, whereas individuals in smaller households must work harder. In effect, household production norms are culturally set at average levels, not at the highest attainable. The maintenance of living standards by some households at a level significantly above that attainable by the majority would lead to social disorder in the absence of more elaborate forms of political control.

The general egalitarianness of tribal cultures is an obvious element in the success of tribal subsistence systems. In the first place, all households enjoy free access to the natural resources needed for their subsistence. Various redistributive mechanisms may be initiated when serious local imbalances result because of random fluctuations in demography or subsistence success. A further stabilizing factor is reciprocal pooling of food and redistribution along kinship networks, which assures a relatively uniform distribution of nutrients. As a result, everyone enjoys the same nutritional standard.

TECHNOLOGICAL ADVANCES IN FOOD PRODUCTION

If population densities are to rise, food production must be intensified either by increased labor or by technological improvements. How this might occur in a tribal culture is an interesting theoretical problem because, as we have seen, food production is relatively frozen by the shutoff factors inherent in the domestic mode of production, in the absence of either political or market incentives, and population growth is normally minimized by the operation of the equilibrium mechanisms outlined in Chapter 6. In effect, there is normally no Malthusian dilemma in tribal culture—the forces of population and food production are continuously kept in check. Thus we must reconsider the old question of whether technological advances in food production cause population growth, or whether population growth itself causes advances in food production. The most basic determining factors would appear to lie in the actual arrangement of the social system. Tribal social systems are, as we have shown, structured to restrain both population and food production. They are, by definition, no-growth systems. Growth of either population or food production, or both, may, however, be deliberately promoted and even institutionalized within more complex social systems.

Within small-scale cultures organized around the domestic mode of production there is a constant struggle to balance the demands of the society at large, which extracts food from individual households by means of kinship obligations, with the immediate self-interest of each isolated household. If growth of either population or food production is to occur, a social system must develop that will tap the "underdeveloped" resources and transform the domestic mode of production into something else. Political authority must overcome the natural tendency of individual households to set their own production goals and to maintain their economic autonomy over and against the interests of the larger society or against the self-interest of aspiring rulers. The political order must establish a public economy. "Big-man" leadership systems, segmentary lineage and clan systems, and hierarchical chiefdoms all represent different sociopolitical strategies for mobilizing productivity above the cutoff point normally operating in the domestic mode of production while still remaining within the limitations of a kin-based, nonstate social system.

Certain cultures seem to respond to the ever-present tendency of population to expand by increasing food production and at the same time developing more complex forms of social organization. These three variables—population growth, intensification of subsistence, and increasing social complexity—are so interrelated that it is not always reasonable to assign priority to any one of them, although a number of theorists place primary emphasis on population growth as the basic determinant. It can be assumed that technological improvements that demand greater intensification of labor will only come about in the presence of population pressure. Conversely, they may be facilitated by the prior existence of certain levels of sociopolitical organization. A complex irrigation system, for example, would probably not be initiated by a society that lacked effective supralocal forms of political control, although a full-time central authority might not be required. For their part, more complex forms of social organization may often become necessary as disputes over access to resources begin to arise under increasing population pressure.

Danish economist Ester Boserup (1965) argued that technological changes in "primitive" agriculture can all be viewed as responses to population pressure. Her approach is very similar to that used in recent attempts by anthropologists to explain the transition from hunting to farming. She assumes that the earliest, simplest farming techniques, such as shifting cultivation, were more productive per hour of labor than the more advanced systems but less productive per unit of land. People would automatically prefer such extensive methods; that is, these methods simply required less work to produce food than more intensive methods. There is indeed a clear relationship between the frequency of cropping in a given unit of land and the density of population. Denser populations require more intensive land use. Fallow periods may well be shortened as a direct response to increased population in local areas, and this shortening of fallow periods or more intense land use will initiate ecological changes that force the use of new technology. Under a typical swidden or "forest fallow" system, a simple digging stick is all that is required for planting in newly cleared, virtually weed-free forest. However, when the fallow cycle is shortened because of the need to increase food production in a limited area, then the increasing appearance of weeds makes hoes necessary. Continued shortening of fallow periods will lead to grasses that can only be cultivated effectively with plows.

From this viewpoint, advances in food production can be seen not as simply brilliant inventions that in turn cause population growth; rather, they were forced on people by prior population growth. It would make no sense at all for shifting cultivators with adequate forest resources to invent a plow, because it would simply not fit their mode of land use and would not be an advantage. It must not be forgotten, however, that intensification in food production will, of course, reinforce the need for further intensification by supporting and amplifying the prior deviation from population equilibrium. This "deviation amplification" is a basic process of population growth, and population growth and subsistence intensification clearly constitute a self-intensifying spiral.

As cultural evolution proceeds the basic trend is for food production to become more and more intensive and for more food to be produced in a smaller and smaller area. Kent V. Flannery (1969) estimated that 35 percent of modern Iran probably would have provided a favorable habitat for Mesopotamian hunting cultures that were able to support 0.1 person per square kilometer in the late Paleolithic period. Ten percent of Iran probably was suited for dry farming and could have supported one or two persons per square kilometer. Highly intensive irrigation agriculture might have been possible over only 1 percent of the total area of the country; but with it up to six or more persons per square kilometer could have been supported even in ancient Mesopotamia. This level of productivity implies both state organization and a totally different kind of food system.

STATE-LEVEL FOOD SYSTEMS

State-level food systems in large-scale chiefdoms and ancient civilizations contrast strongly with patterns characteristic of tribal cultures. Through political coercion states were able to extract food production from local villages and households in the form of taxes or tribute far above the levels that would be required for local needs. Ancient civilizations required permanent administrative bureaucracies, but they also had to support large labor forces on massive construction projects. Most of the grain that fed these non-food producing specialists was extracted from the peasantry or was produced on state-run farms by peasant labor. For example, in Ch'ing dynasty China under the Manchu rulers (1644–1911) some 40,000 people were part of the formal administrative bureaucracy in addition to the 700 people who belonged to the emperor's clan. Another 1.5 million scholar-bureaucrats were a privileged elite with significant degrees of local control (Stover & Stover 1976). Specific data on highly productive wet-rice cultivators in China prior to the Communist government (Harris 1971:203–17) show that 84 percent of their crop was an "exported surplus" beyond their immediate subsistence needs. It took 1,500 men working 10-hour days for 5 years to build the great Ziggurat of Ur III in ancient Mesopotamia (Wheatly 1971:258). In ancient China a vast conscript labor army built the 1,400-mile (2,250 kilometer) Great Wall during the Ch'in dynasty (approximately 215 B.C.). With increased demands of this magnitude, it is not surprising that states may often be much closer to the maximum carrying capacities of their environments than tribal cultures.

Other important cultural features of state-level food systems are allocation of access to productive resources such as land and water according to social class and status, and, as shown above, significant segments of the population often not being involved in food production at all. This arrangement makes it quite likely that nutrients will no longer be equally distributed in the society—some classes may indeed be relatively hungry while other classes are "overnourished." This combination of differential access to subsistence resources and inequitable distribution of nutrients by social class is, as we have seen, one of the basic correlates of hunger in the modern world. However, because ancient rulers derived their power from human labor it would have been counterproductive for them to allow large segments of the population to be malnourished. The rulers of the commercial empires of today's multinational corporations have no such constraints.

Thus, there are three aspects of the food problem that might be considered adverse side effects of evolutionary progress. On the one hand, the adoption of agriculture creates an ecologically less stable food system that is inherently more prone to famine-causing fluctuation. Secondly, as a deviation amplification, technological advances in food production tend to reinforce an accelerating spiral of population and further subsistence intensification that must inevitably place greater strains on the ecosystem and increase the likelihood of further environmental deterioration, and which results in an approach close to, if not beyond, the ultimate carrying capacity of the resource base. Finally, social stratification can create an imbalance in the availability of food to the population, especially when food becomes a commercial commodity.

It would appear from this analysis that many of the food problems the world is now experiencing are merely predictable cultural evolution processes and instrinsic features of large- and global-scale cultures. While some of these difficulties have been with us since the first appearance of agriculture some 10,000 years ago, they were clearly intensified and enlarged by the evolution of states and urban civilization some 5,000 years ago. The fact that they are still unsolved suggests that these may be quite intractable problems that may well only be overcome through a drastic transformation process. The food problem has clearly dramatically intensified over the past 200 years with the emergence of the culture of consumption and its unique food system.

FAMINE IN THE MODERN WORLD

[Despite] the enormous sums invested, the impressive technical progress we have made, and the extraordinary efforts by governments, by international bodies, and by scientific and technical communities—mankind has by and large failed in its supreme effort to feed adequately those billions of people *now* living on earth. Of these, at least one billion are undernourished, and the diets of an additional eight hundred million are deficient in one or several key nutrients.

(BORGSTROM 1967:XI)

Famine is not new. It has been, and continues to be, a chronic hazard of civilization. Famines of varying degrees and intensity were recorded in China at the rate of 1,828 over the 2,019 years up to 1911. Four million people may have died in China in 1920-1921. Three million died in the Indian famine of 1769–1770, 2 to 4 million in West Bengal in 1943. Russian famines from 1918 to 1934 may have claimed 5 to 10 million lives. Famines have ravaged Europe many times and even England counted more than 200 famines between A.D. 10 and A.D. 1846 (Ehrlich & Ehrlich 1972). Since Malthus outlined the dangers in 1798, Europe has moved to the brink of famine, and sometimes beyond, several times. By the middle of the nineteenth century a general food crisis was developing in Europe, but it was alleviated by emigration and food imports from the United States. The most notable problem during this period was the Irish "potato famine" of 1845–1846. The introduction of the potato to Ireland permitted rapid population growth up to some 8 million people by 1841; but a blight struck the monocrop and more than 1 million people died and another million emigrated. The Irish population has since stabilized at half its preblight level. A second European food crisis developed early in this century but famine was averted when vast acreages in Australia, Argentina, and Canada were taken from aboriginal hunting peoples and put into production for the world market.

In 1905 Harvard geologist Nathaniel S. Shaler warned that the world was very near the limits of food production; he doubted that a threefold population expansion could be supported. World population then stood at well under 2 billion. Forty years later the United Nations, declaring that much of the world suffered from malnutrition, launched a major "freedom from hunger" campaign. In 1965 George Borgstrom, a food scientist with twenty years of experience, declared that the world had already failed in its effort to feed itself, and that hunger—"hunger rampant"—was now the great issue of our age. In 1967 William and Paul Paddock, brothers with long experience in tropical agriculture and national food systems in the "developing" world, published a major book in which they predicted that by 1975 U. S. grain surpluses would no longer be able to make up for world food shortages and a period of disastrous famines would begin.

Recognizing the dangers, American President Lyndon B. Johnson declared that the world food problem was "one of the foremost challenges of mankind today;" and in 1966 he directed his Science Advisory Committee to investigate the problem and look for solutions (United States, President's Science Advisory Committee 1967). The committee brought together 115 experts on all aspects of the problem from universities, industry, and government agencies. They worked for a year, with subpanels devoted to such topics as food supply, population, nutritional needs, plant and animal productivity, soils and climate, marketing, processing, and distribution. Finally, in 1967 the committee issued a three-volume, 1,200-page report confirming all the dire predictions that had been made before. Their major conclusion was that ". . . the scale, severity, and duration of the world food problem are so great that a massive, long-range, innovative effort unprecedented in human history will be required to master it" (Vol. 1:11).

The report dealt with the basic problem of the food crisis in the immediate future, the twenty years from 1965 to 1985, on the mistaken assumption, or at least the hope, that effective family planning programs would be initiated immediately and would stabilize the population by 1985. The panelists felt that if the food problem was solved by 1985 it would be manageable well into the future. By 1975, barely halfway to the 1985 safety target, with little hope of stabilizing the population in the near future, it appeared that the predictions of "Famine—1975!" were being fulfilled. At the first Nations World Food Conference, held in Rome in 1974, and sponsored by the United Nations in an effort to deal with hunger as a global problem, experts reported that 460 million people were threatened with immediate famine and 10 million would probably die before the year was out. In 1974 biologist Paul Ehrlich (Ehrlich & Ehrlich 1974) stated flatly that it was already too late for population programs to prevent famine because the great famines were already underway. At the Rome food conference, one American agronomist was quoted as saying that unless something was done to provide better food security for the world, "we may be seeing the end of our civilization." By 1984 it was clear that the food problem was not going away; hunger was occurring throughout the world, although it was perhaps less dramatic than had been predicted.

MEASURING HUNGER

There are several ways to determine whether the world or any given region is meeting its poulation's nutritional needs. One obvious and seemingly simple method is to estimate per capita calorie and protein requirements and to compare these figures with estimates of the availability or the actual consumption of nutrients. In reality, this is a very difficult method to work with because it is not easy to establish a completely adequate basic nutritional standard for the world. In the first place, caloric requirements vary with age, sex, health status, body weight, quality of diet, physical activity, and climate. A world average might have little relevance in any particular area. Furthermore, low body weights in many countries, and their corresponding "adequate" levels of per capita caloric requirements, may be very misleading because these low weights may in turn be a result of nutritional deficiency in children that prevented the population from realizing its genetic growth potential. There may also be a large gap between calories available and calories consumed, because food may be lost in storage, shipping, and preparation, and a further gap between calories consumed and calories absorbed. It is well known that intestinal parasite infestations, common in tropical countries, can divert a significant proportion of the calories an infected individual consumes. Other difficulties involve distinguishing between whether specific applications of caloric requirements are concerned with minimum, average, or optimum allowances and how these are defined.

As interest in these issues began to emerge at an international level, the United Nations Food and Agriculture Organization (FAO 1963) conducted three major world food surveys covering the periods 1934–1938, 1948–1952, and 1957–1959 and more recently has prepared annual world food balance sheets. These data vary widely in quality and have serious limitations but they remain one of the most useful assessments of the world food situation and their conclusions merit careful consideration. The first survey, published in 1946, concluded that immediately before World War II two-thirds of the world had less than a desirable quantity of food available at the retail level. This portion of the world's population fell below a 2,750 daily per capita calorie availability level, then considered a reasonable minimum figure, based on the assumption that probably 10 percent of these calories would be lost before being actually consumed. The postwar survey found that even fewer calories were available per capita than previously; however, a slight adjustment in the calculated average caloric requirements made the gap between adequate and inadequate appear somewhat smaller. A serious decline in the proportion of animal protein in calorie-poor areas was also noted. According to the third survey, published in 1967, calorie availability was only slightly above prewar levels and much of the increase occurred in the already industrialized nations, leaving the rest of the world relatively further behind. The survey concluded that 10 to 15 percent of the world's population was undernourished in terms of caloric quantity and as much as half the population was qualitatively malnourished in terms of protein availability.

Considering these figures at the world level conceals where the real famine problems lie, of course, because nutrients are very inequitably distributed in the world at large and within individual countries. The third FAO food survey indicated that at least 20 percent of the population in poor countries was undernourished, and for 60 percent the diet was qualitatively inadequate. The fifth survey (FAO 1987:22) reported a small increase in the absolute number of undernourished people even though the percentage of hungry actually declined. However, the gap between the well-fed in rich countries and the underfed in poor countries increased:

> . . . the average inhabitant of the developed countries had nearly two-thirds more to eat in 1979–81 than the average inhabitant of the LDCs [Less Developed Countries]; and nearly half again as much to eat as the average inhabitant of the developing countries as a whole.

(FAO 1987:4 ITALICS IN ORIGINAL)

The extent to which a somewhat different interpretation of the caloric adequacy of the diet can yield a different picture of the world food situation is clear when the estimates by the U.S. Department of Agriculture, also published in 1963, are compared with the UN estimates for the same period. In this report Lester R. Brown estimated that nearly 80 percent of the underdeveloped world population, or 56 percent of the population of the entire world, was below acceptable caloric levels. Ninety-two percent of Asia was found to be deficient! Some writers scoff at such figures and argue that much lower average per capita requirements are really adequate. Others feel that these estimates may even be too low.

Whereas there may be honest dispute over the establishment of nutritional standards, there can be little dispute over certain other indicators of major world food problems. One particularly ominous change in the world food system occurred in the early 1950s, when the poor countries became net importers of grain (Brown 1963:76; Paddock & Paddock 1967:41–44). Many of these countries have become increasingly dependent on grain produced by the United States and Canada to make up periodic shortfalls or to supplement regular deficiencies. This dependency is a total reversal of the prior situation, in which these same countries were grain exporters. Furthermore, in the early 1970s the gap between imports and exports of cereals in the poor countries began to widen even more dramatically in spite of the productivity gains attributable to the green revolution (see Figure 4.3).

Perhaps the most directly meaningful indication of food shortages is the occurrence of deficiency diseases and deaths related to malnutrition. Whereas deaths due to actual starvation are rarely recorded, poor nutrition

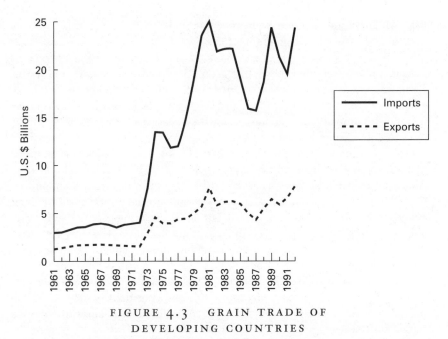

FIGURE 4.3   GRAIN TRADE OF
DEVELOPING COUNTRIES

(Food and Agriculture Organization of the United Nations 1993. *The State of Food and Agriculture 1993*. FAO Agriculture Series No. 26.)

undoubtedly causes dramatic increases in overall mortality rates. It is well known, for example, that the elevated infant mortality rates in much of the world are to a considerable extent due to protein-calorie deficiency. Numerous studies have shown that infant deaths due to common childhood diseases that seldom are fatal in rich countries can be sharply reduced by provision of adequate diets. The most severe and most common protein-calorie deficiency diseases are kwashiorkor and marasmus, which largely affect children and involve a dramatic wasting away of body tissue (Trowell 1954). Protein deficiency is also clearly linked to mental retardation and growth impairment in children (Montagu 1972). The extent of such health problems is impossible to estimate precisely because of inadequate surveys and varying interpretations of clinical symptoms. However, these conditions are clearly reflected in the fact that infant mortality rates in poor countries are often 10 to 20 times higher than the rates of many rich countries. Growth retardation related to malnutrition has been called "almost universal" in poor countries. The World Bank's (1994:214, Table 27) figures show that in twenty-three of the world's poorest countries, on the average, 31 percent of children under the age of five suffer from malnutrition. These countries, which include China, India, and Bangladesh, represent 52 percent of the world's population. Malnutrition rates range from a low of 10 percent in Zimbabwe to a high of 66 percent in Bangladesh.

Many of the symptoms of chronic food deficiency are probably so common in hungry areas that they have become accepted as "normal" conditions. Reduced physical activity and a general physiological slowdown are basic adaptations to starvation (Young and Scrimshaw 1971), but these symptoms may not be immediately obvious when they characterize entire populations or segments of populations.

Another indirect indication of food problems in specific areas is the price of food in relation to income levels, that is, the ability to purchase food. Abundant evidence shows clear relationships between poverty and malnutrition. Below certain income levels it may simply not be possible to obtain an adequate diet. In rural areas formerly self-sufficient farmers with presumably adequate diets have been forced to replace traditional food crops with cash crops that do not generate enough income to allow them to purchase sufficient food (Gross & Underwood 1971). Urban populations must rely entirely on cash to provide their food. The President's Science Advisory Committee report presented data for India showing that in 1961–1962, 20 percent of the population fell within income levels that allowed them to obtain on the average only about 80 percent of their caloric requirements and less than their needed protein. In 1958, in Maharashtra State, poor people at the lowest income levels were consuming only 58 percent of their caloric requirements and 64 percent of their protein needs, whereas those at the highest income levels received 131 percent and 148 percent, respectively. Significantly, estimates of malnutrition derived from income levels correspond quite closely to estimates based on total availability of nutrients in relation to total need, such as those proposed by the FAO Third World Food Survey.

The UN and governmental development agencies have consistently viewed hunger as a problem of technological backwardness and poverty, to be treated with relief operations, new technology, and increased economic growth. A vast institutional structure has developed to implement these solutions. Policies were fine-tuned and targets set by the UN's "Development Decades" initiated early in the 1960s. In order to monitor the food crisis and help individual nations design specific programs to increase their food productivity the UN established four separate bureaucracies, all headquartered in Rome: The Food and Agriculture Organization (FAO, 1945); The World Food Program (WFP, 1961); The World Food Council (WFC, 1974); and the International Fund for Agricultural Development (IFAD, 1977).

There has actually been some improvement in food production on a per capita basis at the global level (see Figure 4.4), but such aggregate figures have little relationship to hunger in local communities. The gap between rich and poor countries remains wide and the inequities within individual countries mean that hunger continues to be a chronic problem. Nevertheless

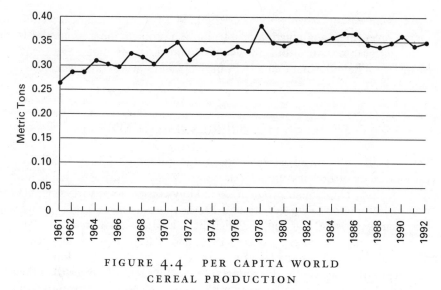

FIGURE 4.4   PER CAPITA WORLD
CEREAL PRODUCTION

(Food and Agriculture Organization of the United Nations 1993. *The State of Food and Agriculture 1993.* FAO Agriculture Series No. 26.)

global patterns do point to stresses in production systems in some cases. Figures published by the World Bank for 1980 showed that the available food supplies of forty-two countries would provide less than 100 percent of the caloric requirements of their populations (World Bank 1983:194–95). Furthermore, fifty-two countries were producing less per capita than they were in 1970 (World Bank 1983:158–159). What we are seeing might be somewhat less sudden and dramatic than some expected, but it is possible that sustainable limits for certain technologies are being reached and exceeded in some cases. For example, the trend in Africa is unmistakable. According to Brown and Wolf (1984:16), "Africa is slowly losing the capacity to feed itself." This is apparent in the increase in grain imports during the 1980s and early 1990s to eight times the levels in the 1960s through 1972 while per capita grain production has steadily declined since 1970 and serious environmental deterioration is occurring.

Development experts recognize that in some sense famines represent the failure of international development policies and also create problems for rich countries. At the World Bank sponsored Conference on Overcoming Global Hunger in 1993, Administrator of the U.S. Agency for International Development (USAID) J. Brian Atwood declared:

> Food is the most basic measure of empowerment, and the hunger and malnutrition of perhaps a quarter of the world's population threaten the developed world and our economies, our interests, and our moral stature.

It is important to remember that the food crisis is not simply a techno-logical problem or a population problem; it is a problem inherent in global-scale cultural organization, in which commercial exchange generates inequality. The following example from Bangladesh makes this clear.

NEEDLESS HUNGER IN BANGLADESH

Bangladesh, the former East Pakistan, is often presented as one of the most extreme cases of hopeless population pressure and Malthusian famine and malnutrition. The human problem is certainly conspicuous, with a popula-tion of 119 million and a density of 2,132 people per square mile. It might not seem surprising that millions died here in the great famine of 1943, 100,000 people died of starvation in 1974, and 131,000 died in the cyclone and floods in 1991. A nutrition survey conducted in 1975–1976 found that over half of the families in the country were eating fewer calories than they needed and suffered from protein deficiencies. Not surprisingly, life expectancy stood at just forty-seven years (Hartmann & Boyce 1982:9). By 1992, after decades of international development assistance, conditions had improved somewhat but still remained grim. According to the World Bank's 1994 estimates, Bangladesh had become the tenth poorest country in the world with a per capita GNP of $144. Life expectancy had risen only to fifty-five years and infant mortality stood at 91 per 1,000, ten times that of the United States (World Bank 1994).

With one of the largest and densest populations in the world, Bangladesh would certainly seem to be a prime example of a Malthusian "basket-case" country. However, when reexamined from a different perspec-tive emphasizing cultural, rather than biological, constraints in the food sys-tem, the picture changes considerably. Such a perspective emerged dramati-cally in 1977 with the publication of *Food First: Beyond the Myth of Scarcity*, by Frances Moore Lappe and Joseph Collins for the Institute for Food and Development Policy, and *How the Other Half Dies: The Real Reasons for World Hunger*, by Susan George. These two books convincingly argue that the world potential for food production is not presently being strained by over-population. On the contrary, grain production is so abundant that wealthy countries can turn vast quantities into animal feed. People are hungry because they have been removed from the land by large landowners and multinational agribusiness interests and because they cannot earn enough to purchase the food they can no longer grow. Poor people's demand for food cannot even be expressed in the marketplace because their purchasing power is too weak.

Paradoxically, Bangladesh is potentially a very rich agricultural land with excellent climate, abundant water, and fine alluvial soils. Before the British arrived in 1757, the region (then called Bengal) supported a prosperous local cotton industry. The peasantry was quite capable of feeding itself because land was not privately owned and was not part of the market economy. The British forcibly introduced cash cropping for export, first of indigo and then of jute, and they made land a commodity to be individually owned. Through a variety of legal and extralegal means the peasantry was steadily deprived of the land. A study published in 1977 (Jannuzi & Peach 1977:xxi, 30) showed that nearly two-thirds of the rural households held less than 10 percent of the land, whereas one-third were totally landless. In this system not having access to land means being unable to eat adequately. Landless peasants were found to consume 22 percent less grain than small landholders, whereas they burned 40 percent more calories because of their increased work loads. Many of the landless worked as sharecroppers, providing labor, and often seeds and fertilizer, while the owner claimed at least half of the crop. Those who worked as wage laborers earned twenty to thirty cents per day. The local elites used their power to manipulate wages and prices to ensure that the peasantry were invariably underpaid, relative to official prices, for the crops they produced, while they were overcharged for the commodities they had to purchase. International development aid and even emergency food aid were invariably monopolized by the landed elite. Researchers Hartmann and Boyce, after two years in the country from 1974 to 1976, including nine months in a representative village, clearly place the blame for hunger on the cultural system:

> Hunger in Bangladesh is neither natural nor inevitable. Its causes are deeply rooted, but they are man-made. The surplus siphoned from the peasants is squandered; land, labor and water are underutilized; and, at the national level, financial resources and skilled manpower are allocated for the benefit of a few rather than for the well-being of the majority.
>
> (HARTMANN & BOYCE 1982:35)

Amaratya Sen (1981) analyzed the Bangladesh famines of 1943 and 1974 and demonstrated that people died because they lacked adequate entitlements to food, not because food was scarce. Entitlement is a person's or household's ability to secure food, either as a *direct entitlement* from primary production, such as from a subsistence crop, or by *exchange entitlement* when food must be purchased or obtained by trade in the market. The 1974 famine was related to a severe flood but production levels were at a decade peak. Prices nevertheless soared and wages dropped, such that many could not afford to buy enough to eat. Those who died were primarily landless laborers or farmers with tiny plots. At the same time the government's stocks of grain for public distribution were low and the United States chose that moment to hold up its deliveries of relief aid until Bangladesh agreed to stop exporting jute to Cuba. Thus, in a market economy, people with weak entitlements to food may be extremely vulnerable to famine if the government is unwilling or unable to supplement their entitlements. Markets will not be particularly responsive to the demands of the poor for food because when the poor lack exchange entitlements, that is, if they have no money, they cannot be part of the market. In contrast, in small-scale cultures each household has virtually the same entitlement to food.

Significantly the food system of prerevolutionary China in 1938 (Fei & Chang 1945, Bodley 1981) was very similar to the situation in Bangladesh in 1974. In a sample village in Yunnaan, 41 percent of the land was owned by 15 percent of the households and more than one-third of the households were completely landless. Landed households were consuming the equivalent of five times the caloric intake of the landless households. Famine was a chronic problem for the impoverished majority. However, after the drastic social leveling by the revolutionary government, China was providing adequate nutrition to its entire population of 800 million, with even less agricultural land per person than Bangladesh (George 1977:36).

Commercial Factory
Food Systems

If we insist on a high-energy food system, we should consider
starting with coal, oil, garbage—or any other source of
hydrocarbons—and producing in factories bacteria, fungi,
and yeasts. These products could then be flavored and
colored appropriately for cultural tastes.

JOHN S. STEINHART AND CAROL E. STEINHART,
"Energy Use in the U.S. Food System"

GLOBAL-SCALE COMMERCIAL FOOD SYSTEMS represent an enormous advance in evolutionary progress and a proportionate loss in long-run adaptive success. Primary technical features of these factory systems are their costly fossil fuel energy subsidies and their reliance on sophisticated biological engineering, which permit very high crop yields for very low inputs of human energy. Other critical cultural aspects are the extreme complexity of the production-consumption market chain and the tendency to increase the per capita energy and resource cost of food consumption through expanded dependence on synthetic and highly processed foods and inefficiently produced animal protein. Because the primary objective of a commercial food system is to produce a financial return to investors, the system's ability to satisfy human nutritional needs on a sustained basis is a secondary, virtually irrelevant consideration. Commercially driven food systems are not only far more costly in per capita demand for energy and resources, they are ultimately less sustainable than small-scale, noncommercial systems and are much less responsive to basic human needs. Global-scale commercial food systems involve substantial social and cultural costs. As noted in the previous chapter, people who lack sufficient financial resources may be excluded from commercial food markets, while at the same time small-scale productive systems are displaced by politically and economically more powerful commercial systems.

Commercial factory food systems involve an enormous concentration of political and economic power that produces vast profits for global elites but they are inherently insensitive to the needs of local human communities and ecosystems. These global-scale systems place great demands on natural resources and consequently have great potential for producing environmental deterioration. Most critically, perhaps, they cannot be sustained indefinitely at present rates of growth, or even at present levels, without drastic restructuring to make them more responsive to basic human needs and the requirements of natural systems. These are critical issues because the present strategy for promoting economic development and reducing world hunger promotes large commercial systems at the expense of locally controlled food systems.

FACTORY FOOD PRODUCTION

By the 1940s and 1950s tractors and farm chemicals were turning farms throughout the world into factories. The demand for farm labor began a drastic decline and development planners everywhere hailed the efficiency of the new technology. If the nonhuman energy expended in the production, processing, distribution, storage, and preparation of food in America is ignored, the system may indeed appear to be very efficient. Before the full costs of the fossil fuel subsidy were widely acknowledged, anthropologist Marvin Harris (1971) originally gave the American food system highest ratings in "techno-environmental advantage" in comparison with the energy efficiency of foragers, shifting cultivators, hoe farmers, and wet-rice growers. His figures were based on a simple estimate of the hours expended per farm worker, multiplied by a fixed rate of 150 calories expended per hour, and divided into the quantity of food calories produced in a given period of time. These calculations may be a reasonable approximation of energy input-output ratios for small-scale foragers and farmers but they are completely inadequate for the American sytem unless they include fossil fuel energy inputs.

Harris corrected his figures in 1975 as shown in Table 5.1. Here are the basic techno-environmental efficiency ratings of the five cultures originally evaluated by Harris, with an adjustment made to the efficiency of the American system by counting separately the nonhuman energy inputs from production to consumption. The surprising fact is that whereas American farm laborers may only expend 1 calorie of human energy for every 210 food calories they produce, approximately 8 calories of nonhuman energy, primarily in the form of fossil fuels, are also required for each calorie produced. It is apparent that the industrial food system is actually operating at an energy efficiency deficit.

TABLE 5.1

Energy Input-Output Efficiency in Five Food Systems

CULTURE	TECHNOLOGY	CALORIES PRODUCED PER CALORIE EXPENDED
Bushman	Hunting/gathering	9.6
Tsembaga (New Guinea)	Shifting cultivation	18.0
	Pig raising	2.1
	Total	9.8
Genieri (Gambia)	Hoe farming	11.2
China	Irrigated wet rice	53.5
United States	Factory farming	
	Human labor	210.0
	Nonhuman energy	0.13

Sources: Data from Harris 1971:203–17; Steinhart and Stainhart 1974:307–16.

Ecologist Howard T. Odum (1971) brilliantly outlined the energy flow systems underlying subsistence patterns at different scales of cultural development using carefully designed cybernetic, circuit-board-like diagrams. Odum used a variety of symbols to represent the pathway of energy through an ecosystem, from the sun through green plants and herbivores to the human consumers. The resulting diagram resembles a complex electrical schematic with switches, gates, and heat sinks, etc., all showing how energy is transformed, stored, and regulated. One need not understand all the complexities of this method of analysis to appreciate how it can illustrate the general design of different subsistence systems and their relationship to the ecosystem. These diagrams dramatically show how commercial food systems use fossil fuels to replace energetic functions performed more efficiently and at lower cost by small-scale cultures that rely directly on natural solar-powered production.

As foragers, humans were dependent for their subsistence on highly complex and stable ecosystems that were largely self-regulating, relatively closed information systems. In a tropical rain forest, for example (see Figure 5.1), the diverse species of the forest do all the work of concentrating energy and nutrients and regulating their flow. Nutrients are largely stored in the living plants and animals and quickly and efficiently recycled after their deaths. Tribal shifting cultivators adjusted to the forest ecosystem by making use of the artificial energy pulse generated each time a forest plot was cut and burned (see Figure 5.2). This pulse temporarily eliminated competitor species and concentrated nutrients to briefly transfer the energy flow into food crops. Except for this minor intervention, the system continued to be basically self-regulating and immediately began to return to its starting point; that is, natural forest succession began at once. Thus, nature did most of the work, and as long as their power base remained restricted to local inputs of solar energy tribal cultures were generally unable to harness enough power to seriously disrupt their supporting ecosystems.

When modern nations began to channel fossil fuel energy into their food systems the picture was suddenly and radically changed. Odum describes the new fossil fuel food systems very neatly:

> One of the results of industrialization based on the new concentrated energy sources was abundant food rolling out from huge fields which were sowed with machinery, tilled with tractors, and weeded and poisoned with chemicals. Epidemic diseases were kept in check by great teams of scientists in distant experiment stations developing new and changing varieties to stay ahead of the evolution of disease adaptation. Soon a few people were supporting many, and most of the rural population left the little farms to fill the new industrial cities.
>
> (ODUM 1971:115)

The greater crop yields that followed industrialization must not be considered simply the result of brilliant inventions, education, determination, and great technological know-how. An enormous energy subsidy was essential. Factory farms do not achieve more efficient rates of photosynthesis and energy conversion. Actually, even some of the most productive factory farms, such as industrialized rice farms, convert only about 0.25 percent of incoming solar radiation into useful energy, whereas a tropical rain forest operates at 3.5 percent efficiency (Odum 1971). Larger per acre yields are possible on factory farms because fossil fuels replace the energy loop the natural ecosystem reserved for its own mechanisms of self-regulation (see Figure 5.3). This system is simply a means of converting oil into food. In effect, as Odum phrases it, in a factory agricultural system "fossil fuel supported works of man have eliminated the natural species and substituted industrial services for the services of those natural species, releasing the same basic production to yield" (Odum 1971:117).

A factory farm is actually an extremely costly, sloppy, and inefficient attempt to replace nature with a very simplified, artificially maintained and subsidized machine. Chemical fertilizers manufactured and transported with fossil fuels replace the tightly calibrated nutrient cycles of the natural ecosystem. More chemicals and machinery control the weeds that in a swidden system are merely part of the restart mechanism and are shaded out as the successional pattern they initiate proceeds. Plant geneticists working in laboratories replace the natural process of biological evolution based on natural selection and species diversity. The delicate natural balances that prevent consumer species from overgrazing are eliminated by heavy application of chemical poisons. Pollution and environmental deterioration are unintended

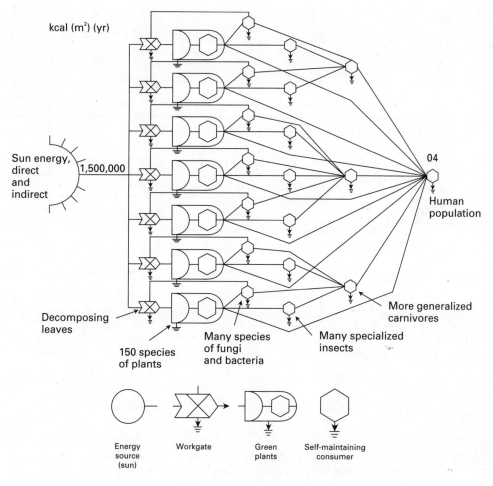

FIGURE 5.1   FORAGING SYSTEMS

Network matrix supporting and stabilizing a tropical rain forest system. People are a minor component but they have integrating and control functions because of the convergence of pathways. (Howard T. Odum, *Environment, Power, and Society.* (New York: Wiley, Inter-Science, 1971), 87.)

by-products of industrial farming because the exotic nutrients and pesticides do not fit into natural ecosystem cycles but instead merely pile up in unexpected places to block these cycles. The massive use of chemical pesticides also has serious direct implications for public health and has stirred widespread public concern and controversy on many occasions, as demonstrated in the Soviet example in Chapter 2.

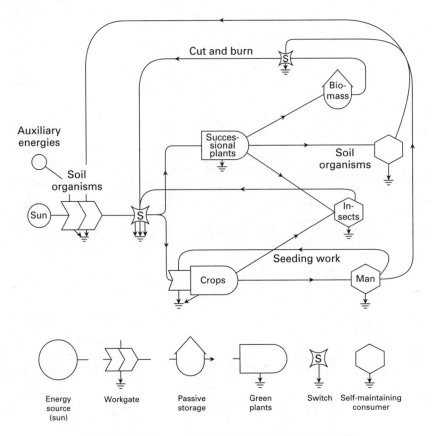

FIGURE 5.2   SHIFTING CULTIVATION

Energy diagram for shifting agriculture. Humans serve as switching timers transferring the flow of energy into food crops made temporarily possible by the material and work accumulated during the long period of plant succession between short agricultural cycles. (Howard T. Odum, *Environment, Power, and Society* (New York: Wiley, Inter-Science, 1971), 113.)

Much of the energy and work force needed to support an industrial food system is disguised by statistics that focus on farm labor and yields per acre. An industrial food system necessarily engages many more sectors of the economy. Harris (1971), in the estimate of the efficiency of U. S. food production cited earlier, used a figure of 5 million farm workers in 1964. Figures presented in Table 5.2, prepared from data in the *Statistical Abstract of the United States: 1994*, suggest that in 1992–1993 there were actually more than 11 million full-time workers in the food system as a whole, including primary producers, food processors, and distributors. These figures show a reduc-

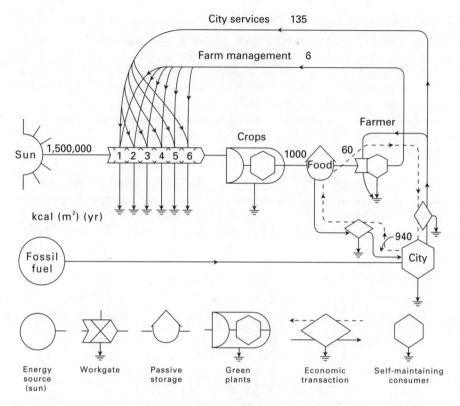

FIGURE 5.3   FACTORY FARMING WITH FOSSIL FUELS

People in a system of industrialized, high-yield agriculture. Energetic inputs include flows of fossil fuels that replace the work formerly done by people, their animals, and the network of animals and plants in which people were formerly nursed. Work flows include the following: (1) mechanized and commercial preparation of seeding and planting, replacing the natural dispersion system; (2) fertilizer excesses, replacing the mineral recycling system; (3) chemical and power weeding, replacing the woody maintenance of a shading system; (4) soil preparation and treatment, replacing the forest soil-building processes; (5) insecticides, replacing the system of chemical diversity, and carnivores for preventing epidemic grazing and disease; and (6) development of varieties capable of passing on the savings in work to net food storages. New varieties are developed as diseases appear, thus providing the genetic selection formerly arranged by the forest evolution and selection system. In this system 170 persons per square mile support 32 times this number in cities. The level of grain production in the United States is about 1000 kcal/(m²)(yr). The fuel subsidy is calculated using 10^4 kcal/dollar. If production yields $60/(acre)(yr) and if the costs are 90 percent of the gross, then $54/acre is the measure to use of materials and services from the industrialized culture. This becomes 54 x 10^4 kcal/acre or 135 kcal(m²)(yr). (Howard T. Odum, *Environment, Power, and Society* (New York: Wiley, Inter-Science, 1971), 119.)

tion of 3 million in the count of actual farm workers, even though there was an increase of 25 million people in the total American population since 1964! Including the 282,000 support workers in the manufacturing of farm machinery and chemicals and the federal Department of Agriculture brings the total number of workers in direct support of food production in 1992–1993 to 2.2 million. Remarkably, there were four times as many people involved in food processing and distribution as in primary production. The U.S. Department of Agriculture's own calculations, which include transportation, estimate that 22.8 million people are employed in the food and fiber sector of the economy.

Anthropologists point out that factory farming's capital intensive dependency on machinery and expensive fossil fuel energy, and the continuing maintenance requirements for specialized technical skills and manufactured imports (Peggy Barlett 1987, 1989), make such production methods a poor choice for the world's small-scale farmers (Netting 1993: 323–324). The massive federally subsidized water development projects that have supported factory farming in the arid regions of the American West lead to soil salination (Reisner 1986) and involve enormous social costs, as will be discussed in a later section.

FACTORY POTATOES VERSUS SWIDDEN SWEET POTATOES

Profit is the only reason for growing potatoes.

(KNUDSON 1972:76)

The extent to which fossil-fuel subsidized factory farming systems have artificially replaced the functions of the natural ecosystem, and the incredible energy and environmental costs of this change, stand out with remarkable clarity when the commercial production of Irish potatoes by large-scale American agribusiness in the 1960s and 1970s (Talburt & Smith 1967, and various *Proceedings of the Annual Washington Potato Conference and Trade Fair,* Washington Potato Commission) is compared with the methods of raising sweet potatoes for local consumption by tribal gardeners in New Guinea, as documented by anthropologist Roy Rappaport (1971) during the same time. Potatoes (Irish or sweet) occupy roughly the same position in each culture, in that they are quantitatively the most important single vegetable consumed and are unquestionably basic staples in the diet. In many American households meat and potatoes were traditionally thought to make a meal complete.

According to Rappaport's (1968, 1971) account of the Tsembaga in highland Papua New Guinea, sweet potatoes directly contributed 21 percent of the diet by weight for the local group of 204 people who were actively culti-

TABLE 5.2

Labor in the United States Food System, 1992–93 (in millions of workers)

Farm labor	2.0 million
Support sectors	.128
Farm machine manufacturing	.097
Agri-chemical manufacturing	.057
Total, primary production	2.22 million
Food processing industry	1.65
Eating and drinking places	4.25
Retail grocers	3.21
Total, processors and distributors	9.11 million
Food system total	11.32 million

Source: United States Bureau of the Census, Statistical Abstract of the United States: 1994, 114th ed. Austin, Texas: Reference Press.

vating about 1,000 acres in 1962. Much of the sweet potato crop was fed to domestic pigs and thus indirectly contributed animal protein to the diet in the form of pork. The basic cultivation system was carried out entirely by hand. The forest was cleared and burned, fences were built to keep out the pigs, and crops were planted with a sharpened stick. Crops were harvested by hand and carried in handcrafted net bags to the house for consumption. There was no elaborate processing; potatoes were simply roasted whole in the fire or steamed in earth ovens. There was also no significant storage, except in the ground until harvest.

Energetically, the system was quite efficient, with approximately sixteen kilocalories of sweet potatoes produced for each kilocalorie of human labor. Only about 10 percent of the easily arable land was under active cultivation at a time and there appeared to be no immediate danger of resource depletion, although in some areas of highland New Guinea there has been a long-term trend toward more intensive cultivation and replacement of forest with savanna. The basic objective of Tsembaga gardening was to meet human nutritional needs, and this was being done very well. No crops were grown for the market, although other New Guinea peoples raised cash crops for local markets and produced coffee for the world market while still maintaining subsistence production for household use.

On a factory farm in the United States, potatoes can be grown as a successful monocrop only with the help of vast energy inputs to maintain correct soil conditions, moisture, and nutrients and to control weeds, epidemic diseases, and insect infestations. On the swidden sweet potato farm all of these functions are carried out by the natural ecosystem and by the diversity of the garden plantings, which imitates the natural system. No irrigation or fertilizer is required on swidden plots, while factory potato farmers must apply chemical fertilizer constantly and in many areas must irrigate to maintain their high yields. In areas where overhead sprinklers are used, special chemicals may be applied to the soil to prevent compaction and lost filtration caused by the perpetual mechanical rain (Hagood 1972). Weeds, insects, and diseases may be variously controlled before planting by chemical treatment of the tubers, by application of chemical herbicides and insecticides to the soil, and sometimes even by soil fumigation that kills virtually all soil organisms. There are specialized pre-emergence weed killers and a wide variety of other herbicides and insecticides that may be applied while the crop is growing. In some cases special chemicals are sprayed on the crop to inhibit sprouting after harvest or to intensify the red skin color of certain potatoes to increase their market value. Note that part of this energy-expensive chemical program is a cosmetic treatment to prevent unsightly blemishes that may lower consumer acceptance but has little effect on increasing actual yields. Where potatoes are contracted to go into chips, the vines must be chemically killed weeks before harvesting to prevent starch buildup in the tubers, which causes an undesirable darkening in the finished potato chips.

The extent of some of this chemical maintenance may be seen in specific production statistics from Washington State, third in the nation for potato production in the late 1960s. In 1969, 60 percent of the potato acreage on farms devoted principally to that crop was chemically sprayed by airplane for insect control and some farms required as many as five to nine separate treatments (United States, Department of Commerce 1969, a, b). Only slightly fewer acres were treated chemically for disease control and 40 percent were treated for weeds. In addition to the tractors and trucks normally required on farms, there were hundreds of specialized machines on Washington farms in 1967 to cut potato seed and for use as potato harvesters, windrowers, diggers, and planters. In 1969 more than 36,000 tons of liquid and dry fertilizer were applied to 62,500 acres of potatoes—more than 1,000 pounds per acre—and virtually the entire crop required both fertilizing and irrigation.

With this kind of treatment it is not surprising that yields increased from a national average of 65 hundredweight per acre in 1920 to 480 hundredweight in Washington in 1982. This means that over 12 million calories were being produced per acre (United States, Bureau of the Census 1983, Table 1204), in comparison with New Guinea sweet potato farmers, who were producing approximately 5 million calories per acre with more than a dozen major crops combined. In addition to the direct energy subsidy from fossil fuels, Washington potato farmers were passing on other hidden costs, making full assessment of the costs impossible in the short term. For example, extensive irrigation already seemed to be causing microclimatic alterations in the region. There is also the danger that irrigation will lead to soil salinization. Fertilizers and other chemicals will in time increasingly leach into rivers and underground water sources, killing susceptible species and overnourishing others. In addition, intensively cultivated areas are more subject to wind erosion.

SOCIAL COSTS OF THE FOOD PRODUCTION SYSTEM

> The growth of corporate agriculture is not inevitable nor simply a product of efficiency, but it is rather a result of the emergence of national policies favorable to large scale enterprises. Some of these policies were promulgated by corporate interests. Others, ostensibly at least, were formulated in the desire to protect the family farmer, but have had the opposite effect.
>
> (GOLDSCHMIDT 1978:XLVIII)

The growth of factory farming has dramatically transformed rural society throughout the world, generally reducing the number of people supported directly from the land, increasing inequality, and often lowering the quality of life for those at the bottom of the economic hierarchy. This process can easily be documented in the United States, where there has been a steady decline in rural population and a decrease in the number of farms as farming has become a business rather than a way of life. Between 1930 and 1990, in the United States as a whole two-thirds of the farms disappeared while those that remained increased in size more than threefold. This transformation occurred within less than a single lifetime. By 1987 just 8 percent of the farms controlled 62 percent of the farmland and more than 40 percent of farm products were produced by corporately owned farms or business partnerships rather than by family farms (*The American Almanac 1994*). This situation mirrors the distribution of land in Scotland but contrasts sharply with countries such as Norway where a more equitable distribution of ownership has been a national policy. In 1989 the largest 12 percent of Norwegian farms controlled only 25 percent of the agricultural land (United Kingdom, *The Digest of Agricultural Census Statistics 1992, Statistical Yearbook of Norway 1992*).

Contrary to popular wisdom, this dual process of economic concentration and impoverishment is not solely driven by economies of scale resulting purely from improvements in technology. We have seen that less fossil fuel intensive food production systems are energetically both more efficient and more sustainable. Furthermore, a wide-ranging comparative study published by the U.S. Department of Agriculture demonstrated that fully mechanized farms operated by one person were economically more efficient than much larger operations (Madden 1967, cited Goldschmidt 1978:xxx–xxxi). Anthropologist Walter Goldschmidt, who studied California agribusiness, emphasized that smaller farms maximized income for the maximum number of people more effectively than larger farms. Smaller farms also supported more prosperous farm towns. Goldschmidt (1978:xxxii–xxxix) attributed the concentration of American farm ownership to public policies that for decades systematically favored large owners over small. Giant corporate farms did not emerge because of the efficiencies of nature. Goldschmidt observed that under federal subsidy programs larger owners received larger support payments. The progressive income tax encouraged high income people to acquire farms as tax shelters so they could write off losses, while reductions in capital gains taxes made farms attractive investments for wealthy financiers and giant corporations. Farm labor has also been a special bonus for large farm operators because seasonal farm workers have few legal protections, especially when, as is often the case, they are not citizens. Goldschmidt also noted that agricultural research sponsored by the federal government through the Department of Agriculture and the land grant universities has often been directed toward the needs of agribusiness rather than the family farm.

In 1940 Goldschmidt was commissioned by the federal Bureau of Agricultural Economics to study the effects of limiting the size of farms using federally subsidized irrigation water. This was a special issue in central California where a few very large estates, a heritage of Spanish land grants and nineteenth-century railroad grants, were monopolizing the Bureau of Reclamation's water projects. Subsidizing large farms seemed to contradict the Bureau's mission, which since 1902 had been to promote water development to support family farms on arid Western lands. In order to assess the social impact of farm size, Goldschmidt selected two communities in the central valley of California, Dinuba and Arvin. Both had approximately 4,000 people, the same environment, and the same overall level of agricultural productivity. Dinuba and Arvin differed only in farm size. Goldschmidt found that Dinuba, surrounded by small farms, had twice as many local businesses as Arvin and two-thirds more local retail trade. Dinuba's farms averaged only fifty-seven acres, but supported a richer community life with more people and a higher living standard per dollar of agricultural production than Arvin. Dinuba had better community infrastructure, including streets, sidewalks, sewage disposal, and recreational facilities; better schools; more civic organizations; more churches; and more democratic local government. The farms around Arvin averaged 497 acres and individually they generated more dollars, but income was skewed toward the upper end of the social hierarchy and their wealth was more externally directed. In Dinuba more than half the workforce were business professionals and farm operators, while in Arvin 80 percent were low-paid farm laborers.

The policy implications of Goldschmidt's research were obvious and the local elite attempted unsuccessfully to use their political influence in Washington, D.C., to stop the project. They then tried to publicly discredit Goldschmidt and suppress his findings and succeeded in closing down the

Bureau of Agricultural Economics and blocking a follow-up study. However, a repeat study thirty and forty years later (MacCannell & White 1984) found that social conditions in portions of the Central Valley Water Project had deteriorated even further than in the 1940s. Researchers Dean MacCannell and Jerry White investigated the federally supported Westland Water District developed in Fresno County in the 1960s. They found sharp class divisions, with a small prosperous elite and an impoverished majority. Many of the wealthy farm owners lived in Los Angeles or in lavish houses on their 2,000-acre estates, while community infrastructure in the district's towns declined. In 1970 farm worker housing was often overcrowded and grossly inadequate and in some communities more than half the population lived below the official poverty level. Not surprisingly, MacCannell and White advocated land reform and adherence to the acreage limitations as a solution.

In the United States overall, where the economic interests of agribusiness and corporate food processors and distributors have prevailed, the food system has become remarkably centralized. For example, in 1990 California produced well over half the nation's vegetables, including some 90 percent of its tomatoes and more than 75 percent of its lettuce. In 1982 Fresno county, discussed above, produced nearly $1.5 billion in crops, the highest in the state. Land ownership in Fresno county was extremely concentrated, with 7.6 percent of the farms, a mere 568, controlling more than 80 percent of the land (U.S. Department of Commerce 1983). In 1990 just 513 corporations, less than .5 percent of the nation's 126,423 agricultural corporations, held one-third of the nation's corporate agricultural assets. Food processors are also highly concentrated. In 1989 nearly 90 percent of America's wholesale beef was sold by the three largest packing houses. In 1992 the 59 largest of some 1.4 million American food manufacturing companies accounted for some 75 percent of sales. At a global level the marketing and intercontinental movement of grain is now controlled by five privately held corporations (Morgan 1979, Sewell 1992). The directors of such giant oligopolies have enormous decision-making control over the industrial food system and are far removed from the social and environmental consequences of their actions on specific local communities and ecosystems.

ENERGY COSTS OF THE DISTRIBUTION SYSTEM

In a tribal culture, as we have seen, food is largely produced by the households that consume it. Only small quantities are normally distributed beyond individual households and this distribution occurs within a framework of reciprocal sharing between close kinsmen. In small chiefdoms, the simplest large-scale cultures, production and consumption still remain largely at the household level, although some foodstuffs may be concentrated by chiefs as tribute to be redistributed at feasts or in times of crisis and to support craft specialists for the production of sumptuary goods. With the evolution of the state and the establishment of politically centralized governments, large quantities of food had to be transferred from the rural subsistence farmers or peasants to the cities to maintain permanent food storehouses for state use. This transfer has been variously effected through the payment of taxes, through the operations of special trader classes, or through well-developed market exchanges. Reliance only on solar energy powered agriculture apparently placed severe limitations on the extent to which the population of a given culture could be concentrated in cities, especially because of the energy costs of transportation relative to the cost of food production. With the tapping of fossil fuels and the rise of industrialized urban centers, where up to 95 percent of the population in particular countries became concentrated, the energy costs of the food distribution system have suddenly come to totally overshadow the costs of primary production.

It is only possible to make a very rough estimate of the total energy costs of the American food system. In a now classic study, John D. Steinhart and Carol E. Steinhart (1974) calculated that in 1970 eight to twelve calories were expended in the production, distribution, and consumption of a single calorie of food. This figure includes such energy costs as the manufacturing and operation of farm machinery, fertilizer, irrigation, food processing, packaging, transportation, manufacturing of trucks, and both industrial and domestic cooking and refrigeration (see Table 5.3). Higher estimates would include the energy cost of shipping food by rail, ship, and air; disposal of food-related wastes; maintenance of buildings and equipment; a percentage of highway construction costs; agricultural research; and domestic use of private automobiles to move food from supermarket to home. Other estimates have placed the figure as high as twenty calories in for one calorie out, and this may be far more realistic.

According to Steinhart and Steinhart's conservative estimate, less than 25 percent of the total energy expended in the American food system actually went to support primary production on the farm; the other 75 percent plus went to processing, marketing, and domestic uses. Significantly, more work force was also engaged in the food distribution network than on the farm, even if labor costs in the transportation system are disregarded (see Table 5.2). Clearly the distribution component of the industrial food system is responsible for much of the enormous energy cost of the total system and for this reason deserves special investigation.

Many of the increased energy costs of the American food system appear to be related solely to the marketing process. Despite the biological limits to per capita food consumption, between 1950 and 1990, under the commercial urging of the food industry, the apparent per capita consumption of calories by Americans increased by almost 20 percent, with protein consumption up 13 percent (*American Almanac 1994*:146). Between 1970 and 1990 soft drink

TABLE 5 · 3   Energy Use in the United States Food System in 1012 Kcal

COMPONENT	1940	1947	1950	1954	1958	1960	1964	1968	1970
ON FARM									
Fuel (direct use)	70.0	136.0	158.0	172.8	179.0	188.0	213.9	226.0	232.0
Electricity	0.7	32.0	32.9	40.0	44.0	46.1	50.0	57.3	63.8
Fertilizer	12.4	19.5	24.0	30.6	32.2	41.0	60.0	87.0	94.0
Agricultural steel	1.6	2.0	2.7	2.5	2.0	1.7	2.5	2.4	2.0
Farm machinery	9.0	34.7	30.0	29.5	50.2	52.0	60.0	75.0	80.0
Tractors	12.8	25.0	30.8	23.6	16.4	11.8	20.0	20.5	19.3
Irrigation	18.0	22.8	25.0	29.6	32.5	33.3	34.1	34.8	35.0
Subtotal	124.5	272.0	303.4	328.6	356.3	373.9	440.5	503.0	526.1
PROCESSING INDUSTRY									
Food processing industry	147.0	177.5	192.0	211.5	212.6	224.0	249.0	295.0	308.0
Food processing machinery	0.7	5.7	5.0	4.9	4.9	5.0	6.0	6.0	6.0
Paper packaging	8.5	14.8	17.0	20.0	26.0	28.0	31.0	35.7	38.0
Glass containers	14.0	25.7	26.0	27.0	30.2	31.0	34.0	41.9	47.0
Steel cans and aluminum	38.0	55.8	62.0	73.7	85.4	86.0	91.0	112.2	122.0
Transport (fuel)	49.6	86.1	102.0	122.3	140.2	153.3	184.0	226.6	246.9
Trucks and trailors (manufacture)	28.0	42.0	49.5	47.0	43.0	44.2	61.0	70.2	74.0
Subtotal	285.8	407.6	453.5	506.4	542.3	571.5	656.0	787.6	841.9
COMMERCIAL AND HOME									
Commercial refrigeration and cooking	121.0	141.0	150.0	161.0	176.0	186.2	209.0	241.0	263.0
Refrigeration machinery (home and commercial)	10.0	24.0	25.0	27.5	29.4	32.0	40.0	56.0	61.0
Home refrigeration and cooking	144.2	184.0	202.3	228.0	257.0	276.6	345.0	433.9	480.0
Subtotal	275.2	349.0	377.3	416.5	462.4	494.8	594.0	730.9	804.0
Grand total	685.5	1028.6	1134.2	1251.5	1361.0	1440.2	1690.5	2021.5	2172.0

Source: John S. Steinhart and Carol E. Steinhart, "Energy Use in the U.S. Food System," *Science* (1974):309.

consumption increased more than 80 percent. It is also estimated that in 1990 nearly one-third of the American population was 20 percent or more above desired weight standards set by life insurance companies.

Between 1940 and 1970 the per capita energy costs of American food doubled. During this period the per capita energy costs of food packaging increased 119 percent while the overall per capita energy costs of processing, packaging, and transportation from factory to marketplace increased by 95 percent (Steinhart and Steinhart 1974). Rising energy costs since 1973 have led to some reductions in energy inputs in the food system, but the scale of energy use is still enormous in comparison with smaller, less commercialized systems.

After 1950 there was a dramatic switch toward the consumption of more energy-intensive processed food. By 1970 America's food was more transported and more expensively processed and packaged than ever before. These changes can be seen in many areas. For example, there was an almost fivefold increase in the per capita production of frozen food in this country. The introduction of these foods raised energy requirements because their distribution required additional preparation and packaging, along with special transportation and storage facilities. Certain new food products, such as potato chips, may be far more costly to transport and store because of their increased bulk and fragility compared with their less processed counterparts. Since 1950 energy costs have risen due to trends in packaging such as the general increase in the use of packaging solely to enhance the consumer appeal of foodstuffs and the switch to more energy-expensive materials. Wood, paper, and reusable glass bottles were steadily replaced by plastic, nonreturnable bottles and aluminum cans. The latter required approximately twice as much energy to manufacture than the steel cans they replaced!

Cultural changes in patterns of food consumption must also account for part of this increase. The per capita consumption of red meat increased steadily between 1940 and 1970, but has declined since. This is important because cattle are relatively inefficient converters of vegetable protein, requiring approximately twenty pounds of protein to produce one pound for human consumption. This ratio would not be critical if cattle were grazed on rangeland that would not produce other food crops, but a high proportion of America's beef cattle are fed high-quality grains in feedlots before being slaughtered. In 1991 approximately two-thirds of the American grain crop was used as animal feed (U.S.D.A., *Agricultural Statistics 1992*). Another important factor is the use of much of the grain crop in industrial products and sweeteners (such as corn syrup in soft drinks) of limited nutritional value (George 1977).

Marketing practices in the American food system were investigated in detail in an important study carried out for the National Commission on Food Marketing at the request of President Lyndon B. Johnson (Marple & Wissman 1968). This study was based on the work of nineteen academicians and seven private researchers and considered the cost structure of food from farmer to consumer, product innovation and competition, and consumer "needs." The findings continue to be useful because they help pinpoint factors in the processing and distribution component of the food system that promote increased energy costs.

It is striking that productivity in the food-marketing industry is not measured by how efficiently human need-satisfying nutrients can be distributed to the population; rather, it is computed by dollar output per hour of labor or return on investment. In this accounting staple foods such as meat, flour, and sugar, which require little processing, are considered less productive because they have a relatively low "value added" in comparison with snack foods, cold breakfast cereals, or other highly processed food "products." If the population is growing very slowly and is already satisfying its basic food needs, then logically the only way for food companies to increase their domestic profits is through increased competition between companies or through the production of increasingly more expensive new food products. Food markets may also be increased through exports in a world market system. Limited increases have also been achieved by raising the nutritional standard for domestic pets. New food products are one of the most important tools used by giant food corporations competing for larger shares of the relatively fixed market. The importance of new food products is underscored by the comments of a president of Campbell Soup Company, cited in the National Commission study, to the effect that a company without new products would see a 50 percent drop in profits within a year and would be losing money within five years.

Thus the introduction of new food items and a corresponding continual upgrading of the energy intensity of subsistence seem to be a logical outgrowth of an expanding economy in a culture of consumption. However, the food habits of any culture, including a culture of consumption, undoubtedly will be relatively conservative and can be changed only with difficulty, regardless of the need for manufacturers to continually create and market new food products. The findings of the National Commission clearly bear out this generalization: Manipulating American tastes in food—introducing totally new foods or even permutations on existing products—has not been easily accomplished. It is instructive that ideas for new products did not normally originate with the consumer. Only 3 percent of the suggestions for 127 new products in a sample examined by the National Commission actually came from future consumers. Consumers were simply not clamoring for new products. New product development is in fact a very expensive, very lengthy, and uncertain process of trial and error, in which most ideas prove unmarketable. In the mid-1960s a typical new cold breakfast cereal product required 4 1/2 years of development activity, and nearly $4 million invested in physical design, market research, and advertising before full distribution could be achieved. Only some 5 percent of new product ideas ever reached full distribution, and only about 10 percent of these ever became well established. Of those products that made it all the way to the test market stage, 22 percent were withdrawn short of full development. Beyond that point, another 17 percent were quickly withdrawn. Manufacturers assumed that every new product had a "life cycle" beginning with a very slow rise in sales or consumer acceptance until it reached a saturation point. A gradual decline would then set in as customers dropped the product entirely or shifted to rival brands.

The amount of money that must be spent on advertising and promotion of new products totally dwarfed expenditures for research and development. Only the largest food corporations could afford to develop new products, but the heavy advertising expenses were made less burdensome because they were tax deductible. Enormous advertising expenditures are an accepted part of the process, as the National Commission study explained, because of the "inertia" of consumers, "arising primarily from reluctance to change established behavior patterns which delays customer acceptance of the new product" (Marple & Wissman 1968:40). The entire process bears a disturbing resemblance to the work of cultural change experts attempting to convince reluctant self-sufficient villagers that they should adopt expensive factory farm techniques. Food manufacturers happily concluded that those products that survive the risky promotion procedure do so because they satisfy a "real" consumer "need."

The nonrandom pattern of advertising expenditures clearly demonstrates that reluctance to change established food habits is strongest when such habits already adequately satisfy basic nutritional needs. Products that appear to be of little nutritional value, or that are at least not a clear nutritional gain over the foods they would replace, often require the most intensive advertising campaigns. The study found this to be true for cold cereals but considered it merely the reflection of "higher-than-average uncertainty as to consumer acceptance . . ." (Marple & Wissman 1968:185). This generalization continues to be valid. For example, in 1992 the Kellog Company, with some thirty-one brands of breakfast cereal on the market, spent $630 million on advertising (*Advertising Age* Sept. 29, 1993).

In general, staple foods such as fresh fruit, vegetables, meat, and milk, which could form the basis of a nutritionally sound diet yet require minimal processing and have little added "value," are promoted very little. "Impulse" items such as soft drinks, candy, and other snack foods, and new products generally, were heavily dependent on continual promotion. Companies spent $1.2 billion advertising candy, snacks, and soft drinks in the United States in 1992. For example, the two largest candy manufacturers, Hershey and Mars, spent $170 million advertising their products. Coca-Cola spent $392 million on its American advertising in 1992 and sold $4.3 billion in soft drinks (*Advertising Age* Sept. 29, 1993). Coke executives calculated that Americans

were drinking an average of thirty-seven gallons of Coke products per capita per year (Huey 1993:46), which is remarkable for a food product whose
only nutritional ingredient, sugar, is often replaced with a non-nutrient substitute. Coca-Cola, which controls 47 percent of the global carbonated soft
drink market, netted $2.1 billion in profit from its 1993 worldwide sales of
$13.9 billion, making it one of the world's most profitable companies. People
must be persuaded to accept food products that are not necessarily good for
them, just as peasant farmers must be urged to accept energy-intensive farming practices that in the long run may prove highly detrimental.

The "need" for new food products was rationalized in an important sociological study by Cyril Sofer (1965), which argued that food habits are not
necessarily "rational" from a nutritional viewpoint, anyway, and that food
may often serve critical nonfood cultural functions other than nutrition. This
generalization is, of course, true; but it seems to be only in global cultures
that nutritional needs become secondary to other cultural functions, such as
maintaining food industry profits. This seems to be a very crucial difference
between major cultural systems. As was noted in the discussion of potato production on the factory farm, profit was the only reason for growing potatoes;
in food marketing the only reason for new food products may also be profit.
As the National Commission study explained: "[The] risky and expensive
venture of new product development and introduction is undertaken in
hopes of finding a new product which yields a higher gross contribution to
overhead and profit on invested assets" (Marple & Wissman 1968:7). This is
the fundamental logic of the market economy as it is presently organized.

A further argument in the Sofer study was that people have a basic
"need" for new products as an escape from food monotony. Variety is, of
course, also a nutritional advantage, and it may be that people have a basic
need for a varied diet to the extent that it is nutritionally adequate. However,
there is no reason to believe that new food products are any advantage in that
sense and there is abundant evidence to the contrary. Sofer indirectly
acknowledged the nutritional shortcomings of new food products by stating
that people often eat food that they know to be harmful, thereby further
absolving the food industry from criticism for actively promoting nutritionally inferior but profitable foods.

POTATO CHIPS AND MANIOC CAKES

Food processing and varied and nutritious diets were not invented by industrial civilization; they have been with us since the beginning of culture and
our first use of fire. There is a clear difference, however, between food
processing in small-scale cultures, where it is unquestionably "consumer-

oriented," and industrial food processing for a profit. Some of these differences have already been demonstrated, but a brief comparison between manioc cakes and potato chips will heighten the contrasts.

One of the finest examples of food processing in tribal cultures can be
seen in the South American manioc complex. Bitter manioc is the staple food
crop for many Amazonian Indians (Dole 1978, Lancaster 1982). Before the
starchy tuber can be eaten it must be peeled, grated, and the pulp squeezed
to separate the poisonous juice from the flour. This process is accomplished
by means of a variety of specialized graters and squeezing devices (see Figure
5.4). The end products may then be further processed into a wide range of
foods. The Waiwai of Guyana have developed at least fourteen different
kinds of bread and thirteen beverages based on bitter manioc and its by-
products (Yde 1965:28–51). The flour may be sifted in various ways, baked
in bread, eaten toasted by itself, or used in soups and stews. The juice is used
in soups and the tapioca extracted from it finds a variety of food uses, sometimes in combination with the flour. All of these processes, of course, take
place in the household. They involve no external energy inputs and no
extended shipping or storage. Tribal diets should not be considered dull and
monotonous because they do not benefit from supermarkets. There is also
no question here of eating potentially harmful food to assure someone else's
profit.

In the United States in 1990, only about half of the potato crop was
shipped to consumers as raw tubers to be processed in the household
(*U.S.D.A. Agricultural Statistics 1992*, Table 230). Even these "unprocessed"
potatoes had to be washed mechanically, chemically treated to inhibit sprouting, in some cases colored or waxed, and transported and stored under temperature controlled conditions. Potatoes destined for chips—and in 1990 this
involved about 20 percent of the crop—would go through the washing,
sprout inhibition, and temperature control and in addition might sit in storage for six to eight months. Further chemical treatments might include gases
or chemical solutions to prevent discoloration of peeled potatoes before
cooking and again to avoid after–cooking darkening that occurs as a natural
enzymatic process and has no effect on taste or nutritive qualities but is
thought to reduce consumer appeal (Talburt & Smith 1967). Oils, salt,
preservatives, and sometimes special artificial flavoring are then added in the
final processing and the end product is packed and shipped in special con-
tainers. Then, of course, millions of advertising dollars must be spent to convince people to eat the product. After critics attacked chips for their high fat
and salt content, an experimental, vitamin-enriched chip made a brief
appearance in 1974. Of course, the success of the potato chip as a food product is not attributable to its nutritional qualities, but rather to the fact that at
the retail level it is many times more expensive per pound than the ordinary
raw potato.

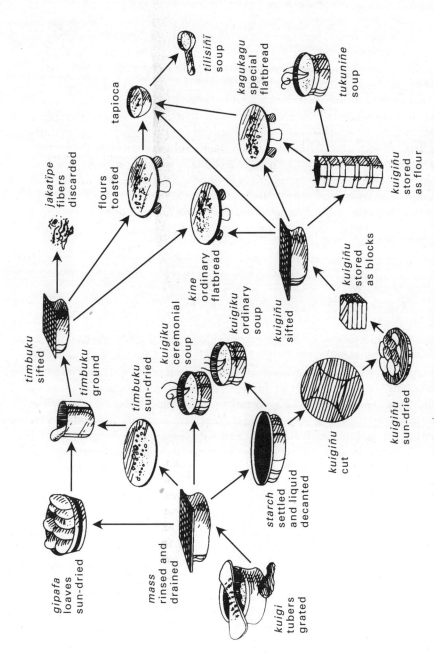

FIGURE 5.4   Steps in the Preparation of Manioc Among the Kuikuru (Dole 1978)

An important dimension of factory food systems that should not be over-looked is that marketing requirements for food that looks attractive, ships well, and can be stored for extended periods in warehouses and on super-market shelves mean that many new chemical ingredients are added for strictly economic, non-nutritional reasons. A bewildering array of food addi-tives, estimated at some 2,500 as early as 1972, are being added to food prod-ucts as coloring agents, synthetic flavors, and preservatives; to prevent cak-ing or separation; to provide body; and for a wide range of other specialized functions (Kermode 1972). Only a few of these additives are used to replace some of the nutrients destroyed in processing. As with pesticide residues, much controversy has arisen over the possible dangers of these additives, but few people would question the basic marketing system that makes them nec-essary. Since 1972 many new additives have, of course, appeared; others have been banned when they were discovered to be harmful. Health authorities and the food industry are engaged in an ongoing struggle over how to con-trol these non-nutritional additives (Freydberg & Gortner 1982, Hunter 1982).

FISHING, GLOBAL TRADE, AND "GHOST ACRES"

Some modern nations have so far managed to keep ahead of their food prob-lems by supplementing their own limited food production capabilities through heavy reliance on fishing and international trade. Fish may be eaten directly or used as a substitute for feed crops for the production of meat, milk, eggs, and poultry. This seems to be a logical step ahead of the Malthusian controls on overpopulation. When the intensification of agricul-ture has reached the point at which further increases can only be achieved if truly prohibitive energy deficits are incurred, then fishing fleets may be expanded and favorable trade agreements reached with nations producing food surpluses.

In 1965 food scientist Georg Borgstrom introduced the concept *ghost acres*, referring to the fact that trade and fishing were ways of gaining extraterritorial acres. Ghost acres were calculated as the amount of land a given country would need to put into production to gain an amount of ani-mal protein equivalent to its net food imports and fishery production. According to this reckoning many nations have far exceeded the carrying capacities of their farmlands, at least given their present culturally prescribed food patterns, and are now precariously dependent on uncertain interna-tional markets and frail marine resources. At that time Borgstrom calculated that Japan's ghost acres exceeded its agricultural acreage by more than six times, and the United Kingdom's effective acres were nearly tripled by ghost acres. Japan's fishing industry was the third largest in the world in 1990, with its fleet spread throughout the Pacific and Atlantic. Fish products accounted for 28 percent of the daily protein supply in Japan, the highest in the world (FAO 1992). Furthermore, in 1992 Japan imported more grain than any other nation, more than double its domestic production (World Bank 1994).

Global trade is not presently operating as a means of allocating food to countries on the basis of critical nutritional requirements; rather, as with other facets of the global market economy, it supports and reflects the interests of the world's financial elite. Scarce protein resources in the form of meat, fish and fish products, nuts, and oilseed cakes move along with bananas, cocoa, coffee, and tea from protein-poor, hungry nations to rich, well-fed nations, propelled by the exigencies of the world's financial markets. Under the General Agreement on Tariffs and Trade (GATT), finance capital will move freely between countries seeking the highest returns on investment. Peru, for example, instead of satisfying the obvious needs of the substantial segments of its population that are protein deficient, finds it more profitable to ship its rich fish meal resource to the United States where it is fed to chickens to subsidize energy intensive egg industries. Likewise, Indian oilseed cakes are fed to European cattle while millions of Indians are starved for protein and Indian cattle scavenge for refuse.

Borgstrom points out that the world's refrigerator ships are almost exclusively engaged in moving bananas and frozen meat from Central and South America, Australia, and New Zealand to Western Europe and North America, where they will bring the highest prices. The curious feature of this trade is that in many cases it does not fill a nutritional need in the rich countries that could not be satisfied by simply replacing the imported supplies with domestic equivalents. Brazilian meat and Peruvian fish meal in the United States might be considered an anomaly, but actually these are the logical outgrowth of a system of world market exchanges between nations that have institutionalized inequality.

In many cases this system quite literally plucks food from the hands of starving people while also indirectly depriving them of the ability to produce their own badly needed food. Millions of acres in Africa, Latin America, and Asia presently devoted to the satisfaction of the culturally prescribed "need" of the developed nations for chocolate, coffee, and tea might instead be converted to the production of food to satisfy local needs.

Anthropologists Daniel R. Gross and Barbara A. Underwood (1971) have shown how such trading patterns may be directly related to malnutrition in Brazil. Vast areas of the Brazilian northeast were converted from subsistence farms feeding peasants to large-scale sisal plantations on which the peasants became poorly paid laborers. The sisal plantations supplied twine to the United States, where it was used to tie bales of hay, which were in turn fed to American cattle. Unfortunately, the former subsistence farmers whose lands were converted from food crops to an export crop found themselves unable to buy enough food with their meager wages to satisfy the minimal nutritional needs of their families. Systematic malnutrition resulted as the peasants were forced to rely on cheap, high-calorie foods that were low in protein. Different permutations of the same situation have occurred throughout the world where the growing of cash crops for export, either to world or to national markets, has replaced food crops grown to satisfy the nutritional requirements of local peoples.

Such disparity between the nutritional needs of people and the distribution of food has no parallel in tribal culture. In fact, while food may circulate between local households according to need, it is very unusual for cultures not to be totally self-sufficient in their subsistence requirements. In a remarkably few cases cultures are unable to satisfy their needs either because of periodic misfortunes or because of peculiarly limiting environmental factors. Food can then indeed be distributed through an "international" trade system that characteristically does not operate by normal market principles that determine prices and profits (Sahlins 1972, Chapter 6). The critical aspect of these systems is that exchange rates are socially prescribed and are not set by market competition. The obvious conclusion is that the market rationale is not always the best means of satisfying human nutritional needs.

In many cases, what can analytically be recognized as "international food aid" between small-scale cultures is actually regulated by ideological aspects of the culture. For example, Australian Aborigines were able to safely share unusually abundant resources with neighbors on ceremonial occasions, and could welcome temporary refugees from drought-stricken areas, because their elaborate system of clan totemism virtually guaranteed that guests would return to their sacred home territories (Birdsell 1971). The rivalrous potlatch feasting characteristic of Northwest Coast chiefdoms may also indirectly help smooth out irregularities in resource availability, fish runs in this case, between groups (Suttles 1960). Tiny, isolated, coral atolls in Micronesia maintained long-distance contacts with other islands, including the large, high island of Yap, by means of an elaborately ritualized tribute hierarchy. In the event of drought or devastating typhoons, threatened islanders could always count on food aid or a temporary refuge (Alkire 1978).

In simple chiefdom societies food consumption patterns may be related to rank. Certain foods may be consumed only by individuals occupying specific ranks as part of a system of sumptuary regulations, but this system is not strictly comparable to the present world food distribution system, which reflects the ranking of nations and rich and poor within nations. In a simple chiefdom individuals are not systematically deprived of their nutritional needs to support the inequity of the social system, but this is now what happens on a global scale. In 1965 Borgstrom computed agricultural self-sufficiency ratings for various nations on the basis of their reliance on ghost acres and showed that poor Asian nations such as China and India were more than 90 percent self-sufficient, whereas the wealthy Western European nations such as England, the Netherlands, Belgium, and West Germany were only

37 to 60 percent self-sufficient. Clearly these "developed" nations are being supported by a food system that could not long be sustained if world fisheries declined from over-fishing, or if the world trade system were to break down.

In effect there is an international series of trophic levels in which the nations at the bottom are supported by high-calorie, low-protein diets while supplying their high-protein resources to the nations at the upper levels. The upper nations are able to consume the highest quality animal protein and a wide array of very costly sumptuary foods imported from nations where these foods are economically inaccessible to the bulk of the population.

The continued expansion of world trade and the proliferation of new food products in rich nations add enormously to the energy costs of food, not only because of additional processing, but also because of the further requirements of storage and transportation. There are also diminishing energy returns due to increasing waste and losses. Normally at least 10 percent of the food supplies of a given nation is lost annually to spoilage and pests before it even reaches consumers. This loss may be serious enough in a market system that moves food from one end of the country to the other through complex networks of intermediary wholesalers and retailers. It becomes critical in a system in which food may be shipped halfway around the world.

THE LIMITS OF FOOD PRODUCTION

World leaders seem to be committed to increased food production as the perpetual solution to the Malthusian dilemma and have so far not given sufficient attention to the need to both stabilize population growth and to restructure the food production and distribution system. More intensive subsistence technology has been one of the principal components of international proposals for dealing with the food problem for decades. The famous "Point Four" program of technical assistance launched by the United States in 1949 made this a prime objective. Since then the United States has been heavily committed to speeding the diffusion of agricultural technology through such official agencies as the Agency for International Development (USAID), The Consultative Group on International Agricultural Research (CGIAR), and the Board for International Food and Agricultural Development (BIFAD) working through the U.S. Land Grant Universities. Private foundations such as the Ford Foundation, Rockefeller Foundation, and Kellogg Foundation have devoted millions of dollars since the 1950s to programs of agricultural extension and research designed to raise food production in poor countries. The United Nations Food and Agriculture Organization (FAO) has been dedicated to increasing food production throughout the world since its inception. Agricultural development was a key element in UN proposals for the Second Development Decade (1970–1980) and continues to be a central focus in the Fourth and Fifth Development Decades. In 1969 the FAO unveiled its Indicative World Plan for agricultural development, which continues to form the basis for UN food strategy. The plan, as outlined in 1970 by Addeke H. Boerma, then FAO head, calls simply for "increasing productivity through more intensive use of physical resources and modern agricultural technology." Cereal production, because of its crucial dietary role, has been singled out for special attention. The plan also assumes continued economic growth to support the further development of technology and to help poor nations purchase the food imports they will still require even if agricultural development succeeds.

The strategy of intensifying production was pioneered by the Rockefeller Foundation and Nobel Prize–winning plant scientist Norman Borlaug. It involves simply exporting the fossil-fuel-subsidized factory farm systems of the highly industrialized nations to the rest of the world. More specifically, it means applying biological engineering to the design of specialized plants that will respond to the application of large doses of chemical fertilizer, pesticides, and water with high yields in the tropical settings where most of the hungry people are now located. "Miracle" plants have been designed through selective breeding (or more directly through genetic engineering). These plants divert more of their energy into seed production and less into foliage and may permit multiple cropping. Such plants may give enormous yields, but in some cases the grain is of markedly reduced nutritional quality or possesses qualities that the target people find objectionable. These technical problems are being solved, however.

This so-called Green Revolution was quickly hailed as an enormous success when per acre yields in many countries soared as these new techniques were applied in the late 1960s, and there were many optimistic statements about rapid doublings in food production and a final conquest over all of nature's limitations. Malthus, it seemed, had been refuted. Some of the most enthusiastic observers felt that the new problem of the disposal of crop surpluses would now replace famine as a worry for once hungry nations:

> It is difficult to remember that only a few years ago there seemed to be a very serious prospect of starvation in Asia. Local agricultural yields seemed stationary while population was rapidly increasing. . . . Now only a decade later, the pendulum of anxiety has swung considerably. The apparent success of the Green Revolution, at least in cereal production, is beginning to raise doubts not about famine but about disposal of surpluses to national requirements.
>
> (NULTY 1972)

Many agricultural success stories have been cited as justification for renewed faith in the unlimited power of technology. Mexico, for example, was able to triple its wheat production and double its corn output within roughly twenty years after agricultural scientists financed by the Rockefeller Foundation began applying modern technology toward the development of miracle plants in 1944 (Fabun 1970). World grain production more than doubled between 1962 and 1992, actually staying ahead of population growth. Furthermore, large surpluses in some farm products continued to pile up in the United States and even India has had sporadic surpluses since the late 1970s (Hazell 1994).

Regardless of the outstanding successes, in some countries many problems have arisen that have made implementation of the new technology difficult. Many agricultural extension workers have been frustrated by stubborn peasants who refuse to believe that the new crops would really be an advantage for them because of their obvious vulnerability and the increased dependency on outsiders that they imply. There have also been serious problems in financing the new technology at both national and local levels. Small farmers cannot afford the investment in expensive seeds and chemicals and neither can poor nations. As was noted earlier, this system ultimately depends on a vast fossil fuel subsidy that has seldom been readily available to poor countries. Escalating petroleum prices on the world market since the early 1970s and general increases in the cost of agricultural intensification contributed to the enormous debt burdens that poor nations faced in the 1980s and 1990s.

Even if financing and the energy base were not a limiting factor, water availability and unfavorable weather conditions could be. Even unlimited energy would not solve all the problems involved in getting enough water to enough acres to support an unlimited Green Revolution. Some of the new technology may require so little labor that unemployment results and rural people are forced to move to the cities. In some countries the new crops have been monopolized by large agribusinesses and wealthy landowners, driving small farmers off their lands. In some cases, transportation and storage facilities have not been adequate to handle either the increased crops or the needed fertilizer. High production may reduce prices below the profit margin, but the prices may still be higher than the poor can pay. Indeed, the social and economic barriers to further intensification of food production may be so critical that the ultimate physical limits may never be reached.

Some experts fear that the successes achieved to date in the Green Revolution might be only temporary, and that serious reversals may occur if potential biological liabilities of the high yield varieties emerge. It must be assumed that these plants will turn out to be highly susceptible to many new pests and blights or to minor fluctuations in weather. A further unknown is the extent of the ecological impact of factory farming on a global scale. Further eutrophication will almost certainly clog inland waters as fertilizer use increases and pesticides will threaten marine food resources. With the full application of fossil-fuel powered factory farm food production humanity may be taking an irreversible step with implications fully as grave as when tribal foragers first turned to simple farming. Now, however, the price could be much higher. Optimists argue that with the proper application of technology we can intensify production to feed 10 billion people by 2050 (Bongaarts 1994). The removal of farm subsidies and trade barriers would allow food prices to rise to levels that would no doubt spur production. However, unless these changes also allow the world's poor to participate in the market, billions will be shut out.

The Population Problem

*The explosive growth of the human population is the most
significant terrestrial event of the past million millennia. . . . No
geological event in a billion years—not the emergence of mighty
mountain ranges, nor the submergence of entire subcontinents,
nor the occurrence of periodic glacial ages—has posed a threat to
terrestrial life comparable to that of human overpopulation.*

PAUL EHRLICH AND ANNE EHRLICH,
Population, Resources, Environment

IT HAS BEEN RELATIVELY easy for Americans and citizens of the other
comfortably wealthy industrial nations to see overpopulation as the "root" of
all the world's environmental problems and of many of its other difficulties
as well. In this simplistic view resource depletion, food shortages, and environmental deterioration, along with war and poverty, must all be caused by
the presence of too many people in the world. Birth control and family planning programs are the obvious solutions. In 1968 biologist Paul Ehrlich presented this viewpoint dramatically in his book *The Population Bomb*, which
popularized the expression "population explosion" and focused wide attention on the problem and this particular cause. Ehrlich emphatically linked
"too many people" together with "too little food" as the cause of hunger in
poor countries and environmental troubles worldwide. On the latter issue he
declared: "The causal chain of the deterioration is easily followed to its
source. Too many cars, too many factories, too much detergent, too much
pesticide, multiplying contrails, inadequate sewage treatment plants, too little water, too much carbon dioxide—all can be traced easily to *too many people*" (Ehrlich 1968:67).

In 1972 Paul and Anne Ehrlich (1972:1) declared in "The Crisis," the
first chapter of their human ecology textbook, that the population explosion
was "the most significant event of the past million millennia" and warned
that it was suddenly bringing all life on earth to the edge of extinction. In his

1991 address delivered in London for the Worldwide Fund for Nature's annual World Conservation Lecture, Paul Ehrlich was appalled that world population was reaching 5.5 billion. This represented an increase of 2 billion people in the 24 years since the publication of *The Population Bomb*. He argued emphatically that "the strategic problem for humanity is that the scale of our activities is too large" (Ehrlich 1992:10, see also Ehrlich & Ehrlich 1990). He continued to maintain that sustaining the present population required eating into the world's capital resources and that it was pure folly to suggest that further growth was supportable.

Despite Ehrlich's dire predictions, many other writers reject the notion of a population crisis. They argue that if we simply achieve full economic development the earth can comfortably support many billions more people. Colin Clark even suggested that population growth itself will be the means of bringing further progress to poor peoples:

> It [population growth] brings economic hardship to communities living by traditional methods of agriculture; but it is the only force powerful enough to make such communities change their methods, and in the long run transforms them into much more advanced and productive societies. The world has immense physical resources for agricultural and mineral production still unused. In communities, the beneficial economic effects of large and expanding markets are abundantly clear.
>
> (CLARK 1968, PREFACE)

There can be little doubt that rapid population growth and the absolute level of population are important aspects of the environmental crisis as Ehrlich suggests, but the level of consumption is in many respects more critical than population size alone. At the same time, Clark is correct that population growth has also promoted technological growth and economic development, but when development means growth in per capita consumption the human impact on the earth increases disproportionately, such that greater numbers have a more negative impact in the long run. Ehrlich (1992) calculated that since his birth in 1932 world population has nearly tripled but because of economic development the effective human impact on the planet has increased perhaps sixfold. He estimated that on a per capita basis Americans have a fifty times greater impact on the earth's life support system than people in the poorest countries. As we shall see, quality of life, or standard of living, must be considered in any attempt to assess carrying capacities for given environments. Population pressure is always relative to particular cultural conditions.

Instead of treating population as the overriding problem, this chapter examines population in broad cross-cultural and evolutionary perspectives. The elevated population growth rates that presently characterize world demography will be seen as one problematic symptom of a world dominated by the culture of consumption. Given present consumption patterns it would be misleading to deny the reality of the environmental crisis that accelerates with each increase in either population or consumption. Global economic growth may well be a false hope, both because it may be unattainable and because, if attained, it would only elevate consumption and cancel any environmental gains that may be achieved, even if world population can be stabilized. Rather than focusing on economic growth, the world needs to focus on sociocultural development and the politics of wealth distribution to meet existing human needs. As Ehrlich argued in 1968, rather than planning technological advances to meet the future needs of another 5 or 10 billion people, ". . . it would be more prudent to take proper care of 3.5 billion people [the 1968 population] before boasting about how easy it was to do the same for much greater numbers" (Ehrlich 1992:10).

There is no disagreement on the basic fact that world population has grown enormously since the beginning of the industrial era and that unsustainable growth continues in much of the world. With few apparent exceptions (Simon 1981), most also agree that present growth patterns cannot continue indefinitely. It is easy to demonstrate the impossibility of perpetual growth. For example, in 1968 Paul Ehrlich calculated that, given a doubling time of 37 years, the estimated world rate at that time, there would be 60 million billion people, or 100 persons per square yard over the entire surface of the earth, within just 900 years. In 1971 Isaac Asimov estimated that at growth rates prevailing at that time the human population would equal the mass of the globe within a mere 1,560 years; and within 4,856 years it would equal the mass of the universe. The real question is obviously not whether growth will continue but rather how it will stop. Technological optimists feel confident that the world can support more than 10 billion people (Bongaarts 1994), while some super-optimists feel that we might accommodate well over 100 billion. Predictions of global population based on conditions in the late 1960s warned that there could be 8 billion people in the world by the year 2000. However, the actual rate of increase declined somewhat, and in 1994 the U.S. Census Bureau predicted 6.1 billion for the year 2000, slightly more than double the 1960 population. Obviously, if that growth rate continued there would be 12 billion by 2040.

A major assumption concerning the origin of the population problem, which provides the basis for much current policy making, is that the rapid growth now experienced in the poor countries of the world is simply the result of the combination of traditionally high fertility rates with the sudden lowering of traditionally high mortality rates that has accompanied incomplete economic development. Most of those holding this view feel that values relating to family size have somehow not caught up with the drop in mortality, and that further economic growth and education will correct the situation such that people everywhere will experience the "demographic transition" to low fertility and low mortality enjoyed by rich nations. This interpretation may place too much emphasis on continued economic growth and does not acknowledge the demographic advantages of small-scale cultures and relative social equality.

POPULATION PRESSURE, CARRYING CAPACITY, AND OPTIMUM POPULATION

... preindustrial population rates reflect some form of optimization effort engaged in by individuals and groups, rather than a culturally unregulated surrender to sex, hunger, and death. Among preindustrial populations both age-specific fertility and age-specific mortality could readily be raised or lowered in conformity with optimizing rationalities which maintained or enhanced the well-being of individuals and groups—although seldom with equal or even beneficial results for all.

(HARRIS & ROSS 1987:1)

It makes little sense to speak of overpopulation and the need to halt growth without discussing carrying capacity, optimum population size, and what constitutes population pressure. Surprisingly these topics are often completely ignored in population programs, even though they may be at least implicit in any attempt to regulate population or set demographic goals. This failure to adequately deal with these aspects of the population problem is perhaps understandable when we realize that they are culturally and environmentally relative concepts and directly involve the most basic characteristics of any culture.

An optimum population would exist at what anthropologist Fekri Hassan (1981:167) has called the optimum carrying capacity for its technology and environment—that is, the level of population that could safely maintain itself over several generations without drastic crashes as the resource base fluctuates. This is precisely where a culture concerned with minimizing subsistence risk (Gould 1981, Hayden 1981a) would find itself. Small-scale tribal cultures have been in effect designed by the collective decisions of people organized in independent bands and villages seeking to satisfy their basic human needs on a long-term basis, such that they always have attempted to maintain themselves at optimum population levels. The important thing is that maximum decision making authority for production, reproduction, and consumption is at the individual and household levels. Thus people are free to make the decisions that best meet their needs.

Population pressure is a widely discussed component of the population problem and is frequently assumed to be some readily apparent, absolute quality. However, on closer analysis it proves, like carrying capacity, to be neither easily recognized nor absolute. As Cowgill (1975), Hassan (1981), and others point out, population pressure cannot be profitably treated in isolation from other cultural, demographic, and environmental factors. The problem with the concept of population pressure is that it places undue emphasis on population, while the real issue is how to maintain a balance between the total human demand for resources in a given area and the sustainable supply, given a certain technology. In fact, population pressure is culturally defined and is only meaningful in relation to particular technological systems, environments, and per capita consumption levels.

Raymond C. Kelly (1968) found that in traditional New Guinea cultures population pressure occurred only rarely in an absolute sense but was frequently manifest as a local imbalance between people and land experienced by particular clans. Local imbalances may occur even when the total population is stable simply because random demographic processes, including variation in the sex ratio, birthrates, and mortality, may, under different cultural circumstances, have widely varying impacts on local groups of different size. As a result, certain clans may outgrow their land base while neighboring clans dwindle to extinction. Many cultural devices are employed to relieve this pressure of population on land resources, including transfers of land and people between clans through gifts, adoption, and warfare. Where population pressure is not compensated for by normal redistributive measures it may be felt as a steady reduction in the culturally defined standard of living, with people forced to work longer hours to increase food production. Eventually there may be a switch to less desirable food sources (Bayless-Smith 1974) or a move to marginal ecological zones (Zubrow 1975). Thus, "absolute" population pressure might be relieved by simply redefining what the members of a culture consider an acceptable standard of living, by technological innovation, or by a reduction in population.

Population redistribution has sometimes been developed to a high degree, particularly in island cultures in which adoption is widely used, but it can be only a temporary solution. Resource distribution may help raise regional carrying capacity by evening out local surpluses or seasonal fluctuations; but elaborate redistribution systems are usually dependent on formal political offices and thus can only occur in large-scale cultures. Migration to relieve population pressure is probably a normal response that occurs automatically whenever ecologically similar territory is readily available for occupation (see Dumond 1972).

The final option, population control, has been practiced by virtually all tribal cultures to some degree. Tribal foragers have followed this course almost exclusively and achieved remarkably stable populations that must have maintained a dynamic equilibrium with shifts in their environments. Cultivators may sometimes have established equilibrium systems as well balanced as those of the foragers, but have far more often slipped into subsistence intensification and predatory expansion against their neighbors as their populations have gradually increased.

POPULATION CONTROL AMONG FORAGERS

Whereas many demographers believe that the human population has grown at a slow and steady rate from its very beginning to the origins of agriculture, anthropological research suggests that the thousands of years before domestication were characterized by relative population equilibrium, punctuated by only occasional and unusual growth phases as people pioneered new territories. By the eve of the transition to settled farm life the human population had grown to an estimated 8–9 million over a span of perhaps 3 million years (Hassan 1981:199, see also Deevy 1960, Coale 1974, Demeny 1990). Much of this increase represented expansion into empty lands. Only very slight local increases in density occurred prior to the introduction of agriculture. As a general principle it can be assumed that tribal cultures quickly established a culturally regulated equilibrium as soon as their populations had grown to a culturally defined carrying capacity within specific environments.

It seems that cultural factors, not food shortages or high mortality rates, were the primary factors in setting limits to population growth in tribal cultures. This is a particularly significant point, because it is still widely assumed that small-scale cultures were characterized by uniformly high fertility and mortality rates and a precarious food supply, but such was decidedly not the case. Tribal cultures were generally stabilized at levels considerably below the maximum population densities that their technologies and environments might potentially have sustained if increasing absolute population was a cultural objective. Even Paleolithic hunters, if their political structures had forced them to work harder and if they would have adjusted their food preferences away from big game toward a concentration on small mammals, might have increased their population densities many times over. This is, of course, precisely what happened during the Mesolithic period. It is also likely that real famines were rare during the Paleolithic period although it has been established both archaeologically and ethnohistorically that hunting peoples did sometimes starve in the Arctic when relatively minor shifts in climate made critical food resources unavailable. In such unstable and marginal environments population equilibriums were very dynamic (Smith & Smith 1994). Dramatic shifts in the environment probably occurred throughout the last great Ice Age, such that population/resource balances were continuously interrupted. Nevertheless, while the availability of game certainly did influence population densities among hunting and foraging peoples, food shortages per se definitely appear not to have been the primary factor limiting population growth; rather, as we will show, it was the organization of the cultures themselves.

There is overwhelming evidence to suggest that mortality was also not a significant limiting factor for tribal hunters and foragers. Deaths due to epidemic disease were apparently far lower before the establishment of permanent villages than at any time thereafter. Tribal hunting peoples were consistently well nourished, they led physically active lives, and they apparently avoided most infectious epidemic diseases by maintaining dispersed populations so that these diseases could not become established and spread. Foragers may also have developed high levels of natural immunity thanks to strong selective pressure enforced by relatively high infant mortality rates and constant exposure to endemic pathogens. Deaths due to warfare were probably rare during the many thousands of years that people lived as foragers and homicide and suicide are both decidedly uncommon among undisturbed ethnographically described foraging peoples. The probable occurrence of accidental deaths is more difficult to evaluate, but it seems reasonable to assume that they were not a major factor. Demographic data based on age estimates of selected prehistoric skeletal populations and modern ethnographic data reveal that foragers at age fifteen could expect to live an average of twenty-six additional years. This is, of course, about half the average for peoples in industrialized nations today but it is roughly the same as life expectancy at age fifteen in thirteenth-century England and higher than has been described for some Neolithic populations (Hassan 1981:118).

Tribal cultures held in reserve an enormous potential for rapid population growth that was activated only under special conditions. Even if mortality rates as high as 50 percent to age fifteen are assumed to have been typical for foraging peoples (half of the population dying before reaching reproductive age)—and this is by no means easily demonstrated (Weiss 1973)—it still would have been quite possible for the population to have doubled each generation if high fertility was culturally encouraged. Such rapid growth probably did occur at times but was only common when previously unoccupied territory was first entered or when a population was recovering from some natural disaster, such as an unfavorable shift in the ice in the Arctic (Smith & Smith 1994). In the New World, for example, people were well established in North America by 10,000 B.C. and were settled in the southern tip of South America by 9000 B.C. Such a rapid spread could hardly have been achieved by cultures that were barely keeping ahead of extinction.

The full significance of this picture of the demography of early foraging peoples can perhaps best be appreciated when considered in contrast to the grim view presented by modern demographers in their assessment of the history of population growth and the origin of our present dilemma. Paul Ehrlich (1968:29), for example, in *The Population Bomb*, states that "our ancestors were fighting a continual battle to keep the birth rate ahead of the death rate." The distinguished demographer Donald T. Bogue summarizes this period in his major textbook, *Principles of Demography*, as follows:

> During the many thousands of years of man's existence on the earth before the beginning of civilization, the population problem facing most communities was that of survival—to offset successfully the terrible attrition of death on their numbers. . . . When population did manage to grow, there was always the

threat of famine, war, and epidemics. Such a situation is the only conjecture that is consistent with the facts. . . . We are forced, therefore, to conclude that the human race has been required by circumstances of high mortality to reproduce at near-biological capacity and that a whole system of fertility-promoting practices has evolved as an integral part of every culture.

(BOGUE 1969:53–54)

In fact, precisely the opposite situation now appears to have been the case and the problem that remains is to outline precisely what fertility-dampening practices maintained tribal populations in dynamic equilibrium.

Among hunters, density limits seem to have been set by the availability of cultural recognized food sources and by the lack of formal political structures to deal with conflict. Small local bands of twenty-five to fifty people were apparently the most efficient hunting and gathering groups. Fewer people would have difficulty feeding themselves because of random accidents and runs of bad luck, whereas larger groups would experience diminishing returns as local resources were depleted too quickly. Expansion of subsistence through intensified collecting or domestication was apparently rejected as a solution far more often than not and seems to have been a course that was only reluctantly followed in the face of either political pressures or environmental changes. Migration certainly occurred among hunters as new bands on the fringes of occupied territories moved steadily into vacant lands, but this would not have been at the expense of other groups already firmly in possession of their territories (Krantz 1976). There is little evidence of warfare or territorial conquest between bands. Perhaps most critical was the fact that there was no culturally encouraged reason for increasing population density beyond the minimum needed to reproduce healthy domestic units and local communities. Birth spacing by deliberate abortion and infanticide seem to have been the primary mechanisms of fertility regulation, although indirect physiological factors must have played a role.

Infanticide has received much attention as the basic method of population control among foraging peoples, but this is a complex issue and many questions remain unanswered. Some writers argue that baby girls were killed or neglected so that boys could be raised to become warriors or hunters (Riches 1974, Divale & Harris 1976). However, computer simulations suggest that selective female infanticide could never have been very common because it would easily cause an irreversible decline in a small population (Schrire & Steiger 1974). It has also been argued that detailed census data provide no real evidence for selective female infanticide (Yengoyan 1981, see also Smith & Smith 1994). Furthermore, both the actual rates and individual motives for even general infanticide are not well recognized. Birdsell (1979) suggests that 15–30 percent of births in aboriginal Australia ended in infanticide, but convincing supporting evidence has not been provided and is unlikely ever to be obtained. Some authors offer antagonism between the sexes as an important motivation for infanticide (Freeman 1971, Cowlishaw

1978), but it seems more likely that it occurs primarily as a birth-spacing mechanism when a woman realizes that attempting to raise a new baby might threaten the welfare of her older child.

It has been assumed that women in nomadic foraging societies were forced to space their children approximately four years apart because of the difficulty of carrying two dependent children on daily foraging expeditions and on the frequent moves to new camps (Sussman 1972). This may be a critical consideration motivating, or at least rationalizing, the family planning decisions of individual women; but if it were an absolute necessity it would be difficult to explain the rapid growth known to have occurred when virgin territories were occupied. Whatever the motivation for such spacing and regardless of the method employed it will yield a stationary, no-growth population, assuming that an average woman attempts to raise four children and that half of them survive to reproduce.

POPULATION EQUILIBRIUM IN ABORIGINAL AUSTRALIA

One of the most provocative and best documented arguments that tribal foragers maintained culturally regulated optimum populations is presented in J. B. Birdsell's analysis of Australian Aborigines, based on twenty-five years of intensive research. According to Birdsell's (1953, 1971, 1979) estimates, Australia supported a constant population of 300,000 Aborigines, the maximum that could be sustained by a hunting and gathering technology, for perhaps 30,000 years, with only minor fluctuations related to overall changes in the environment. They were not constantly tottering on the edge of disaster with their numbers held in check by high mortality rates and they did not continually outstrip their meager resources only to crash precipitously and later rebound. In contrast, the commercial culture now controlling Australia had grown to 17 million within 200 years of the first European settlement and continues to grow at more than 1 percent per year.

The forces that may have contributed to the relative stability in the aboriginal population involved not only environmental factors but included culturally defined territorial spacing mechanisms as well. According to Birdsell's analysis, Australian cultures were organized into linguistically distinct tribal groups averaging 500 people, that were in turn divided into bands of 25 people composed of individual families of 5 persons. Tribal territories were large enough to provide a reliable subsistence base for the population roughly 98 percent of the time, while individual band territories might be somewhat less self-sufficient, so that resources from neighboring bands might be needed in 10 to 15 out of every 100 years. Band territories were carefully laid out to ensure that they allowed access to all critical food resources in sufficient quantity for long-range survival. In some coastal regions, where a tribal territory included several diverse ecological zones with different resource potentials, each band territory would include portions of each zone. Interband and intertribal ceremonies normally occurred in times of plenty. These ceremonies helped distribute seasonal or random concentrations of food and served to equalize resources, thus helping to bring population densities closer to the maximum carrying capacity for the technology. Bands in drought-stricken areas might be temporarily taken in by more comfortably situated neighbors. Individuals were so emotionally attached to the sacred sites within their traditional territories that represented their totemic origin points that there was no danger that they would ever choose to remain permanently in their refuge. Boundaries were also clearly defined by the wanderings of spirit beings, which were recorded in myths and commemorated in intergroup ceremonies. The religious and ceremonial system played a vital role in supporting population balances through boundary maintenance and resource redistribution.

The upper limit for tribal population was set by the density of the communication network that could be supported by foragers restricted to foot travel. As tribes grew larger, it became more difficult for the bands within them to remain in contact. When more bands appeared, the frequency, intensity, and length of interactions such as joint ceremonies and intermarriage declined and linguistic diversity increased, making further communication more difficult. Tribes that grew too small, that lost bands until they dropped below 500 members, would automatically interact more with bands in neighboring tribes and would eventually be absorbed into them. Bands needed to include at least twenty-five people in order to maximize the availability of food, given random variations in hunting success; to provide task groups of optimum size; to ensure demographic viability, given gender variations at birth; to defend themselves; and to ensure a large enough pool of marriageable individuals to meet the cultural requirements of band exogamy, that is, marriage outside of the band. Upper limits to band size were apparently set by the absence of strong political controls, which meant that increased conflicts that might arise with denser population could only be adequately controlled by fissioning, or splitting a large band into two or more smaller bands. The need to minimize the strain on local ecosystems also determined maximum band sizes. Random fluctuation in local band size was regulated through selective infanticide, adoption, and transfers of people in "violation" of normal residence and exogamic norms. Local boundaries were also adjusted by means of occasional duels and skirmishes.

Actual tribal densities varied from lows of perhaps eighty square miles per person in the interior deserts, where rainfall might drop to a mean of only four inches per year, to densities as high as two square miles per person in rich coastal or riverine environments. Optimum carrying capacities for tribal territories remained within 10 to 20 percent of the maximum density that could be supported in the best years, thanks to the cultural mechanisms that helped level out the long-range fluctuations in resources due to droughts and other unpredictable events.

It is uncertain what means of birth spacing were most common but it is clear that infanticide was often practiced by Australians; abortion and contraception may also have been important spacing mechanisms. It is important to note in this context that the distinction between abortion and infanticide may not be culturally meaningful. Some tribes may induce labor in the third trimester of pregnancy and then kill the fetus if it survives. "Birth" itself, and "humanness," may be culturally defined at a quite different point than that normally recognized by state legal systems (Neel 1968).

It appears from the data that Birdsell presents that a system of density equilibrium was indeed operating among Australian tribes and bands. The primary density determinant seems to have been environmental, as reflected by a statistically significant inverse relationship between rainfall and size of tribal territory. Deviation from this mathematical relationship can be accounted for by the presence of extra water and consequently greater biological productivity in riverine or coastal regions, where carrying capacity is higher than would be expected otherwise. Further evidence is provided in the reports that large tribes were in the process of splitting into small tribes of 500 members when they were first contacted by Europeans. It has also been shown that tribes that were initially fragmented by the acquisition of new initiation ceremonies quickly returned to their original size after the diffusion wave had passed.

Some authorities argue that Aborigines did not quickly establish an equilibrium, but rather steadily but gradually expanded both population and technology (Bowdler 1977, Lourandos 1985, 1987). This viewpoint is supported by the appearance in Australia of some technological improvements, such as the spear-thrower and the dingo, only within the past 5,000 years. However, as noted in Chapter 2, there is little evidence that Aborigines exterminated the Pleistocene megafauna (Horton 1984), and Aborigines were in contact with gardeners and pig raisers in New Guinea for thousands of years without borrowing their more intensive production techniques.

THE NEOLITHIC POPULATION EXPLOSION

The relatively rapid growth in population that accompanied and perhaps contributed to the adoption of farming is one of the most significant demographic events in human history. It marked the end of the long period of relative population equilibrium that foraging peoples established and initiated a period of almost continuous population growth and a rapid series of interrelated changes that led successively to politicization, the emergence of large-scale urban culture, and finally the rise of industrial global cultures. It has been estimated that world population suddenly jumped from approximately 8 million in 8000 B.C. to 86 million by 4000 B.C., a tenfold increase (Deevy 1960, Polgar 1972, Coale 1974, Hassan 1981). The fourfold increase related to industrialization between 1650 and 1950 seems relatively minor in comparison, although, of course, this later increase did occur over a much shorter time period. The scale of the Neolithic expansion is even more dramatic in specific countries. France, for example, experienced a hundredfold population increase by 3000 B.C. over densities obtaining during the Upper Paleolithic period and only a tenfold increase between 3000 B.C. and the twentieth century.

Explaining the breakdown of "Paleolithic" dynamic population equilibrium mechanisms and the subsequent transition to sedentary village life must surely be one of the most critical theoretical problems in anthropology. Numerous specific explanations have been proposed for the Neolithic transition that occurred in different parts of the world independently about 5,000 to 10,000 years ago. The common element is the enormous environmental changes that occurred in the post-Pleistocene world at the end of the last Ice Age. Climate became milder, especially in the temperate zones; vegetation zones shifted; many large animals became extinct; and sea levels rose, flooding many coastal plains and separating many formerly connected land areas. Many authors explain the Neolithic as a relatively gradual process of subsistence intensification designed to increase food production in the face of dwindling resources and great instability (Cohen 1977, see also Hayden 1981a). More intensive use of local resources may involve sedentism, with people maintaining a relatively fixed residence throughout the year. Sedentism could in itself encourage population expansion because it eliminates at least one incentive to birth spacing—the inconvenience of more than one dependent child that would need to be carried every time camp was moved. However, Barry Hewlett (1991) argues that foragers and simple horticulturalists do not differ significantly demographically. It is quite possible that foragers spaced births to protect the health of mother and child as well as to maintain mobility, and thus the practice might have been continued even after sedentarization. It is well known that many settled village peoples space births four years apart, or even longer, for precisely this reason. Late weaning can be very important to the health of the infant, particularly where protein is scarce. Furthermore, there is some evidence that prolonged lactation may suppress ovulation and thus serve as a natural contraceptive.

Some writers attribute population growth to the increased food supply made available by domestication. This argument is the opposite of the Boserup subsistence intensification theory discussed in Chapter 4, and in the preceding paragraph, which sees population pressure or resources/population imbalance leading to more intensive resource use, including sedentism and domestication. Increases in food production in a given region are thus more likely to be results rather than causes of imbalances in the resources/population equation.

Randel A. Sengel (1973) has suggested a rather novel solution to this vexing problem. He argues that in the Near East an increased reliance on wild grains, ultimately caused by climatic changes that increased their prevalence, may have resulted in a significant augmentation of the protein intake of the population, which in turn lowered the age of menarche and increased the reproductive span of the women. Empirical evidence from Europe indicates that nutritional improvement has apparently had that effect in modern times and it is by no means certain that the age of menarche is a constant in all human populations. Some writers, however, suggest that the domestication process resulted in the displacement of wild plant foods that were richer in protein than domesticated varities, so the question is by no means settled (Flannery 1969).

It is clear that even a slight increase in the reproductive span could result in a gradual population growth even if the original pattern of birth spacing were retained. It might be assumed that such increased growth would quickly be recognized and the birth-spacing mechanism would be adjusted to restore equilibrium. However, it is not likely that population control in tribal cultures was actually carried out with long-range social goals in mind; rather, individual women made "family planning" decisions that were for their immediate self-interest and in the aggregate these decisions proved to be highly adaptive for the entire culture.

Although these demographic changes, whatever their causes, were in the long run revolutionary in impact, they were so slow that, like the domestication process, they would have been imperceptible to the actors. In the Near East, for example, the population may have grown from 100,000 in 8000 B.C. to 2.5 to 12 million by 4000 B.C., an annual growth rate of only 0.08–0.12 percent (Carneiro & Hilse 1966). At such gradual rates a tribe of 500 people would add only about 12 people in a generation.

POPULATION CONTROL AMONG
TRIBAL VILLAGE FARMERS

Population growth was a much more difficult force to contain for sedentary or semisedentary cultures based on domesticated, and thus inherently more elastic, food sources. Tribal farmers certainly have in many cases achieved remarkable population equilibrium, as will be shown in the following sections. In general, however, domestication touched off a period of great cultural instability throughout the world. Suddenly expanding cultures pushed hunters out of the most fertile lands only to be themselves incorporated into expanding conquest states and ultimately into an expanding global culture.

Foragers, newly transformed into farmers, found their resource bases increasingly inadequate for the support of their growing populations and were forced into more difficult environments or into cultural transformations that they might not otherwise have chosen. In some cases growing populations simply expanded beyond the carrying capacities of their environments and collapsed without the development of complex political systems or more "advanced" technology.

The American Southwest affords an example of this latter outcome. From approximately 7000 B.C. to A.D. 100 that area was occupied by hunters and seed collectors that made up what archaeologists have called the "desert tradition," which must have constituted an enduring, relatively stable adaptation. Toward the end of that period domesticated plants from Mesoamerica were gradually adopted and by A.D. 400 farming villagers were becoming established.

Through an intensive analysis of the archaeological record in one small valley in Arizona, Ezra B. Zubrow (1975) has reconstructed 1,400 years of population history from the beginning of domestication up to A.D. 1400. His study shows a steady increase in population within the valley and a continual expansion into more marginal environments as the carrying capacities in the most favorable zones were reached. The population peaked shortly after irrigation was introduced in approximately A.D. 1000 and then began to decline as pressure on the resource base and a change in the rainfall pattern beginning in A.D. 1150 drastically lowered the carrying capacity of the valley. Population densities plunged rapidly between A.D. 1100 and 1200 to a small fraction of the peak and by 1400 the valley was abandoned completely. Thus a culture of village farmers expanded for perhaps 700 years and then totally collapsed. This record stands in striking contrast to the 7,000 years of success that foragers previously enjoyed in the same general environment.

The archaeological and ethnographic record contains many other examples of village farmers who were able to support their population growth by pushing out their neighbors. The Neolithic population expansion carried speakers of Indo-European languages with their farming village life-style based on sheep, cattle, and grain crops throughout Europe over a 2,000-year period beginning about 6500 B.C. or earlier. The fate of the prior European foragers is uncertain. Although some may have adopted farming or been incorporated into the invading culture, it seems more reasonable to guess that many resisted the change and simply moved into marginal environments and gradually declined. Austronesian speakers carried taro, bananas, breadfruit, and pigs from Southeast Asia to the most remote parts of the Pacific from about 4000 B.C. to A.D. 600. Bantu-speaking peoples carried cattle and millet throughout Central and Southern Africa beginning about A.D. 200. In East and South Africa, Bantu farmers and herders were still expanding into territory occupied by the San Bushmen foragers in the seventeenth century. Their growth was not halted until the militaristic Zulu empire was finally overwhelmed by the British army in the late nineteenth century. Marshall Sahlins (1961) has shown how growing African tribal cultures such as the Nuer and Tiv have utilized their segmentary lineage systems as a means of mobilizing on their boundaries, in the absence of formal political leadership, to expand their territory against weak neighbors.

Archaeologist Don W. Lathrap (1970) argued that village farmers were well established in the central Amazon Basin, utilizing manioc as their primary staple, by 3000 B.C. Almost from that point on the evidence suggests that a continuous period of population growth, migration, displacement, and differentiation of cultures began that continued into modern times. However, many uncertainties remain. More recently archaeologist Betty J. Meggers (1995) has attributed prehistoric population movements in Amazonia to the peridiodic effects of long-term climate fluctuations, thus emphasizing population equilibrium rather than continuous population expansion. In contrast, Lathrap felt that cultures existing in relative equilibrium, or those with comparatively small, slow-growing populations, were simply pushed up the smaller tributaries of the Amazon, and finally into the interfluvial hinterlands, by successive migration waves from the expanding centers. Among these expanding Amazonian village farmers the best known historically were Tupi speaking peoples. They, like the Zulus in Southern Africa, were still spreading south and east up the Amazon and even down the Brazilian coast, pushing aside prior foragers and more stable farmers, when the Spanish and Portuguese arrived in the sixteenth century. The difference between the migratory expansion waves of small-scale Amazonian and African tribes and large-scale chiefdoms and European colonialism is that the former were driven by demographic and political processes, whereas Europeans were primarily motivated by commercial economic forces as the global culture developed.

Chronic raiding and head-hunting recorded for shifting cultivators in many other parts of the world, including New Zealand and Southeast Asia, may also be viewed as responses to a failure to maintain population equilibrium. The Ibans in Borneo were actively expanding against their neighbors, some of whom were foragers, in the late nineteenth and well into the twentieth century. Traditionally oriented hill tribes in northwestern Thailand were growing rapidly in the 1960s but maintained their cultures intact without warfare by crowding out neighbors and through high rates of migration into lowland areas, where excess population was absorbed into other ethnic groups (Kunstadter 1971).

In spite of these examples of population growth among village farmers, considering the time periods involved it is apparent that very few such cultures reproduced at maximum feasible fertility rates for more than a very brief time. Cultural regulation of population growth certainly continued to be a very significant factor even after domestication began. As with foragers, fertility control was probably the most important regulating mechanism for village farmers, although increased mortality through raiding was at times an additional means of control. Abortion, infanticide, contraception, and birth spacing remained the primary means of limiting fertility, although many specific cultural practices that limited the frequency of coitus, or shortened the fertile period by delaying marriage, also became important.

One of the most common birth-spacing practices is the long postpartum taboo on sexual intercourse that occurs widely among shifting cultivators in tropical climates (Whiting 1969). The taboo often extends for more than a year after the birth of each child and has been shown to be related to reduced fertility rates in cultures that practice it. The taboo correlates with a number of other cultural practices and elaborate causal explanations for its occurrence have been proposed (Saucier 1972). It is quite possible that this is not always practiced as an intentional means of birth spacing; but whatever its "cause" it does serve as a critical check on fertility.

THE TSEMBAGA EQUILIBRIUM MODEL

The 225 Tsembaga people of the New Guinea highlands, a Maring speaking subgroup, are a frequently cited example of a small-scale horticultural group with a culturally regulated relationship between population and resources. The Tsembaga ritual system may help reduce a buildup of population pressure on the land that might otherwise lead to famine, technological intensification, or forced migration. The Tsembaga system has been described in detail by anthropologist Roy Rappaport (1968) in his now classic monograph *Pigs for the Ancestors*. His data were reduced to a computer simulation by systems researchers Steven B. Shantzis and William W. Behrens III (1973) of the Massachusetts Institute of Technology. While there are many weaknesses in the model, it nevertheless merits careful consideration because it highlights the complexities and possibilities of locally managed ecosystems.

The critical component of the system is the growth of the pig herd to a point that triggers a ritual cycle involving raiding and pig slaughters, which balance both human and animal populations. A growing pig herd is highly desirable because pigs are important as status symbols and as sources of high-quality animal protein; but a pig consumes as much of the cultivated crops as an average adult and the herd quickly becomes more bother than it is worth. A growing pig herd means that people must devote a larger and larger proportion of the cultivated land to raising pig feed and more labor must be expended per capita to tending pigs and gardens. Increases in both the human and pig populations cause a sharp rise in internal conflicts, not only because competition for resources increases, but also because the pigs themselves are a perpetual source of disputes. When these disturbances become intolerable, a ceremonial pig slaughter is held. In a pig feast that Rappaport

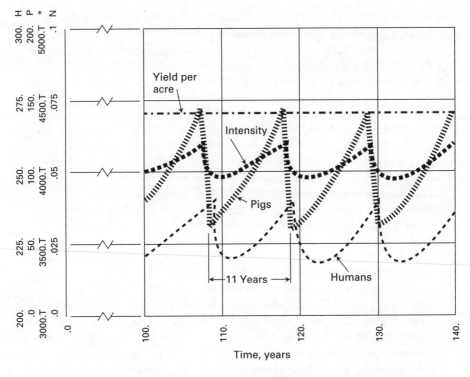

FIGURE 6.I   THE TSEMBAGA MODEL

Steven B. Shantzis and William W. Behrens III, "Population Control Mechanisms in a Primitive Agricultural Society," in *Toward Global Equilibrium*, edited by D. H. Meadows and D. L. Meadows (Cambridge, Mass.: Wright-Allen Press, 1973)275.

observed in 1963, the Tsembaga pig herd was reduced from 169 animals to 60 and the area of new garden plots was reduced by more than a third below what had been required earlier to support the full herd.

In the simulation model constructed by Shantzis and Behrens (1973), the human population maintains itself indefinitely, fluctuating in eleven-year cycles between approximately 220 and 230 persons, while the pig herd fluctuates between 60 and 145 (see Figure 6.1). Both populations remain in dynamic balance well below the point at which destructive shortening of the fallow cycle would become necessary. The slight increase in normal human fertility rates that might result from the intervention of modern medicine would, if not compensated for by other cultural controls, reduce the ritual cycle to ten years and shift population levels much closer to the critical carrying capacity. If new health programs were to raise the annual population growth rate from 1.3 to 2.0 percent per year, the control mechanisms would quickly break down and the human population would peak at over 400 within 120 years, forcing people to intensify their production system still further. A permanent end to intergroup raiding would have a similar drastic impact. Historically, the extension of government control in the New Guinea highlands has intensified pressure on the land by reducing mortality and encouraging cash-cropping of coffee and other crops for export to global markets.

If we assume that the Tsembaga kept no pig herds, held no festivals or raids, practiced no population control through infanticide or contraception, and experienced no migration, the dynamics of their population would be far different from that predicted by the ideal equilibrium model. Shantzis and Behrens constructed a computer simulation of just such a case that dramatically illustrates the inherent imbalances that unrestricted growth would permit. Under such conditions population growth would be constrained only by the availability of land and productivity per acre. Given a modest rate of uncontrolled population growth based on average fertility and life expectancy rates drawn from UN estimates for similar peoples, and starting with only 196 people and 972 acres of potentially arable land, it quickly becomes necessary to shorten the 125-year fallow period to put more land into production to feed the growing population. Within less than sixty years, this intensification of food production surpasses the carrying capacity and initiates a continuous decline in yields per acre, reflecting a progressive degradation of the land. Within approximately eighty years, the population would peak and then suddenly plunge to near zero as a result of famines and an almost total decline in soil fertility. This, of course, unrealistically assumes no technological innovation to increase per acre yields. It seems obvious that under these conditions the Tsembaga would recognize the declining yields within two or three years and would be confronted with the choice of either reducing population growth or working harder to intensify production to prevent the collapse that would be barely three generations away.

Rappaport's original presentation of the Tsembaga equilibrium model touched off a lively debate among anthropologists. Some critics argued that the model was based on simple functionalism and could not explain how the system came about—that is, Rappaport described how the system worked, or might have worked, but did not account for how it got that way (Rappaport 1979). Others argued that environmental limits were not really operating; rather, political factors overshadowed any ritual that might have operated (Friedman 1974). Some writers suggested that the pig-feasting system originated and persisted as a means of awarding allies in the raiding system (Peoples 1982). More detailed computer simulations indicated that the demographic impact of intergroup conflict was probably overstated (Samuels 1982). Perhaps the most important criticism is that the Tsembaga were part of a much larger open system and any model focusing on the fate of one small subgroup could not be accurate. The Tsembaga model was, of course, highly idealized and no empirical data demonstrates that it operated as described for any length of time into the past. In addition, many other highland New Guinea peoples are known to have moved to much more intensive production systems. However, the Tsembaga example demonstrates that small-scale systems are more likely to maintain decision making power over local ecosystems under the control of local domestic units rather than remote government centers or foreign markets that have little concern for the quality of local ecosystems.

THE HAVASUPAI INDIANS

Well-documented cases demonstrating population equilibrium in tribal populations and the mechanisms involved are uncommon because normally historical depth is absent from the anthropological record. However, historical data on the Havasupai Indians of Arizona shows that they have maintained a relative population equilibrium for at least 200 years (Alvarado 1970). Since the first census of this small tribe of farmers and hunters in their Grand Canyon home in 1776, well into the twentieth century, their population fluctuated between a low of 166 (due to a measles epidemic) to a high of 300. The modern high of 350 only occurred after outside intervention increased over a forty-year period.

Such stability, in spite of abundant food resources, led anthropologist Anita L. Alvarado to investigate possible explanations. She determined that cultural factors limiting fertility were largely responsible. Among these cultural factors were an imbalanced sex ratio with a preponderance of males, perhaps because boys received subtle advantages, and a significant delay in age at first marriage. Women traditionally did not marry until age twenty-five to thirty and men not until thirty-five to forty. The combined effect of these customs is to reduce fertility by not only reducing the number of years when a given women would be at risk for pregnancy but also by structuring it so that men would be married during their least fertile adult years. The Havasupai also tolerated a rather high proportion of unmarried, widowed, and divorced individuals who would otherwise have been marriageable. Furthermore, they made use of herbal contraceptives and abortion and nursed their babies for approximately two years, thereby undoubtedly delaying the resumption of ovulation. Extensive use of the steam bath by the men, followed by a dip in very cold water, might well have been an important spermicide. The testes produce viable sperm only within a very narrow temperature range and extremes can produce temporary sterility. Mortality rates do not appear to have been significantly high in pre-European times. Warfare was virtually unknown and the people appeared to be exceptionally healthy.

ISLAND POPULATION PROBLEMS

Perhaps the severest test of a culture's ability to regulate population growth was the problem of maintaining equilibrium on the small islands and coral atolls of the Pacific. Certainly cultures with such restricted land bases would run up against physical limits to population expansion much more quickly than would cultures in continental areas.

The general process of adjustment to island environments was outlined in a theoretical model by Tim Bayliss-Smith (1974) that recognized three phases of population growth and cultural response. Following the initial settling of an island, there may be rapid expansion and an extensive—that is, low labor input—subsistence system, which continues until the available land base is filled. Intensification of the food production system may then follow, with greater labor inputs and new technology, or "lower" dietary standards may be introduced. Finally, emigration and direct cultural controls on population growth become necessary. Many of these islands have been settled for a very long time; much of Micronesia, for example, may have been occupied for 1,000 years, and the maximum practical limits of technological intensification of food production must have been reached very early, so that this solution would have been quickly exhausted. Actually, many of the coral atolls required an extremely high degree of technological development before any kind of gardening could have been established because of the absence of soil and the shortage of fresh water.

In practice, various cultural controls helped maintain population well below any theoretical maximum carrying capacity based on the ultimate limits of food production. In the Polynesian outlier atolls, the critical population ceiling seems to have been set by the environmental limits to taro production. Taro was a daily element in the diet and a prime measure of the overall adequacy of the food supply. If cultural preferences were not a factor then presumably these cultures might have simply switched to crops that provided more calories per acre or per unit of labor, such as coconuts, and supported even denser populations. However, it appears that the ideal was for taro to supply approximately 50 percent of the caloric intake and it was culturally intolerable for it to drop below 25 percent. Coconuts were not expected to constitute more than 25 percent of the diet. Population pressure was clearly present to the extent that the proportions of these critical foods deviated from the cultural ideals. A further form of cultural control of carrying capacity was the planting of nonsubsistence crops, such as ritually important turmeric, which displaced food crops, and the social and ceremonial stress placed on certain marine resources.

Various social and political adjustments helped maximize available resources while minimizing possible ecological stresses to the food systems from overuse. For example, large-scale cultures, with higher levels of social stratification in which political leaders were given authority to regulate production and distribution of food, seem to have arisen in both Micronesia and Polynesia wherever resources were sufficient to support such developments. Shortages of food and "overpopulation" here, as in the New Guinea example, were in effect treated as problems of allocation; but in this case they were critical enough that political authority was needed to solve them. Other social mechanisms for allocating people to land, and vice versa, were also widely employed. For example, cognatic descent systems, which allow descent to be traced through either parent, were common in the Pacific and were easily manipulated to relieve local pressures. Adoption was also practiced; in some Micronesian islands as many as half of all children were actually adopted (Knudson 1970).

At the interisland level, various cultural practices helped relieve local problems and permitted larger densities than might have otherwise been possible, in much the same manner as intertribal relations in aboriginal Australia. For example, if typhoons temporarily destroyed the food resources of a particular atoll, the residents might be temporarily taken in by the residents of unaffected high islands or they might be sent emergency food. Likewise, if a critical imbalance in the sex ratio developed, individuals might in effect be exported or imported as needed.

Virtually the entire range of fertility control mechanisms were practiced by Pacific island cultures. In Micronesia a woman was often restricted to no more than three children and abortion, infanticide, coitus interruptus, and frequent periods of ritual celibacy all occurred. In Tikopia (Firth 1957), in addition to these controls, complete celibacy was sometimes required of the younger males in a family if productive land was not available. These unmarried men often set out on overseas voyages and never returned, although if they remained extramarital access to women was not denied them. When population pressures became intolerable on Tikopia, an entire clan or other social segment was simply driven away, although that was a very rare event. Raymond Firth's conclusion for Tikopia is probably applicable to the Pacific as a whole before European intervention: "It can be safely said that until recent years the population of Tikopia was normally in a state of equilibrium with its food supply" (Firth 1957:414).

Archaeological research carried out by Patrick Kirch and Douglas Yen (1982) revealed 3,000 years of continuous human occupation on Tikopia. During that time the population of the three-square-mile island probably did not exceed its historically known population range of 1,000 to 1,700 people. However, maintaining this balance required converting virtually the entire island to human use. Shifting cultivation eventually gave way to permanent gardening and selectively planted domesticated forest replaced the original forest cover. In the intensification process, erosion from the island's volcanic slopes filled in part of the lagoon and increased the land area. At least one wild bird species was locally exterminated but supernatural sanctions mediated by the island chief apparently protected some of the marine life from over-exploitation. Tikopia's extremely remote location and small size allowed its people to maintain their autonomy and self-sufficiency.

THE STATE INTERVENES

When autonomous small-scale cultures came under the influence of the global system three things drastically modified the demographic picture. In the first place, traditional population control mechanisms invariably dropped out. The disappearance of these control measures may be due to deliberate pressures aimed at eliminating them, as when missionaries halt abortion and infanticide or the government forbids raiding and warfare. Many important regulating practices may simply be abandoned as other practices that support them are modified. For example, the traditional religious system provides essential support for the postpartum taboo and a variety of other ceremonial regulations. If the Tsembaga were converted to Christianity they might voluntarily abandon pig sacrifices and many of their control mechanisms would collapse. Even if no other modifications in the culture occurred the elimination of traditional population controls would be certain to lead to rapid population growth.

The second factor affecting small-scale cultures under the influence of the global system was that the politicization process that created the state initially provided positive incentives for population expansion, through conquest and internal growth, because a growing population was the primary way in which political rulers extended their power. Furthermore, the extraction of taxes and tribute from formerly autonomous villages and households increased the demand for labor at the domestic level and made larger families a rational choice. Mahmood Mamdani (1973) pointed out that villagers in India and other poor countries were especially pleased to add sons to their families, as they could help on the farm. Extra children contributed more to the labor force than their maintenance cost, at least until the limits of labor intensification were exceeded. Anthropologist Clifford Geertz (1963) provides a well-documented case study of such a situation in Java. It is not surprising that other researchers have found that cultures based on intensive agriculture, which is likely to be associated with state organization, show higher fertility rates and higher population growth than either foragers or simple horticulturalists (Bentley, Goldberg, & Jasienska 1993).

The third effect of the incorporation of autonomous groups into the global system was the reduction of traditionally high mortality rates. This process has received the most attention as the principal cause of the modern worldwide population explosion, but this common interpretation needs to be qualified in important ways. As argued earlier in this chapter, the mortality rates of independent small-scale cultures may not have been as high as commonly thought and high mortality was clearly not the primary mechanism of population control. During the early phase of state intervention with tribal cultures, mortality rates are typically elevated because of frontier violence and the disruption of forced cultural change. In many cases tribes were simply exterminated at this point (Bodley 1988, 1990). Extinction has sometimes actually been accelerated by the retention of traditional fertility checks even in the face of severe depopulation. Examples of this process can be drawn from South America (Wagley 1951) and Micronesia (Schneider 1955). Jane Underwood (1973) argues that Schneider mistakenly identified the continuation of traditional abortion practices as a factor in the depopulation of Yap in Micronesia but other traditional controls could certainly have come into play.

When it has been advantageous to retain a native labor force, however, the cultural change process has usually been regulated to minimize undue increases in mortality; and new health measures reducing infant mortality and controlling endemic diseases such as malaria have in the long run succeeded in lowering overall mortality rates. It is quite possible that if the traditional culture remained intact, and new incentives for population growth were introduced, a reduction in mortality rates might be easily countered with an adjustment in fertility control mechanisms and no dramatic population explosion would need to occur. Unfortunately, a real test of this hypothesis might never be possible, because modern medical technology has invariably been accompanied by both a loss in traditional fertility controls and the appearance of new incentives for growth. The main point is clear, however—traditional cultures are not in themselves the primary cause of the present population explosion.

POLICY IMPLICATIONS

Modern population policy has largely been based on the demographic transition model, which described the way population growth first soared and then declined in Europe and North America as economic growth occurred. Improvements in public health and the availability of antibiotics reduced mortality rates, making it more likely that each child would survive, while increasing numbers of urban workers found large families to be a disadvantage as their material conditions improved. Therefore family size declined rapidly and population growth slowed. It was widely believed that the same demographic pattern would occur in the rest of the world as the global economy grew and many planners argued that promoting economic growth everywhere was the best way to reduce population growth. However, the developing world is still growing rapidly and at present rates total world population could reach 10 billion by 2050. Population did grow rapidly throughout the "developing" world when mortality rates began to drop with improvements in health and since the 1970s fertility rates have in fact also declined dramatically. This was not the "demographic transition" that demographers predicted because rather than improving, living standards actually declined for most people in poor countries, especially during the 1980s (Robey, Rutstein, & Morris 1993). Worsening living standards in urban settings may make large families a liability, while at the same time the availability of new contraceptive technologies makes family planning more attractive.

The key element that may contribute to a reduction in world population growth is fertility decision making control by women. It seems likely that women exercised such control in autonomous small-scale cultures but tended to lose control when male dominated large-scale civilizations developed. The increasing use of contraceptive technology by urban women in poor countries and the related reduction in family size has been called an unexpected "demographic revolution" (Robey, Rutstein, & Morris 1993) that may significantly reduce population.

Poverty and Conflict in the Global Culture

*A large number of people on this planet, to whom the comfort
and stability of a middle-class life is utterly unknown, find war and
a barracks existence a step up rather than a step down.*

ROBERT D. KAPLAN,
"The Coming Anarchy"

IN ADDITION TO ESTABLISHING a successful adaptation to the natural
environment, every human society must maintain a certain minimal level of
internal order and security to survive. Conflict and violence, both internal
and external, must be carefully regulated. Individuals, households, and other
social units must have access to basic resources and sufficient involvement
with decision-making processes to protect their self-interests. During the
thousands of years before the first large-scale, politically centralized societies
appeared, small-scale tribal societies successfully minimized these universal
problems by maintaining the household as the primary institutional structure, with decision-making power widely dispersed throughout society and
therefore highly responsive. Differential access to wealth and power was
unlikely to provide a systematic source of conflict, because individuals' social
action occurred in small, face-to-face communities, where everyone could
participate according to their individual abilities. Poverty and powerlessness
were not institutionalized. Feuding and raiding were chronic problems but
they usually took the form of interpersonal conflicts and were unlikely to
represent serious challenges to the established social order. There were no
professional armies and no permanent war leaders.

With the arrival of politicization and the resulting social stratification
and economic specialization that accompanied the appearance of the first
states a mere 6,000 years ago, social order became a far more difficult and
dangerous problem. Whole segments of a society were sometimes denied

direct control over their basic subsistence requirements, and real political power came to rest with an elite few. Monumental royal tombs, palaces, and temples were constructed to reinforce the legitimacy of the ruling elite and the social order. For the first time in human experience, political power and religious ideology were used to compel households to provide labor and to produce basic subsistence for an elite few who controlled the political system and its supporting institutions. However, because human labor was the primary source of energy in ancient civilizations it was crucial that the peasantry remain healthy. Thus, it would have been counterproductive for ancient rulers to have ignored the basic needs of the populace that ultimately sustained them. Although they sought to meet the basic needs of their populations, pre-capitalist states were precarious systems because they engendered internal political conflict and external wars and because they depended on intensive agriculture operating close to the regional carrying capacity. Throughout history states have been subject to frequent collapses of social order through civil wars, peasant revolts, and popular uprisings, which, in combination with foreign invasions, have destroyed many individual states. Indeed, seldom have any states survived more than a few centuries.

The social order problem changed with the recent emergence of a globally organized culture because the scale of elite power is now far greater than in any ancient civilization. The institutions that the elite control have enormous power over the daily lives of people everywhere. Commercially controlled and highly concentrated communication systems, including radio, television, cinema, and the print media, now shape virtually everyone's thought and behavior, creating passive consumers and wage laborers worldwide. At the same time, industrial technology reduces the requirement for human labor and makes the basic welfare of millions of people irrelevant to those in power. Relative and absolute poverty and powerlessness are intrinsic aspects of the global culture that continue to threaten the internal security and domestic tranquility of virtually all states.

The potential collapse of democratic political systems and their replacement by overwhelmingly powerful and oppressive totalitarian forces would represent the ultimate global political crisis. Such an event would mean the curtailment of many of the individual freedoms now enjoyed in most industrial nations and might be followed by a period of intensifying civil strife. Such an outcome might occur independently of international conflict. Disastrous internal disorders could be precipitated by a major downturn or collapse of our precarious consumption-based economic system, by unresolved urban stresses, or by unresponsive political processes. Terrorist acts and civil disturbances on the part of dissident political groups, spontaneous urban riots and looting, labor strife, organized crime, corruption among high political officials, illegal use of power, rising rates of violent crime and juvenile delinquency, drug abuse—all are symptoms of serious underlying conflicts and contradictions in globally organized cultures.

Anthropologists have traditionally been concerned with a variety of problems relating to social order that are directly relevant to a better understanding of our present crisis. However, before considering the anthropological perspective in detail, a brief historic review of the social order crisis in America will be presented to clarify both the nature of the crisis and current attempts at its solution. The United States provides an excellent starting point for any treatment of this topic because culturally it has long been a world leader—yet its violent crime rate is far higher than that of any other modern nation. Perhaps even more importantly, in recent decades the American government commissioned several major studies of the problem in an attempt to pinpoint its causes and to work toward the prevention, or at least the reduction, of violence and disorder.

VIOLENCE AND INSECURITY IN AMERICA

Violence is dangerous to our society. It is disfiguring our society—making fortresses of portions of our cities and dividing our people into armed camps. It is jeopardizing some of our most precious institutions—poisoning the spirit of trust and cooperation that is essential to their proper functioning. It is corroding the central political processes of our democratic society—substituting force and fear for argument and accommodation.

(U.S. NATIONAL COMMISSION ON THE CAUSES
AND PREVENTION OF VIOLENCE 1969)

Violent crime, political terrorism, assassinations, riots, and various other forms of social disorder have always been part of the American scene. It was not until the assassination of President Kennedy in 1963 and the outbreak of widespread urban rioting in 1967, followed in 1968 by violent political demonstrations, campus disturbances, and the assassination of Martin Luther King, Jr., and Senator Robert F. Kennedy, that the government began to ask serious questions. Several national commissions were convened in the late 1960s to examine various aspects of the crisis. Perhaps the most comprehensive of these commissions was the National Commission on the Causes and Prevention of Violence, established in June 1968 by President Johnson. He directed it to "go as far as man's knowledge" could take it in the search for the causes and prevention of violence.

The thirteen-person commission, headed by Milton S. Eisenhower, worked for eighteen months. It had a research staff of 100 at its peak and was divided into eight major task groups. More than 200 leading scholars assisted the commission with the preparation of 150 separate papers and projects. These were published in thirteen volumes of task force reports, five investigative reports, and a final commission report. This massive project surely represents the single most ambitious attempt by any modern nation to understand the problem of violence and social disorder and its conclusions merit careful consideration in the light of more recent developments.

The final report of the National Commission (United States, National Commission on the Causes and Prevention of Violence 1969) concluded that while the United States has always been a relatively violent nation, the 1960s saw virtually all types of violence increase dramatically over the levels of prior decades. This increase was not merely a reflection of population growth, changes in the demographic structure, or changes in detection and reporting procedures. Over the decade between 1958 and 1968 the rate of reported violent crimes (homicide, forcible rape, robbery, and aggravated assault) doubled, reaching nearly 300 cases per 100,000 people. After the commission report was published, the violent crime rate continued to escalate, more than doubling again until by 1992 it had reached 758 per 100,000. These are truly astounding statistics. For example, in 1960 there were 9,100 murders, a rate of 5.1 per 100,000 people. In 1992 there were 23,800, 9.3 per 100,000 (*The American Almanac 1994–1995*). By comparison, in Norway there were only 55 homicides in 1990, a rate of 1.1 per 100,000.

Between mid-1963 and mid-1968 nearly 2 million people were involved in group protests, urban riots, and various political demonstrations that resulted in an estimated 9,000 casualties, including nearly 200 deaths. This relatively sudden increase in group disorders caused widespread alarm and spawned several other special commissions. Such group disorders were not unique in American history, however. For example, during labor violence between 1902 and 1904 200 persons were killed and 2,000 injured.

In view of the overall increase in violence in America, the commissioners felt that the basic foundations of our society were clearly being threatened and urged immediate action to control the problem. The dangers of internal disorder were considered fully as serious as any external threats, requiring a reassessment of national priorities along with a scaling-down of military expenditures for national defense. As the commissioners stated: "We solemnly declare our conviction that this nation is entering a period in which our people need to be as concerned by the internal dangers to our free society as by any probable combination of external threats."

The commissioners called for a doubling of expenditures on the criminal justice process and greater coordination and efficiency in law enforcement activities in general. They also recommended that firearms be regulated and the availability of handguns restricted. If drastic action was not taken quickly, they foresaw a bleak future for Americans. Our inner cities would be dotted with isolated "safe" areas occupied by upper-income families protected by armed guards and electronic surveillance equipment, while crime and terror would prevail for the poor at night, when there would be no possible security. Public facilities such as schools, libraries, and playgrounds would also require armed guards. Commuters from safe suburban compounds would travel carefully patrolled and "sanitized" corridors in armored cars, while guards would "ride shotgun" on public transportation. These defensive measures would in turn lead to further intensification of terror and violence as those at the bottom of the social order became increasingly desparate. This picture has proven to be remarkably prophetic.

The commissioners recognized that merely increasing the efficiency of law enforcement was not sufficient if the underlying causes of violence were not corrected. In their view, violence was a sickness, a social pathology: "Necessary as measures of control are, they are only a part of the answer. They do not cure the basic causes of violence. Violence is like a fever in the body politic: it is but the symptom of some more basic pathology which must be cured before the fever will disappear" (United States, National Commission on the Causes and Prevention of Violence 1969:xix).

To discover the underlying causes of violence, the report attempted first of all to pinpoint where crimes were committed most often and who committed them. It confirmed that violent crimes were most prevalent in cities of over 50,000 people, where crime rates were eleven times greater than in rural areas. Crimes were most often committed by young, low-income males living under urban slum conditions. An earlier national commission (United States, National Advisory Commission on Civil Disorders 1968) had declared that this association between crime and slum living conditions was "one of the most fully documented facts about crime." The Violence report agreed with this assessment and specifically listed poverty, poor housing, and unemployment among the most important factors in an interrelated combination of "powerful criminogenic forces" present in urban slums. The general conclusion was that the urban poor were trapped in a situation from which they could not easily escape because of their inability to earn adequate income. This led to frustration and violence because the dominant culture measured success by material wealth, which, in the popular ideology, was equally available to all who put forth the individual effort to achieve it. The final commission report summarized some of these criminogenic forces as follows:

> To be a young, poor male; to be undereducated and without means of escape from an oppressive urban environment; to want what the society claims is available (but mostly to others); to see around oneself illegitimate and often violent methods being used to achieve material success; and to observe others using these means with impunity—all this is to be burdened with an enormous set of influences that pull many toward crime and delinquency
>
> (UNITED STATES, NATIONAL COMMISSION ON THE
> CAUSES AND PREVENTION OF VIOLENCE 1969:XXI)

The commission argued that economic progress brought rapid social change and greatly increased wealth for some persons while denying it to others. At the same time, it weakened traditional mechanisms of social control and led to frustrations due to inequities in wealth distribution.

Inadequate law enforcement and reduced respect for elected authority and established institutions were thought to encourage further crime. All of these causes were concentrated in urban centers.

Other studies on violence and disorder in America often emphasized the "deviant" aspect of this behavior, and explained it—at least in part—as a problem of faulty socialization or inappropriate values fostered by a subculture of poverty. From this viewpoint, causes are seen to lie largely with the poor themselves, and the recommended solution becomes "education" in the broadest sense. This view represents a misunderstanding of the adaptive value of deviant behavior under poverty conditions and seriously overemphasizes the role of "values" in initiating such behavior. It also mistakenly equates such behavior with criminality. Cross-cultural research reveals a common pattern of noncriminal behavioral coping responses to material deprivation throughout the underdeveloped world and in urban slums in developed nations that is strikingly similar to the behavior patterns of the urban poor in early industrial England (Eames & Goode 1973). Nontraditional marriage arrangements; the matrifocal family; various forms of petty marketing practices, such as children hawking gum on the streets; and many other patterns are simply ways of making the best of a difficult situation. Poverty behavior, indeed, presents a consistent picture, but it is because people are adapting to the same problems—not because they are locked in their own self-replicating culture of poverty.

The commission recommended that various steps be taken to eradicate the basic causes of violence and disorder. These included a major restructuring of urban life, greater expenditures on welfare and improved housing, and so on. Unfortunately, as promising as these recommendations may have sounded, they still left unchallenged the fundamental structures of American culture that continue to produce great social inequality. The law enforcement approach to the problem has produced a fourfold increase in our prison population between 1970 and 1992 and a tripling of the incarceration rate, from 96.7 per 100,000 in 1970 to 330.2 in 1992. In comparison, in 1990 Norway imprisoned its people at 72.8 per 100,000.

SOCIAL ORDER IN EGALITARIAN SOCIETIES

Solving our social order crisis is indeed a formidable task, particularly in view of the fact that the most humane societies known are institutionally far different from the highly stratified urban societies that we often mistakenly assume are based on the fundamentals of human nature. A very high level of social disorder is not just a problem of human nature. It is a cultural problem whose solution may require drastic cultural change. More egalitarian modern nations, such as Norway, clearly show levels of violence that are dramatically lower than America's. Furthermore, it is instructive to note that most of the criminogenic factors identified in the report just discussed are absent in tribal cultures. The key factor seems to be the relatively greater level of basic equality and democracy in tribal cultures in comparison to politically centralized states. With low population densities, no emphasis on material wealth as a source of status, and all households enjoying access to subsistence resources, tribal societies face very different social order problems and are able to solve them very effectively.

Anthropologists who have observed the most autonomous foraging cultures have generally been impressed with their relatively low levels of internal violence. Some societies, such as the San Bushmen of Southern Africa and the Semai of Malaysia (Dentan 1968), have been characterized as almost totally nonviolent, but it would be misleading to assume that all tribal peoples lead perpetually harmonious social lives. Some tribal societies, such as the Yanomamo Indians of the upper Orinoco rain forests, have been described as highly violent (Chagnon 1968). Anthropologist Napoleon Chagnon (1988) has estimated that up to 30 percent of Yanomamo men die violently. Chronic feuding is characteristic of tribal societies, but it is usually externally directed. The very existence of the Yanomamo is threatened by violence related to the intrusion of global-scale cultures and it is likely that external factors may have greatly increased the levels of violence that Chagnon found in Yanomamo life. The basic survival of autonomous tribal societies was seldom threatened by internal conflict. It could hardly have been otherwise, considering the thousands of years that tribal societies endured. There was no "war of all against all" that Thomas Hobbes (Leviathan [1651], Part I, Chapter 13) envisioned, nor was there total harmony. Strictly speaking, tribal societies are anarchic, in that they lack government (Barclay 1982). However, they maintain internal order without formal legal codes and specialized law enforcement institutions and even without formal political offices invested with coercive authority. Tribal societies are dramatic proof that the expensive law and order machinery that we now require is not the only route to social order.

The maintenance of social order by tribals is not a result of any moral superiority of "noble savages." It is due to cultural conditions. In tribal societies individual self-interest is unlikely to conflict with the long-range interests of society. Excessive conflict, theft, use of force, or hoarding of resources for exclusive use would all be self-defeating in a tribal society in which everyone's survival ultimately depended on mutual trust and cooperation. As noted in earlier chapters, this same correspondence of interests has also contributed to the ecological success of tribal societies and to the maintenance of population equilibrium.

In low-density tribal societies, conflict is unquestionably further minimized by extreme flexibility in group membership and by the small size of the local, face-to-face residential group. A typical hunting band averaged only approximately twenty-five people, including children; thus, relatively few adults were ever forced into close interaction. Camps shifted location every few days or weeks and such moves were often used as an excuse for changing band personnel. Careful studies of modern hunting bands such as the San Bushmen have revealed that individuals and families constantly shuffle between bands and that many of these shifts are simply a means of resolving interpersonal conflicts without violence (Turnbull 1968:132–137, Woodburn 1968b:103–110.)

The Importance of Equality

The concept *equality* is critical to an understanding of the differences between tribal cultures and large- and global-scale cultures. No one is, of course, ever totally equal with anyone else in any society; but in tribal societies the differences that separate people are age, gender, and unique personal qualities exclusively. Positions of prestige and influence are open to all persons qualified to occupy them. For example, anyone with sufficient skill may become a respected hunter or a band leader. Anthropologist Morton Fried defined an egalitarian society very concisely, as follows:

> An egalitarian society is one in which there are as many positions of prestige in any given age-sex grade as there are persons capable of filling them. Let it be put even more strongly. An egalitarian society does not have any means of fixing or limiting the number of persons capable of exerting power. As many persons as can wield power—whether through personal strength, influence, authority, or whatever means—can do so, and there is no necessity to draw them together to establish an order of dominance and paramountcy.
>
> (FRIED 1967:33)

Of equal importance is the distribution of basic physical necessities. No one in an egalitarian society is denied access to the means of production. Fried is emphatic on this point:

> In no simple society known to ethnography is there any restriction on access to the raw materials necessary to make tools and weapons. This statement can be made flatly about resources in the habitation area of a given unit. . . .
>
> (FRIED 1967:58)

Land, water, and game are always open for use. This is the "irreducible minimum" referred to in Chapter 2. Although boundaries may be recognized for tribal, band, and occasionally family territories, trespass regulations usually mean that permission to use an area must be requested but cannot reasonably be denied (Myers 1982). Group membership also fluctuates widely. The trespass rules themselves often serve the important function of helping people monitor who is using resources to better manage their availability. Among tribal horticulturalists access to land may be regulated by descent groups, but these are not rigid organizations and membership changes may commonly occur if land shortages arise. Individual ownership of property certainly does occur, but it is normally restricted to personal weapons and artifacts, game killed, herd animals, and crops—things in which personal labor has been invested. With use-access to basic resources open to all, and particularly when residential shifts are part of the subsistence round, there are no real advantages to be gained by asserting individual title to land. In regard to movable property, one can only make practical use of so many goods; and given both the need for mobility and the cultural emphasis on generosity there is no incentive either to hoard or to steal property. Furthermore, in a small society a thief would be unable to hide. All these factors almost certainly minimize interpersonal conflict.

Many anthropologists describe differences in age and gender status in tribal societies as "inequality" and these differences are occasionally described as oppressive and exploitative. For example, Bern (1979) uses such language to describe the dominance of the old men in Australian aboriginal society. Many observers recognize the differences between the sexes and between individuals of different ages in tribal societies. However, any inequities do not deny anyone the opportunity to marry, raise a family, and make a living. We can say that, in spite of age and gender differences, everyone is guaranteed the irreducible minimum. Age differences are, of course, only temporary and tribals themselves usually do not consider different gender roles to be oppressive. Two women anthropologists, Phyllis Kaberry (1939) and Diane Bell (1982), conducted field studies to investigate the position of aboriginal women in Australia and specifically rejected the charge that women were exploited by the traditional system. In virtually all tribal societies women do tend to work closer to the home and care for children more than do men and their work is often more routine. Men often do heavier work and their work can carry them far from home. However, where detailed time-expenditure studies have been carried out (Johnson 1975, 1985, Lee 1979, Modjeska 1982) they indicate that the total work load appears to be relatively equitable between the sexes.

Thus, there are cultural conditions in tribal societies that reduce the basic causes of violence and disorder and specific mechanisms to reduce the frequency of otherwise unavoidable problems. There are also direct and effective means of handling any trouble that does arise and specific mechanisms to channel conflicts. Serious breaches of tribal norms could result in expulsion from the society—which would mean the loss of all physical and emotional support for the recalcitrant individual. Survival without kinspeople is virtually impossible and an exiled troublemaker would have difficulty being accepted by other groups in a society in which there is no anonymity. Such a drastic sanction rarely needs to be applied, but the threat is always in the background. In many societies the threat of witchcraft accusation may be an effective means of compelling conformity. Chronic troublemakers might find themselves accused of witchcraft and possibly blamed for a variety of sicknesses and community misfortunes. In extreme cases, accused witches are publicly executed.

Conflict Resolution

In addition to simply moving away egalitarian tribal societies often employ highly ritualized methods of conflict resolution. Ingroup interpersonal violence may even be encouraged by some cultures but it is usually very carefully regulated. The Yanomamo (Chagnon 1968), for example, recognize several distinct levels of violence in a carefully graded series of increasing intensity. Their disputes might be settled by ritual duels that range from chest pounding (in which two men exchange bare-fist blows to the chest) at the lowest level to spear-throwing duels at the highest. Intermediate duels involve blows to the side and club fighting. Minor injuries and prominent scars may result from these actions, but deaths are uncommon. More pacific ritual forms of conflict resolution in egalitarian societies include Eskimo song duels in which the disputants publicly insult each other until the loser is laughed down by the audience. Generally, when disputes in these cultures are not settled by the individuals most directly involved they are resolved by community consensus. The objective is merely to restore order, not to punish. Abstract notions of justice are quite irrelevant in this situation.

Leadership

Although there is no concentration of coercive power in political offices in egalitarian societies this does not mean that there is no leadership or political organization. Headmen have been found in some of the most simple foraging bands, but their authority is severely limited. For example, among the Nambikuara Indians of Brazil, described by Claude Levi-Strauss (1944), the band headman is delegated primary decision-making responsibility for band subsistence activities, selection of routes and campsites, and interband relations. However, he is only a leader as long as his followers consent to his leadership and he must not recommend actions that band members would not choose. A chief's success is measured by his ability to see that the band is well fed. He is also expected to excel in generosity and constant demands are made on him for food and small articles.

Thus a Nambikuara headman must be an especially skillful, dedicated, and hardworking individual. He bears a heavy responsibility for band well-being and security, but his position is always tenuous. If his leadership qualities falter, the band may simply disintegrate as disgruntled individuals and households seek out other band leaders with whom to align themselves. A headman is generally allowed a young second wife to ease the burdens of leadership. The only other rewards appear to have been highly personal and

few persons desired the position. Band headmanship in tribal society, therefore, is not the kind of political office found in larger-scale cultures. In fact,
Levi-Strauss had a difficult time explaining why anyone would even aspire to
such a position in Nambikuara society. He concluded that "there are chiefs
because there are, in any human group, men who, unlike most of their
companions, enjoy prestige for its own sake, feel a strong appeal to responsibility, and to whom the burden of public affairs brings its own reward"
(Levi-Strauss 1944).

Richard Lee's (1981) description of leadership among the !Kung
Bushmen presents a similar picture. He found that the !Kung went to such
lengths to prevent the accumulation of power in a leader and were so fierce-
ly egalitarian that it was not always obvious that "headmen" even existed. In
fact, when he asked a Bushman whether the !Kung had headmen, the man
replied, "Of course we have headmen! . . . Each one of us is headman over
himself" (Lee 1981:93–94). Lee concluded that leadership existed but it was
very diffuse, totally noncoercive, and represented a form of "political reciprocity" much like the reciprocity characteristic of tribal economics.

SOCIAL ORDER IN LARGE-SCALE CULTURES

Chiefdoms (Service 1962, Carneiro 1981) are the simplest nonegalitarian
societies and many ethnographic examples are known from the Pacific,
Africa, and the Northwest Coast of North America. Chiefdom societies
restrict the number of individuals who can occupy important positions within the society but still permit relatively free access to basic natural resources.
Social control remains largely a matter of kinship but true political offices
exist. Ranking within a chiefdom may be highly elaborated, with a hereditary
chief at the top and each corporate descent group ranked both relative to
each other and internally. The authority of the chief is defined by the position he (most often a male) occupies and his personality and special skills are
a relatively minor aspect of his qualifications. The office of chief is ritually
set apart and reinforced by a variety of sumptuary regulations or taboos, such
as the right to eat special foods or to own special articles. Conflicts may
become intense as individuals vie for status and rebellions may occur when
particular chiefs overstep the customary bounds of their office; but, in general, the social order problem is qualitatively much simpler, even given ranking, than in societies with full stratification.

Stratified societies, most fully represented by ancient civilizations, kingdoms, and centralized states, begin with the potential social order problems
implied by ranking in chiefdoms but add the critical element of restricted
access to strategic resources. According to Morton Fried's (1967:186) definition, "[a] stratified society is one in which members of the same sex and

equivalent age status do not have equal access to the basic resources that sustain life." This involves the arrangement of people into classes according to their degree of access to power and resources. There is also a pervasive division of labor by economic specialization such that no one except certain rural peasants can directly provide for more than a very small proportion of their basic needs. The ruling elite at the top of the hierarchy can effectively regulate access to and use of both critical natural resources and the technological means of production. Control over water, soil, and air may in this way be denied to large segments of society.

With the development of stratification, for the first time in human history cultural conditions permitted exploitation of one subgroup within a society by another. Exploitation is an emotional and value-laden concept that many social scientists might prefer not to deal with but in discussing problems of social order it cannot be avoided. *Webster's Dictionary* defines exploitation as "unfair utilization." The catch here is in the meaning of *unfair* because no one would dispute that there is utilization of one class by another in a stratified society. Certainly the members of the ruling class are dependent for their welfare on the lower classes because they draw their labor force and all their food, goods, and services from them. The fairness of this arrangement may be judged from both an inside and an outside view. This is where Antonio Gramsci's (see Chapter 1) concept of cultural hegemony comes into play. If the elite, through their manipulation of the dominant ideology, can convince the commoners of the legitimacy of the system, then no one will feel exploited. An outsider, unmystified by culturally shaped beliefs, might label the system exploitation if the commoners are deprived of basic physical necessities while the elite bask in luxury.

Material deprivation can be objectively measured by health status, food supply, clothing, housing, and other indicators and may relate to both a minimal *survival level* and a culturally defined minimum *comfort level*. Material deprivation of either sort is absolute deprivation and is encompassed by the popular concept *poverty*. Relative deprivation, or the feeling that one is not as "well off" as one would like to be in comparison to the next higher class, may be found whenever there is an inequitable distribution of wealth and power and can occur above the absolute level. Deprivation of some kind seems to be a universal feature of all stratified societies. Some socialist countries have succeeded in easing the absolute deprivation of different classes but classes exist in these countries nonetheless, along with the potential for disorder.

Anyone viewing a particular stratified society from the outside finds it difficult to understand why the impoverished lower classes so often seem to accept their lot without a struggle. Yet such systems could not exist without the threat of physical coercion and the use of powerful forms of thought control, or cultural hegemony (Harris 1971). The use of police force, brutality, and imprisonment in support of the political power, wealth, and property rights of the ruling class is certainly a familiar element in the history of all states. However, in many of the ancient agrarian civilizations, such as those in Egypt, Mesopotamia, Mexico, and Peru, the need for such force was minimized by the great state religions that encouraged the lower classes to accept their positions as part of a divinely established order. An elaborate esoteric priesthood, awesome pyramids, and complex, dramatic ritual would certainly have intimidated those who might have doubted their place in the divine scheme. In fact, many impoverished peasants may never have considered themselves exploited.

The recommendation of the National Commission that police forces be strengthened clearly indicates the continuing importance of physical coercion in modern industrial societies such as the United States. The mass media and the institutions of formal education may also be interpreted as forms of thought control that replace the role of state religion in their support of the established order. Anthropologist Marvin Harris (1971) suggested that television may be a very important means of minimizing social disorder in highly stratified societies, as it occupies peoples' minds and provides them with at least vicarious involvement with all levels of the society. A further stabilizing factor, as noted earlier, has been continuous economic growth, which has helped convince people that they are moving up even though their relative position within the social hierarchy has remained constant.

CROSS-CULTURAL PERSPECTIVES ON WAR

A knowledge of how and why primitive peoples made war may shed light on the prospects for war or peace in our own time.

(NAROLL 1966:14)

Perhaps the single most important perspective that anthropologists can bring to the study of war is the contrast between tribal and nation-state war. In fact, depending on how it is defined, war may be said to be totally unknown among many of the organizationally least complex cultures; and even where it does occur in tribal cultures, there are significant qualitative differences that make tribal war profoundly different from its nation-state counterpart. These points are critical because they bear directly on the central question— can modern war be prevented? The evidence strongly suggests that war is an inherent feature of large-scale, politically centralized cultures but is not characteristic of small-scale cultures. Military conquest is a form of economic growth that helps sustain wealth inequality. In global-scale cultures war may not be inevitable between nations integrated within a decentralized global market economy, although civil war may be a persistent problem when social inequality is high.

The most widely accepted definitions of war would automatically exclude much of the intergroup conflict that typically occurs between tribal communities. War is generally considered an organized armed conflict between political units in pursuit of a group goal. To the extent that organization and group objectives are emphasized, this kind of war is usually absent in small-scale cultures. Anthropologist Bronislaw Malinowski, writing during the Second World War, was emphatic on this point: "[We] do not find among these lowest primitives any organized clash of armed forces aiming at the enforcement of tribal policy. War does not exist among them" (Malinowski 1944:277).

Many writers would further restrict the definition of war to armed conflict between nation-states carried out for national objectives. Quincy Wright, unquestionably one of the world's leading authorities on war, used the term in its widest meaning to include violent intergroup conflict or armed aggression in any form; but in his monumental work *A Study of War* he strongly emphasized the qualitative differences between tribal and civilized war:

> War in the sense of a legal situation equally permitting groups to expand wealth and power by violence began with civilization. . . . Only among civilized people has war been an institution serving political and economic interests of the community, defined by a body of law which states the circumstances justifying its use, the procedures whereby it is begun and ended, and the methods by which it is conducted.

> (WRIGHT 1942:39)

Certainly, the major conclusion of any evolutionary study of intergroup conflict, whatever we choose to call it, is that its form is strongly related to the political organization of a given culture. As an empirical generalization it can be stated that as a culture's political system becomes more centralized its military organization becomes more complex, its weapons and tactics become more effective, and individual engagements become more costly in casualties (Otterbein 1970). Predictable shifts in the immediate goals for fighting and in the supporting ideology also occur. The nature of the interrelationship between political centralization and war cannot yet be precisely explained, but they have evolved together. The state makes war and war helped to create states.

If the immediate objectives that commonly motivated political communities to fight with their neighbors are analyzed, they can be grouped into four major categories, following the work of several researchers (Wright 1942:278–283, Naroll 1966, Otterbein 1970). These categories are defense, plunder, prestige, and political control. Presumably they reflect considerations that both military decision makers and the combatants have in mind when they go to war. Anthropologists also recognize many other "functions" of war; they do not pretend that these four categories include all the psycho-

TABLE 7.1

Political Organization and War Motives

	DEFENSE	PLUNDER	PRESTIGE	CONTROL
Uncentralized:				
Bands				
Copper Eskimo	0	0	0	0
Tiwi	+	0	0	0
Tribes				
Somali	+	+	0	0
Wondi	+	+	+	0
Centralized:				
Chiefdoms				
Sema	+	+	+	0
Mutair	+	+	+	0
States				
Thai	+	+	+	+
Aztec	+	+	+	+

Source: Data from a worldwide sample of forty-six cultures in Otterbein 1970:148–49.

logical factors that may motivate particular individuals to fight. What is significant about these categories is that they do not occur in different cultures in a random, unpredictable manner; rather, they tend to be distributed in an orderly arrangement that reveals a great deal about the nature of war and its relationship to political organization. There are cultures in which no organized fighting occurs for any of these reasons and such societies may justifiably be said to lack war.

In general, the motives for war tend to be cumulative so that, for example, if a culture goes to war in order to extend political control over a neighbor, it will probably also fight for defense, plunder, and prestige. However, if a culture fights for plunder, it may not fight for political control and those cultures that do not fight for defense do not fight at all. This property of related variables is called scalability and is demonstrated for a few selected cultures in Table 7.1. It will be noted that those cultures showing the most motives for war are politically centralized, or large-scale, and usually states, whereas those with the fewest motives are politically uncentralized, or small-scale. Figure 7.1 illustrates this relationship more accurately, drawing on data from a worldwide sample of forty-six cultures examined by Keith Otterbein (1970) in his cross-cultural study of the evolution of war. Significantly none of the politically decentralized cultures in his sample used war for purposes

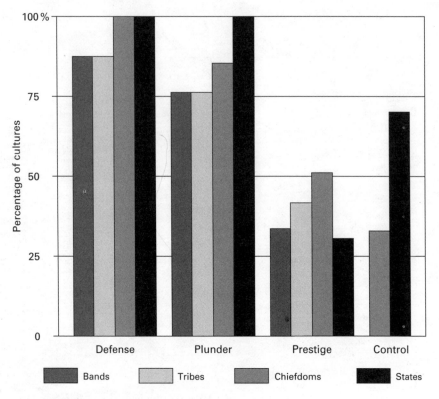

FIGURE 7.1   MOTIVES FOR WAR

(Data from a worldwide sample of forty-six cultures examined in Otterbein 1970: 66–67.)

of political control and whereas all centralized cultures fought for defense and economic advantage, many uncentralized cultures did not.

Otterbein also worked with a composite scale of military sophistication that reflected the general military effectiveness of cultures. For example, cultures with standing armies, or age grade societies that group young men into even-aged cohorts of warriors, were considered militarily more effective than those lacking such organization. Likewise, more flexible tactics, more deadly weapons, the presence of fortifications, negotiations with military foes, and war for political domination were all treated as indicative of greater military sophistication. Here again, the split between decentralized small-scale cultures and centralized large-scale cultures was striking. Table 7.2 presents the data from the cross-cultural sample that confirm the generalization that more politically centralized societies tend to be more sophisticated militarily.

TABLE 7.2

Political Organization and Military Sophistication

POLITICAL ORGANIZATION	MILITARY SOPHISTICATION		
	LOW	HIGH	TOTAL
Centralized	3	13	16
Uncentralized	24	6	30
Total	27	19	46

Source: Data from a worldwide sample of forty-six cultures in Otterbein 1970:74.

Attempts to estimate and compare casualty rates are difficult and often misleading but some trends are obvious (see Table 7.3). Otterbein rated casualty rates as high if a third or more of the forces engaged in given battles were killed and was able to show that as military sophistication increases, so do battle casualties. Thus, to the extent that military sophistication is related to political centralization, more politically centralized cultures will tend to have higher casualties. Cross-cultural comparisons rating the frequency of war have also been used to test the validity of the argument that a high degree of military sophistication acts as a deterrent to war. Actually quite the opposite is more likely. The more sophisticated a community is militarily the more frequently it engages in aggressive war and is itself attacked in turn. Thus, we may cautiously generalize that as cultures become more politically centralized they become more militaristic, fight more often, and have higher casualty rates.

The nature of the relationship between war and human nature has been a widely debated topic for many years. Quincy Wright, who directed the University of Chicago's Social Science Research Committee project on the causes of war from 1926 to 1941, took the following position:

> [It] is meaningless to say that war is inevitable because of the pugnacity of man as an animal. While man has original drives that make war possible, that possibility has only been realized in appropriate social and political conditions.
>
> (WRIGHT 1942:5)

Prominent anthropologists such as Bronislaw Malinowski (1941) and Margaret Mead (1940), who joined the debate during World War II, took much the same position; and this view remains the general consensus among anthropologists today. Humans may indeed possess an innate capacity for aggression but this capacity must be culturally shaped.

TABLE 7.3

Military Sophistication and Casualty Rates

| | CASUALTY RATES | | |
MILITARY SOPHISTICATION	LOW	HIGH	TOTAL
High	7	8	15
Low	13	5	18
Total	20	13	33

Source: Data from a worldwide sample of forty-six cultures in Otterbein 1970. Data were not available to evaluate all forty-six cultures on these variables.

"ROOTS" OF THE SECURITY CRISIS: OVERPOPULATION OR INEQUALITY?

Future wars will be those of communal survival, aggravated or, in many cases, caused by environmental scarcity. These wars will be subnational, meaning that it will be hard for states and local governments to protect their own citizens physically. This is how many states will ultimately die. . . . peoples and cultures around the world will be thrown back upon their own strengths and weaknesses, with fewer equalizing mechanisms to protect them . . . To the average person, political values will mean less, personal security more.

(KAPLAN 1994:74)

The evidence of worldwide social disorder is overwhelming. For example, in 1991 there were forty-eight regional wars and civil wars underway in the world. Together these had already led to the deaths of some 5 million people (George 1992:140–141). Other estimates place the human toll of all armed conflict since 1945 at 40 million, with civilians comprising 75 percent of this figure (Code of Conduct on Arms Transfers Act of 1993, before U.S. House of Representatives). There were 17.5 million refugees seeking international protection and assistance at the end of 1992 (*World Almanac 1994*:831). With the end of the Cold War, strategic planners in wealthy nations began to view social disorder in the impoverished world as the primary threat to global security. They began searching for the basic causes of conflict in much the same way as the National Commission on Violence, discussed earlier, looked for the causes of domestic disorder within the United States. However, in the case of the global security crisis there has been a clear tendency for analysts to identify overpopulation and resource scarcity as the root problem rather than inequalities within the structure of the global culture itself.

Many observers are quick to attribute contemporary conflicts to "pent-up ethnic hatreds," as Brian Beedham (1993:14), associate editor for *The*

Economist, states in a survey of the prospects for future wars. He declares, "The world has too many countries where different peoples who do not like each other live within the borders of the same state." This trivializes ethnicity and makes cultural difference a threat rather than a hopeful basis for organizing people to confront human problems. Anthropological researchers have shown that many cases of supposed ethnic conflict can be interpreted very differently. For example, Mary Kay Gilliland Olsen (1993) shows that even in the former Yugoslavia, a much publicized symbol of ethnic conflict, the real causes of conflict between Serbs and Croats are national level "competition for power and control of economic wealth" waged between elites who have used ethnic identities to further their own political agendas.

The above opening quotation by *Atlantic Monthly* editor Robert Kaplan on "future wars" is taken from an article titled "The Coming Anarchy," which presents the "overpopulation" perspective on social disorder. Kaplan (1994:46) picks West Africa in the 1990s as "*the* symbol of worldwide demographic, environmental, and societal stress, in which criminal anarchy emerges as the real 'strategic danger.'" Describing civil wars, throngs of refugees, crime-ridden urban slums, high rates of population growth, and a breakdown of national boundaries in Sierra Leone and other West African countries, Kaplan argues that many countries are becoming "ungovernable" because of the press of population on a deteriorating resource base. This perspective is also expressed by Thomas Fraser Homer-Dixon (1991), an authority on peace and conflict, who developed a formal theoretical framework to examine the relationship between environmental change and acute social conflict. Homer-Dixon theorized that poor, rather than rich, countries would be especially vulnerable to environmental pressures that would lower agricultural productivity and cause economic decline, population dislocation, and social disorder. These problems would in turn lead to international conflicts, ethnic conflicts, and civil wars that would become security problems for the wealthy nations of the world.

Although Homer-Dixon acknowledges that cultural institutions and ideology are important variables, his position is that "Population size and growth are key variables producing the syndrome of environmental scarcity. . ." (Homer-Dixon 1991:102). He treats per-capita human activity multiplied by population as the prime determinant of the "environmental effects" thought to cause social upheaval and conflict. His view is that culture is what makes some societies less able to adapt to environmental stresses. There is little concern with the way in which the organization of the global culture itself may underlie all of these problems because the objective of his research is to identify ways in which policy makers can intervene to minimize the negative social effects and conflict caused by "environmental stress."

Homer-Dixon identifies the full range of global environmental concerns, such as climate change, rising sea levels, and resource depletion, that would almost certainly produce enormous social upheaval. What he does not address are the ways in which the organization of the global market econo-my systematically produces "environmental stress" and shifts the costs to the poor. For example, he attributes conflict generating poverty, or "relative deprivation," to the environment, not to the political economy. He states: ". . .as developing societies produce less wealth *because of environmental problems* [my emphasis], their citizens will probably become increasingly dis-contented by the widening gap between their actual level of economic achievement and the level they feel they deserve" (Homer-Dixon 1991:109). He warns that disaffected groups might resort to revolutionary insurgencies to establish "distributive justice." A new regime would likely be "extremist, authoritarian, and abusive of human rights" (1991:113). Homer-Dixon notes that a repressive regime might defeat an insurgency, but even a democratic regime would need to use distraction and persuasion to maintain its legiti-macy in the face of "environmentally induced economic decline" (1991:114).

While it is obvious that environmental degradation underlies much con-temporary social conflict, it must also be recognized that since World War II the economic structure linking rich and poor countries has produced extreme poverty and environmental deterioration in the "developing" world. The liberalization of global markets, which has allowed the relatively free flow of investment capital from rich to poor countries and which favors the business enterprise of giant multinational corporations, may accelerate the problem.

THE FINANCIALIZATION PROCESS
AND THE DEBT CRISIS

> If the goals of official debt managers were to squeeze the debtors dry, to trans-fer enormous resources from South to North and to wage undeclared war on the poor continents and their people, then their policies have been an unquali-fied success. If, however, their strategies were intended—as these institutions always claim—to promote development beneficial to all members of society, to preserve the planet's unique environment and gradually to reduce the debt bur-den itself, then their failure is easily demonstrated.
>
> (SUSAN GEORGE 1992:XIII-XIV)

Since the end of the eighteenth century the commercialization process of capital accumulation directed by business enterprise led to rapid industrial-ization and generated economic growth for favored groups in the wealthy "core" of European and North American states. A new hierarchy of states emerged in which formerly independent large-scale cultures on the "periph-ery" were locked by colonialism into unequal economic exchanges with the industrial core (Wallerstein 1974). Finance, or money and banking, was the cultural foundation of the commercialization process from its beginning, but when the 1944 Bretton Woods Conference established a global monetary system based on the American dollar *financialization* itself began to emerge as the dominant cultural process worldwide (Phillips 1994). Initially, capitalists borrowed to build industrial factories, but increasingly finance has become an autonomous "paper" or electronic economy, only remotely connected to the "real economy" of factories, goods, and human services. Researchers Richard J. Barnet and John Cavanagh (1994) estimated that only 10 percent of the trillions of dollars that daily flow through the world's computerized foreign exchange markets involve actual goods and services. Speculators who play the money game in this "casino economy" can profit handsomely from tiny shifts in interest rates or spreads in prices between markets because of the staggering scale of the monetary sums involved in these transactions.

In this financialization paper economy, mortgages, bonds, and creditor-debtor relationships have become more important than ownership of equity shares in industrial corporations. For example, as early as 1979 the total market value of debt instruments was 3.5 times the value of corporate stocks in the United States (Greider 1987:30). Since the early 1970s the value of the dollar has not been fixed to gold and financial markets have been deregulated in ways that make financial speculation even more profitable for a wealthy minority. Surprisingly few individuals participate directly in the financialization process. For example, in 1981 the *Wall Street Journal* reported that there were 405,830 finance professionals and 1.7 million of its subscribers owned financial securities (Greider 1987:735, 37). In 1994 only 3.4 percent of American households owned any corporate or municipal bonds, even fewer held government securities, and only 20 percent held any stocks or mutual funds.

The new global financial order works to benefit the world's wealthy investors, wherever they are located. It seems to be a much more efficient way of transferring wealth from rich to poor than the old colonial systems because the wealthy let the national governments of poor countries deal with the social control problems that exploitation inevitably generates. Money temporarily shifted from rich to poor countries to finance their economic development creates a gigantic debt yielding a rich return for investors in the financial community. According to Susan George (1992) of the Transnational Institute, during the nine years from 1982 through 1990 poor debtor countries in the South transferred $706 billion in interest payments to rich creditor countries in the North and a total payback of a staggering $1,345 billion. This was equivalent to more than $1,000 for each of the 600 million people living in Europe and North America. To put these figures in perspective, George shows that all of the financial resources transferred from rich to poor countries from 1982 to 1990 totaled just $927 billion, including all forms of economic assistance, charity, private investment capital, and bank loans. Subtracting the $927 billion in support from the $1,345 billion in payback reveals a balance of $418 billion actually returned to the rich creditor countries. This return is roughly six times the amount (in 1991 dollars) that the United States spent rebuilding Europe after World War II under the Marshall Plan. George calls this "unprecedented financial assistance to the rich from the poor" and points out that the beneficiaries were the elites of poor countries and wealthy investors in the rich countries.

After nearly a decade of work on the debt issue, researchers at the Amsterdam-based Transnational Institute concluded that Third World debt is a "central factor in the overall crisis of the third world" and a "major contributing factor" to much of the ecological devastation, especially deforestation, that has accelerated worldwide since the late 1960s and 1970s (George 1992:1-2). George points out that huge lending programs for massive capital projects, such as dams, highways, power plants, manufacturing facilities, and vast agricultural enterprises, were in themselves often highly destructive and unsustainable forms of development that served the immediate interests of national elites. Much of the money actually returned quickly to the banks in core countries either as payments to multinational development corporations or as the personal wealth of corrupt national elites. Furthermore, these development projects displaced and impoverished the small landowners and squatters, many of whom became the "shifted farmers" referred to in Chapter 2, who are being forced to cultivate fragile marginal environments. By the 1980s, servicing the debt proved to be an insurmountable problem. The "structural adjustments," or austerity programs, imposed by the international financial agencies such as the World Bank and the International Monetary Fund (IMF), involving currency devaluations, reduced social welfare programs, and increased resource extraction for export, caused enormous human suffering and dramatically intensified the deterioration of ecosystems.

In order to meet the structural adjustment goals imposed by the official debt managers, countries must export more than they import to produce a positive balance of payments as a condition for short-term loans to help debtors meet their payments. This approach, which is called "export-led" economic growth, requires debtor nations to extract as much as possible from their labor force and their natural resources and provides no incentive for sustainable resource management or social equity. George is especially critical of development policies that are driven by the debt problem because they tend to ignore other issues, such as:

> . . . equitable land tenure, aid to small, food-producing farmers, credit for the poor, education for women, child survival/family-planning programmes and the like; much less sustainable environmental policies.

(GEORGE 1992:18)

It is probably no accident that Brazil, the country with the largest international debt, was also the top ranked deforester. In general, countries that were heavy deforesters were also transferring one- to two-thirds of their returns from exports to the wealthy in the form of debt service (payments of interest and principal). Thus, neither the resources themselves nor the income from them benefited the majority of the population. Ironically, many of the giant corporate developments that deforested the Brazilian Amazon actually proved uneconomical. Yet they served as profitable tax write-offs for wealthy investors, much like many agribusiness developments in the United States.

The international debt crisis began in 1982 when Mexico, second largest debtor nation after Brazil, declared that it was about to default on its debt payments. The International Monetary Fund's structural adjustment, export-led plan that followed was a prime incentive for the development of the *maquiladora* zone along the border with the United States. Hundreds of foreign manufacturing companies were attracted to the border zone by the promise of a very cheap labor force and lax environmental and worker safety laws. The "winners" in this situation were: 1) the Mexican financial elite; 2) the companies that gained a competitive edge in the global "free market;" 3) the American banks that received most of the interest payments from the Mexican debt; and 4) the investors who received a hefty return from their holdings in maquiladora companies and creditor banks. The "losers" were: 1) the Mexican workers who must accept wages as low as $26 per week, and who cannot escape their badly polluted environment; 2) the 11.5 million American workers whose jobs disappeared between 1979 and 1984 alone; and 3) those American communities negatively impacted by the influx of desperately poor Mexican immigrants.

Speaking for the Transnational Institute, Susan George is emphatic about assigning responsibility for both the debt crisis and the social and environmental problems that have followed:

> ". . . we believe that it is above all the actions of the Northern [Europe and North America] creditor governments, and those of the international institutions [World Bank and IMF] they largely control, which drive the forces behind this destruction. They invented the initial "development" model which has led to ecological disaster. They have used the leverage provided by the debt crisis to perpetuate this model. We have indeed met the enemy and he is not so much "us" as the people and the institutions we have allowed to speak for us. Only informed and active citizens can call them to account.
>
> (GEORGE 1992:32–33)

EXPORT SUGAR, STARVATION, AND INFANT MORTALITY IN BRAZIL

Anthropological research reveals the human side of the global economy's harsh realities as experienced by the world's impoverished majority. Anthropologist Nancy Scheper-Hughes worked as a Peace Corps health worker near Recife in northeastern Brazil from 1964 through 1966. She returned between 1982 and 1989 to conduct research on the effects of chronic hunger and infant death on maternal love. Her account (Scheper-Hughes 1992) of the lives of the residents of a squatter slum in a town she called Bom Jesus is a moving portrayal of how the poor coped with the enormous suffering that accompanied Brazil's economic "miracle."

The economy in this corner of Brazil is based on monocrop sugar production for export and is dominated by the landed aristocracy who own the giant sugar mills and the vast *latifundia* estates. The fifty largest estates range in size from 5,000 to 50,000 acres, dwarfing the largest California agribusinesses described in Chapter 5. Since the 1950s, continuous expansion by the large estates at the expense of small holdings and the conversion of all land into sugar production have made it virtually impossible for the underclass, who constitute roughly 80 percent of the population, to raise subsistence crops or even gather firewood. They must purchase all their basic needs. Food prices are high because even beans are imported from the south.

In 1989 those men lucky enough to find seasonal work on the sugar plantations could earn the legal minimum of $10 a week cutting cane, while women were earning $5 a week. Comparing these weekly wages and the $26 Mexican maquiladora wages to the $170 legal minimum in the United States, it is clear why American labor is no longer "competitive" in the global economy. The critical point in Bom Jesus is that the minimum food needs for a household with four children cost $40 a week. Thus, even if both husband and wife had permanent minimum wage work they could not provide basic subsistence for their family. In contrast, the severely depressed wage scale made it possible for a Bom Jesus middle class professional earning just $175 a week to spend $62.50 weekly to feed his household of three and five additional domestic servants.

The sugar barons at the top of the social hierarchy married within their own class in order to protect their wealth. They hired armed security guards twenty-four hours a day and maintained a residence on their plantations, in the town of Bom Jesus, and in the city of Recife. Their children might be sent to Europe for school and they would go to the United States for medical attention. A shantytown resident accurately described the elite as follows:

> The rich are the owners of the city. They are the people who don't have to work for a living, who are "excused" from the daily struggle that is life. For the rich, living in their mansions and big houses, nothing is ever wanting. Every wish is satisfied. They are our bosses, our *patroes*. They don't owe anything to anybody. Everybody owes them.
>
> (SCHEPER-HUGHES 1992:80)

From the viewpoint of the wealthy, there is no real hunger in Brazil. Malnutrition exists because people have poor dietary habits and need to be educated. People are poor because they are unwilling to improve themselves and don't like hard work.

James Scott (1985) points out that the weak have many "weapons" for dealing with their exploiters, but they are unlikely to succeed in direct confrontations with the institutions of oppression. The poor of Bom Jesus survived by putting everyone in the family to work, by maintaining a collectivist and egalitarian ethic with kin and within the poor community, and by cultivating their own dependency relations with the wealthy. Even with all these efforts, physical starvation was a chronic problem. Nutritional surveys in the 1980s showed that cane workers averaged only 1,500 calories per day, less than the 1,750 calories the Nazis gave the residents of the Buchenwald concentration camp during World War II and just 40 percent of the daily U.S. average of 3,700 calories. With some justification the Brazilian northeast could be considered a concentration camp for 30 million people, as some have charged. Two-thirds of rural children showed clinical evidence of undernutrition and one-fourth were nutritionally dwarfed (Scheper-Hughes 1992:153). Chronic undernutrition contributes to overall poor health, low energy, low self-esteem, and high rates of miscarriage and underweight babies. Most importantly, starvation is a prime reason why official figures showed that 116 out of 1,000 live births were dying within the first year in the Brazilian northeast. This is twice the 1993 national average for Brazil and twelve times the average for the United States.

Not satisfied with the aggregated regional and national infant mortality rates, which she felt were deceptively low, Scheper-Hughes obtained the handwritten birth and death records from the registry books in Bom Jesus, which would more accurately reflect local realities. She also collected full reproductive histories from 100 women. These data revealed that in 1965, shortly after the military took power in Brazil, infants were dying in Bom Jesus at a staggering 493 per 1,000, nearly 50 percent in their first year of life. By 1987 infant mortality stood at 211 per 1,000, well above any national level rates in the world. On the average, an older woman had seen 4.7 of her children die.

The women Scheper-Hughes questioned about the general causes of infant mortality correctly blamed social conditions, environmental factors, and poor medical care. As one woman said, "Our children die because we are poor and hungry" (1992:313). However, the poor were also culturally conditioned to attribute the deaths of their own children to "weakness," just as they blamed their own poor health on "nerves." Thus, what was actually a problem generated by the political economy was viewed as a medical problem to be treated with tranquilizers and vitamins from the pharmacy rather than through social change. The medical profession in Bom Jesus supported this "medicalization" of starvation, helping to obscure its roots in the class structure and the global economy. This was a form of cultural hegemony in which the underclass came to rationalize their own exploitation. Scheper-Hughes is emphatic about the real causes of sickness and death in Bom Jesus:

> I do not want to quibble over words, but what I have been seeing on the Alto de Cruzeiro [the slum in Bom Jesus] for two and a half decades is more than "malnutrition," and it is politically as well as economically caused, although in the absence of overt political strife or war. Adults, it is true, might be described as "chronically undernourished," in a weakened and debilitated state, prone to infections and opportunistic diseases. But it is overt hunger and starvation that one sees in babies and small children, the victims of a "famine" that is endemic, relentless, and political-economic in origin.
>
> (SCHEPER-HUGHES 1992:146).

The connection between Brazil's high infant mortality rates, as seen in Bom Jesus, and Brazil's position in the global economy are probably not a coincidence. Scheper-Hughes points out that Brazil's enormous borrowing to finance its economic miracle caused interest on the debt to soar by 1985 to nearly one-third of the government's total expenditures, forcing it to cut expenditures for public health. At the same time wages dropped by one-third and food costs soared. It is instructive to note that in 1986 Cuba, another Latin American sugar economy, but one that had remained isolated from development loans and the global market, showed infant mortality rates of 13.6 per 1,000 and life expectancy at birth of seventy-six years, virtually equalling the U.S. figures.

STATE TERRORISM AND INVESTMENT RISK IN GUATEMALA

> Counterinsurgency violence escalated in geometric proportions. It began with abductions . . . The escalation of repression gave way to selective massacres . . . repression reached its peak when the massacres were no longer selective but indiscriminate . . . no discrimination was made between civilians and combatants, or between collaborators, sympathizers, and people indifferent or opposed to the insurgency. Distinctions were not made between men and women . . . between young and old, between children and adults. The entire population was seen as "a rotten orange," in the words of the San Luis officer, and everyone, absolutely everyone, should be thrown onto the demolishing fire . . . thus the massacres were genocidal.
>
> (FALLA 1994:184)

In a global market economy, prudent investors seeking the highest returns and the lowest risks from their financial capital must consider social and political conditions wherever they invest. National and international business interests will likely fear adverse effects whenever oppressed people demand respect for their basic human rights and press for land reform, social security, higher wages, and improved working conditions. The annual editions of the *Political Risk Yearbook* (Political Risk Services 1994) rate virtually every country in the world on its eighteen-month and five-year potential for political turmoil and give letter grades from A+ to D- for specific risks to international finance, direct investment, and exports, much like Standard & Poor's AAA to D bond rating system. With the liberalization of global markets in full swing, the 1994 yearbook gave only a handful of mostly African countries D grades for "hostility to foreign business" and "serious security concerns" or for making "foreign business a handy scapegoat in politics." Even modest increases in labor costs or higher taxes to fund public health and education could threaten international corporate profits and shake "investor confidence." In a tightly integrated world economy the possibility of adverse changes in the business climate of any country could cause declines in foreign exchange rates and in the value of government and corporate securities. As international finance capital moves more freely, social "unrest" in any corner of the world might be felt as a ripple in financial markets everywhere as worried investors shuffle their assets to safer havens. The global market produces strong incentives for governments to suppress disruptive public opinion even as increasing economic inequality makes public dissatisfaction more likely.

In countries that lack genuine democracy, brutal regimes, backed by well-armed military forces, have frequently used internal violence and terror to block social reform and thereby safeguard the interests of the global financial elite. Linguist Noam Chomsky has persuasively argued that governments have often used labels such as "national security" and "counterinsurgency" to mask human rights violations by military forces against dissident domestic political groups (Chomsky & Herman 1979, Chomsky 1989, 1991,1993). Since the end of World War II, the United States has selectively provided decisive military assistance and development aid to many antidemocratic regimes, such as Brazil under military rule, that maintained "favorable attitudes" toward international business. The American government used Cold War fears of Soviet or Cuban communist subversion to justify its support of pro-American Latin American dictatorships.

In a more humane world, truly democratic processes, not political terror, would arbitrate the legitimate interests of competing social groups. Because it is a democracy, America's foreign policy can be shaped by public opinion, but it is often difficult for the public to get accurate information on issues involving powerful special interests. Guatemala is a case in which anthropologists have helped to publicly document the community and personal impact of human rights violations committed by a U.S.-supported government in the name of national security. Anthropologists, with their knowledge of the indigenous languages and cultures and their personal contacts stretching over many years, were in a position to see firsthand the realities that official information sources denied.

Guatemala is the largest Central American country. In 1992 over half of its 10 million people were Mayan Indians, speaking twenty different languages and living in rural communities based on subsistence agriculture, migratory wage labor, and production for local markets. During the civil war of the 1970s and 1980s, when leftist guerrilla forces of the Guatemalan Army of the Poor (EGP) and the Organization of the People in Arms (ORPA) began to gain popular support, the Guatemalan army responded by indiscriminantly killing tens of thousands of Indians in a scorched earth campaign of terror. An estimated 440 villages were destroyed. In some cases their residents were systematically murdered, in others they were relocated into strategic hamlets (Falla 1994:8). People were tortured, mutilated, and killed in the most gruesome ways, recalling the holocaust of the original conquest. In 1992 200,000 Guatemalan refugees were living in Mexico, while many others fled to the United States.

The government and its American supporters claimed that the Guatemalan army was simply responding to Soviet and Cuban communist subversion and that the guerrillas were primarily responsible for atrocities against civilians. Reports by anthropologists, missionaries, development workers, and human rights organizations strongly refuted the official accounts.

The roots of the conflict are found in the centuries-long political and economic domination by the *ladino* (non-Indian) elite over the Indian majority. Population growth also plays a role, as Homer-Dixon would predict, because rich agricultural soil is in short supply in the Guatemalan highlands and many Indian farmers are landless, but inequities in the political economy aggravated the problem. In the 1980s 2 percent of the landholders controlled 70 percent of the land and 72 percent of the population could not afford a minimum diet (Chomsky 1993:173). The primary problem was the government's unwillingness to respond to the legitimate grievances of the Indian community. Ladinos have long used their political influence with the government to expropriate Indian land and keep wages low. For example, in 1978 more than 100 Indians were killed by the army for marching on the town hall in Panzos to demand land titles to defend their lands from expropriation by large landholders (Davis 1988, IWGIA 1978).

Political violence was also occurring in El Salvador, Brazil, Argentina, Chile, and other Latin American countries at the same time, but what made the Guatemalan case especially noteworthy was that the villages and people destroyed were not anonymous. Places such as Chichicastenango and Huehuetenango are famous in the anthropological literature and are personally known to many anthropologists, including the present author. Many of the Indian people who died horrible deaths at the hands of the Guatemalan army had for decades assisted anthropological field researchers who knew their lives and their families. Outraged by the unspeakable atrocities, eleven anthropologists, a geographer, and a political scientist, all with extensive experience in Guatemala, published their own highly personal accounts of the death squads, disappearances, tortures, and massacres in *Harvest of Violence* (Carmack 1988). They reported that the guerrillas also used political violence but it was very selective, while the army killed indiscriminantly. In 1983 and 1984 Ricardo Falla, Guatemalan anthropologist and Jesuit priest, lived with Indian survivors hidden in the Guatemalan rain forest and interviewed others in the refugee camps in Mexico. He obtained detailed eyewitness accounts of army atrocities against noncombatant men, women, and children. Painstakingly reconstructing specific military operations, he listed names and ages of 773 civilian victims murdered by the army in the Ixcan region (Falla 1994). Myrna Mack, another Guatemalan anthropologist, was killed by the army in 1990.

In 1992 the American Association for the Advancement of Science's Committee on Scientific Freedom and Responsibility sponsored a special training program for human rights workers and government officials in Guatemala. Forensic anthropologist Clyde Snow demonstrated how to properly exhume mass graves, identify victims, and find physical evidence of "extra-judicial executions" and torture. This kind of work will make it much more difficult for anyone to use political terrorism with impunity.

America's interest in Guatemala is easily documented. Guatemala's total external debt in 1992 was $2.7 billion and roughly one-third of its foreign trade was with the United States. Coffee is its primary export crop. Between 1966 and 1975 the United States provided $16.7 million in military assistance and shipped $23 million worth of military equipment to Guatemala. From 1966 to 1985 the United States gave Guatemala $430 million in grants and credits. The country received an additional $370 million in economic assistance from 1988 to 1991. In 1980 Americans had direct investments of $229 million in Guatemala but given continued political "instability" that figure had dropped to $105 million by 1991 (*The American Almanac 1994–1995*). In the 1994 *Political Risk Yearbook* Guatemala was thought to have high short term risk for "turmoil," defined as "economic disruption due to war, insurrection, demonstrations, or terrorism." Consequently it received a B for direct investment potential and exports because of the risk of "possibly dangerous turmoil or moderate restrictions on business activity" and restrictions on trade and payments. Fortunately for the international finance community, the five-year outlook for Guatemala predicted only moderate turmoil and an A- for direct investment, suggesting a "favorable attitude, especially with respect to equity, loan participation, and taxes" and "restraint" in fiscal and labor policy.

OPULENCE AND DEINDUSTRIALIZATION IN AMERICA

In the United States, just as in the poor countries of the world, economic growth and the globalization of the economy have disproportionately benefited the few while the majority have steadily lost wealth and control over their lives. Various measures of wealth and income distribution suggest that since approximately 1970 changes in American economic policies have worked to redistribute wealth to the richest at the expense of middle- and lower-class households (Phillips 1990). The most dramatic evidence of this is seen in the increase in the number of the super-rich relative to the poor. Economic growth during the two decades between 1969 and 1989 was reflected in a ninefold increase in the number of millionaires while at the same time the number of poor increased by approximately 25 percent. According to the Census Bureau, in 1969 there were only 143,000 millionaires. Twenty years later in 1989 there were 1.3 million people worth more than $1 million. In 1993 *Fortune* magazine (June 28) listed twenty-five American individuals or families with assets of more than $2 billion each. Their collective holdings were worth more than 2 percent of America's GNP. The Waltons, principal owners of the Wal-Mart retail empire, were ranked as the wealthiest American family. Their fortune was estimated at $23.5 billion, the second largest in the world after the Sultan of Brueni, whose personal fortune was some $37 billion.

In 1992 the wealthiest 20 percent of American households received 51 percent of aggregate pre-tax income in the country while the poorest 20 percent received less than 1 percent. Income distribution was relatively more equitable in 1970, when the poorest received more than 5 percent and the richest 41 percent of the income (*American Almanac* 1977, 1994). In 1970, 25 million Americans, 12.6 percent of the population, fell below the poverty level. In 1992 36.9 million Americans, nearly 15 percent of the population, were living below the official poverty level. This figure includes the 21 percent of American children under the age of eighteen who were living in poverty.

Another measure of economic inequality in the United States is the excessive spread in income between minimum-wage workers and the salaries of top corporate executives. In America as in Brazil, because wages have fallen relative to the cost of living minimum wage workers cannot support a household unless both husband and wife are employed. In 1992 the poverty level for a family of three was set at $10,292, well above the minimum annual wage of $8,840. Plato recommended that the highest salary in a community should not exceed five times the lowest. More expansive American authorities suggest that a twentyfold top to bottom salary spread would be reasonable, and that is the range in Japan (Crystal 1991:23–24). However, in 1993 the highest paid American corporate chief executive officer earned $41.3 million in salary, bonuses, and extra compensation—more than 935 times a minimum wage of $8,840. The average compensation of top executives in 200 of the largest American corporations was $4.1 million in 1993, 463 times the lowest annual wage (Dumaine 1994).

Encouraged by changes in the tax laws and economic policies that favored the rich, excessive salaries have helped concentrate wealth at the upper levels of American society (Phillips 1990). From the 1940s through 1964 the highest tax rate stood at 91 percent for the top bracket and thus set a practical ceiling on income. By 1973 the top income bracket had dropped to 70 percent for households with incomes of over $200,000. Under the tax "reform" of 1986 the highest incomes were taxed at no more than 28 to 31 percent. Thus, in 1992 any household earning over $86,500 was taxed at just 31 percent, effectively removing any incentive to limit personal wealth accumulation. Corporate taxes were also reduced, raising returns to wealthy stockholders, while reductions in the capital gains tax meant that the wealthy could keep more of their "unearned income" from investments. These reductions in combination with increases in social security payroll taxes meant that wage earners paid a larger proportion in total taxes.

During the 1980s the federal government doubled defense expenditures, providing a profitable bonanza to the arms industry while amplifying human problems and shifting more wealth to the American economic elite. The global arms trade drains critical economic resources away from human needs and makes conflicts more destructive. Many weapons, such as land mines, do not discriminate between combatants and civilians. Furthermore, armaments are frequently used to suppress domestic political opposition, as noted in the Guatemalan example. After the Cold War ended in 1990–1991, many American defense contractors with large investments in nuclear weapons actively promoted the export of conventional weapons to keep profits high. The United States became the world's largest exporter of arms. Significantly, in 1991 eight of the top ten armament companies in the world were among the 500 largest American industrial corporations. General Motors, the world's largest industrial corporation, was also the world's fourth largest arms producer. General Electric, America's fifth largest industrial corporation, was the world's sixth largest armaments company (*Arms Trade News* 1993, Nov).

In 1990 American defense contractors received $144.7 billion from the government, 10 percent of the federal budget, only slightly less than the $146 billion the government spent in that year on all public assistance (welfare), food stamps, supplemental income, and medical and social programs for the poor. For many reasons the deficit between revenues and expenditures soared, such that the total federal debt quadrupled between 1980 and 1992. The United States became the world's largest debtor nation. The value of the dollar declined on international markets and a large trade imbalance developed as the country began to import far more than it exported. Foreign interests began buying up American real estate and businesses (Phillips 1990, Barnet & Cavanagh 1994). The rising deficit forced up interest rates on borrowing, further increasing investment income for the wealthy 2.2 percent of American households holding government securities. Leveraged buy-outs and mergers further concentrated the ownership and control of corporate assets. Many American corporations kept profits high by "downsizing;" firing employees; hiring lower wage, nonunion, or part-time employees; and moving factories overseas. America's heavy industries were increasingly being replaced by highly mobile light manufacturing and service industries in a process that has been called "deindustrialization" (Bluestone & Harrison 1982, see also *Urban Anthropology* 1985, Vol. 14 nos. 1–3).

Anthropologist James Toth (1992) has documented the impact of deindustrialization on Carlisle, a small town in Pennsylvania where economic growth occurred in a way that removed decision making power over capital and profits from local businesspeople to remote corporate offices. Toth and his researchers found that small businesses, small manufacturing plants, and independent contractors that had formerly provided steady, secure employment for local residents were replaced by electronics firms, shopping malls, banks, and realty agencies that were subsidiaries of conglomerates headquartered elsewhere and that effectively drained the community's capital resources. As Toth explains:

> . . . as Carlisle loses its isolation and becomes integrated into larger financial, commercial, and labor markets, local economic and government leaders become middlemen and brokers for higher layers of authority located in corporate centers and company headquarters in Pittsburgh, Philadelphia, Baltimore, New York and even outside the country. City government and local business leaders continue to administer to the various needs of the community, but real power has shifted to those living far from Carlisle.

(TOTH 1992:13–14)

The largest beneficiaries of global financialization and American deindustrialization are those "super-consumer" Americans in the top .5 percent of the population who can afford to purchase costly luxuries, such as $21,995 IWC Da Vinci wristwatches, the $189,000 Rolls-Royce Silver Spur III, or a $6 million winter residence on Fisher Island in Florida, those who travel in private jets, and those "high net worth individuals" who can take advantage of Citibank's private banking, "integrated wealth management," and "global asset management" programs. The primary concern of these fortunate families is personal security. For example, Fisher Island, a 216-acre "sanctuary" off the coast of Florida, is described in an advertisement as home to "four hundred of the world's most prominent families" and boasts ". . . perhaps most important of all, an atmosphere of security that allows residents to lead a life of privacy and pleasure" (*Architectural Digest* 1994 February, p. 99). In 1987 the seaside luxury homes, yachts, private racquet clubs, golf course, marinas, shops, and bank on "Fortress Fisher" were protected by a forty-person security force and electronic security systems. The island was accessible only by private ferry to those with security clearances (Flanagan 1987).

Even this kind of sheltered enclave does not fully protect the wealthy from their own domestic employees. Former FBI official James Fox (1994) advises that anyone hiring gardeners, nannies, chauffeurs, live in nurses, private airplane pilots, or personal trainers needs to check out the employment agency and then insist on a pre-employment physical, drug testing, a written integrity test, and a nondisclosure agreement (signed loyalty oath). Finally, the personal background of any prospective employee must be examined by a private investigator. It is hard to hire reliable domestic help in a country like America, where 15 percent of the population live in poverty.

Anthropologist Katherine Newman (1988, 1993) has described the 1980s as a period of "declining fortunes" for many middle- and working-class Americans who are "falling from grace." During the decade between 1981 and 1992 10.6 million adults lost their jobs because of plant closings or force reductions and most suffered drastic reductions in income when they found lower wage jobs (Newman 1988, *American Almanac* 1994–1995). This downward mobility has affected up to one-third of the American population, many of whom were not previously poor. In 1992 dollars, median income in America declined by 10 percent during the 1980–1993 period, from $35,839 to $32,241. In order to learn how the realities of America's political economy were impacting downwardly mobile Americans, Newman conducted intensive "focused life history" interviews with more than 300 people. In 1982–1983 she interviewed diverse groups of professionals, managers, skilled blue-collar workers who had lost their jobs, and divorced women. In 1988–1990 she interviewed 160 people from 60 families representing the high school classes of 1970 and 1980 in a single New Jersey suburban community. She found that many people believed the American Dream of a steadily improving standard of living was no longer attainable. Generations were being pitted against each other. People she interviewed were coming to resent economic elites they considered to be illegitimate.

Newman found that downsized managers sometimes blamed their fates on powerful external forces but the dominant culture of capitalist meritocracy provides them little support. Success in the corporate business world ideologically defines the moral worth of the meritorious individual. In this survival of the fittest view, people who lose their jobs deserve their fate. As one former executive declared:

> I have to accept my firing. . . . The people who were involved in it are people
> I respect for the most part . . . They are successful executives . . . So I can't
> blame them for doing what they think is right. I have to say where have I gone
> wrong.

(NEWMAN 1988:78)

This "blame the victim" acceptance of one's personal fate at the hands of corporate decision makers was echoed by a member of a self-help club for fellow unemployed executives, who declared:

> I believe in the capitalist system. Private industry should make the products and the profits, and we'll all prosper. *If people at the club are not prospering, that's their problem.* . . . There's a place out there for all of us, it's just a matter of finding it.
>
> (NEWMAN 1988:76)

Anthropologist June Nash (1989, 1994) found a similar acceptance of job loss by the former workers of a Massachusetts General Electric plant that was moved to Canada in 1986, eliminating 5,000 jobs. Former employees questioned by Nash rejected the notion that General Electric had any responsibility to the community even though it had been its principle employer for over a century. They justified the plant closing by referring to the company imperative to make a profit and did not take the position that organized labor or local governments should have any control over such capital investments. Nash attributes this passivity on the part of displaced workers to the ideological hegemony of the corporate elite. Those holding real power in the world would prefer to continue making decisions in their own immediate interests. They want ordinary people to believe that their fates are determined by inherently uncontrollable "natural" forces. Newman explains this as follows:

> ". . . American culture tends to subtract large forces from our lives—economic trends, historical moments, and even government policies that privilege one group over another—and looks instead to the individual's character traits or values for answers.
>
> (NEWMAN 1993:221)

In fact there are many alternatives to unbridled corporate power. Public policies can be democratically shaped in ways that strengthen the power of local communities. For example, sociologist Denny Braun (1991) argues that in an economic democracy people would question

> whether the real interests of Americans can be served by policies aimed at maximizing the profits of huge, conglomerate corporations. . . . Is the overseas expansion of American multinational firms of any benefit to U.S. citizens? Does it instead harm us, reduce our incomes, and increase inequality?
>
> (BRAUN 1991:277)

He thinks that an informed answer would be *no* and advocates reductions in defense spending, changes in the tax structure, and improvements in education, arguing that everyone's minimal needs would be met in an economic democracy.

8

The Future

*Obviously we stand on the threshold of postcivilization. When we
reach solutions to today's problems, the society and culture that we
will have built for the purpose will be of a sort the world has never
seen before. It may be more, or less, civilized than what we
have, but it will not be civilization as we know it.*

PAUL BOHANNAN, "BEYOND CIVILIZATION"

FOCUSING ON ALL OF the world's problems at one time can be an overwhelming and depressing task, but identifying common causes and seeking
solutions from an anthropological perspective can be a source of new opti-
mism and hope. Indeed, there are common causes to our problems and there
can be common solutions. Previous chapters necessarily treated the specific
human problems of environmental deterioration, resource depletion,
hunger, overpopulation, poverty, and conflict as if they were discrete issues,
but an anthropological perspective requires us to look for interconnections.
A broad overview is important because the way policy makers conceptualize
problems and their causes will obviously influence the solutions that they
propose. The future will be shaped by the decisions of today's policy makers,
and judging from humanity's evolutionary history, today's solutions will create new problems for the future. National and international policy makers
and disciplinary theorists have reached a popular consensus that "underde-
velopment" is the world's problem and "sustainable development" the solution to be worked out in a world dominated by "free market" capitalism.
However, there are persuasive alternative views, based on different, often
broader perspectives that could help shape a more just and more sustainable
future.

Culture process and culture scale have served throughout this book as
organizing devices to help identify connections between problems and to
point the way to possible solutions. From this viewpoint the problem
becomes how to design a global system that will permit small-scale,

community-based cultures maximum autonomy to thrive within large-scale states interconnected by a global, capitalist market system that is itself sustainable. The dilemma is that capitalism assumes perpetual economic growth driven by material inequality and profit-seeking individualism, while small-scale cultures emphasize community, stability, and equality. The following sections will examine different views of the future taken by various environmental organizations, indigenous peoples, "free-market" capitalists, and futurist thinkers in a search for possible solutions to contemporary problems. United Nations initiatives such as the Rio Declaration, Agenda 21, and the Biodiversity Treaty will be considered in some detail as important global responses to contemporary problems.

THE DILEMMA OF SCALE

Previous editions of this text presented the argument that the world's major problems are different manifestations of a single crisis and that civilization itself is the most basic problem. Our problems are all extremely complex, interrelated, and in a general sense multicausal, but many of the most critical are obvious products of different cultural processes and correlates of scales of cultural complexity. Over and over in preceding chapters it has been shown that a specific problem is either totally absent or at least not a serious problem in small-scale cultures. Many problems did not arise or become critical until the appearance of globally organized cultures. Particular problems also often show a peculiar cause-and-effect relationship with advances in culture scale and complexity. For example, war, population growth, and technological development are all causes of and results of increases in cultural scale. Any attempt to single out causes is further complicated by the fact that individual problems are themselves interrelated in similar feedback mechanisms—under certain conditions population growth may lead to war, accelerating technological intensification, which promotes population growth, and so forth.

This multicausality and complex interrelationship between problems has important implications for any attempt to identify causes and find solutions. In many cases it is apparent that current problem-solving efforts are inadequate because they treat isolated symptoms and avoid basic underlying factors. An example from the medical field may illustrate this point. In 1956, T. L. Cleave (1974), surgeon-captain of the British Royal Navy, linked together a list of seemingly diverse diseases, including dental decay, peptic ulcers, obesity, diabetes, constipation, and varicose veins, into a single category that he called the "saccharine disease." Using historical data and research on tribal peoples, he argued that all these conditions are caused at least in part by the extensive use of concentrated carbohydrates such as sugar and white flour by modern industrialized populations. This radical change in diet from the patterns that humans had evolved during many thousands of years altered body chemistry and greatly slowed transit times in the digestive tract by reducing dietary bulk, thereby creating many pathogenic conditions. Other researchers had simply not seen the problems as related, perhaps because they did not examine populations in which these pathologies were absent, and they did not seek basic cultural causes, such as the commercialization of food systems. At higher levels of analysis, it may be that virtually all major world problems are connected to the dominant cultural processes of politicization, commercialization, and financialization that have promoted increases in cultural scale.

Two closely interrelated variables, *social stratification* and extreme *specialization of labor*, the most fundamental characteristics of politicized large-scale cultures, were the foundation for the later emergence of the global-scale culture. Stratification and specialization are the basis of political centralization, the market economy, wealth inequality, and the frequent conflict between individual and subgroup self-interest, on the one hand, and societal interest on the other. All of these cultural features, although they are not in themselves crises, do tend to promote overpopulation, overconsumption, and other symptoms of the environmental crisis and are clearly linked to poverty, war, and crime.

Continued specialization may be a fatal flaw. Specialists are now busily treating symptoms as causes; and in many cases, certain groups even have a special stake in—and indeed may profit by treating—specific symptoms. The defense establishment, for example, "treats" war, the police and legal professions treat crime, and various health and social work professions handle personal crises. The very specialization of these fields makes it unlikely that researchers will perceive connections between deliberately isolated and apparently unrelated symptoms. In many cases, even if a definitive solution were discovered, it would almost certainly be resisted by specialist groups because it might be a clear threat to their job security. For example, the end of the Cold War has caused enormous dislocation for the military-industrial complex and has had ramifications throughout the global economy. It should be no surprise that the discovery of the saccharine disease and its simple cure has led to the addition of fiber content to some food labels and the marketing of certain high fiber foods. These minor changes have not eliminated the saccharine disease because concentrated carbohydrates are produced and distributed by a massive food industry, which in turn is merely one expression of extreme stratification and specialization.

It is possible that the extreme forms of social stratification and economic specialization that characterize global-scale culture may simply be maladaptive. Sustainable development may require sweeping culture change that could be as dramatic as the kinds of change that occurred in Europe and North America during the earlier Industrial Revolution. In fact, economist

Robert L. Heilbroner's early 1960s prescription for development change in the "developing" world may describe precisely the scope of the change that will be needed to solve the crisis of the contemporary world:

> Nothing short of a pervasive social transformation will suffice: a wholesale metamorphosis of habits, a wrenching reorientation of values concerning time, status, money, work; an unweaving and reweaving of the fabric of daily existence itself.
>
> (HEILBRONER 1963:53)

THE GLOBAL FREE MARKET FUTURE

> This Commission believes that people can build a future that is more prosperous, more just, and more secure. Our report, *Our Common Future*, is not a prediction of ever increasing environmental decay, poverty, and hardship in an ever more polluted world among ever decreasing resources. We see instead the possibility for a new era of economic growth, one that is based on policies that sustain and expand the environmental resource base. And we believe such growth to be absolutely essential to relieve the great poverty that is deepening in much of the developing world.
>
> (WCED 1987:1)

The consensus approach adopted by the United Nations and leading governments since the end of the Cold War is that more economic growth is the best overall solution to world problems. This emphasis on growth is reflected in the British government's 1990 environmental strategy, *This Common Inheritance* (United Kingdom, Department of Environment 1990:8). Linking the need for continued economic growth in wealthy nations to environmental concerns, the British strategy argues that further growth is needed to pay for pollution abatement and conservation efforts and to make future industrial production cleaner. The optimistic growth position also appears in the above quote from the UN's Brundtland Commission and is often combined with an emphasis on the need for expanded global trade driven by free-market economic principles. This stress on economic growth and environment, rather than "development" and community well-being, is critical, because, while it does not threaten the interests of investors and the transnational corporate elite, it may stop short of the far-reaching cultural changes that sustainability may actually require.

Many advocates of continued economic growth correctly argue that environmental problems are caused by the failure of price structures to properly reflect the full costs of production. As Frances Cairncross (1993:63), environment editor for *The Economist*, explains: ". . . one of the principal reasons for environmental damage is the failure of markets to provide the right signals." Poorly functioning markets discount ecosystem damage as an "externality" that no one takes responsibility for. Certainly government subsidies that mask the costs of improper use of agricultural pesticides or that fund otherwise "uneconomical" water development projects or deforestation are sending the wrong cost signals. Enthusiastic advocates of free-market economic principles feel that, if all costs are properly accounted for, economic growth can continue indefinitely. Thus we see attempts to place dollar values on people's "willingness to accept" various levels of pollution, or for nature protection, such as a study that found a grizzly bear fifteen times more valuable than a whooping crane, or that the lions in Kenya's Amboseli Park are each worth $27,000 per year in tourism (Cairncross 1993:45, 50). Measures of this sort have been used to show that the market value of sustainably harvested commodities such as nuts and timber from a given tract of rain forest would be worth more than the economic value of the same land as a cow pasture (Peters, Gentry, & Mendelsohn 1989).

Market principles have also been applied to environmental protection in the form of green taxes, carbon taxes, energy taxes, marketable pollution rights, or emission reduction credits. Free-market advocates prefer these approaches over more direct forms of government intervention and certainly consider them preferable to limiting the scale of the global economy itself. Many market-based approaches may indeed help limit environmental damage. For example, the *Intergovernmental Panel on Climate Change* (IPCC), established in 1988 by the World Meteorological Organization and the United Nations Environment Program, recommended such special taxes and subsidies to limit emission of greenhouse gases to slow global warming (IPCC 1991). "Debt for nature" swaps might also help protect vulnerable resources in poor countries. Similar proposals were incorporated into the American *Blueprint for the Environment* (Comp 1989), "a plan for federal action" compiled by a task force of eighteen American environmental organizations that offers detailed recommendations for policy changes to be implemented by specific federal agencies. The difficulty with many of these proposals is that politically they have been very difficult to enact, because they are often perceived as being against the short-term interests of powerful corporations.

While market-based approaches to environmental problems do show promise, there are more fundamental limitations to market principles that must be addressed. For example, while economic theorists assume perfectly competitive markets, in real markets competition tends to be self-limiting as monopoly power increases. Giant corporations work hard to reduce competition. Herman E. Daly and John B. Cobb (1989) stress that the market system is directed by government policies that are in turn guided by economic theory that is inherently unconcerned with human communities, justice, fairness, or the well-being of nature. There is no market incentive for producing public goods that contribute to community welfare but generate no profit because they are freely used by everyone. Free-market theory may not be the best guide for the future. Daly and Cobb observe:

> Just as policies derived from a discipline that knows nothing of human community are destructive of that community, so policies derived from a discipline that knows nothing of the physical world are destructive of that world.
>
> (DALY & COBB 1989:100)

Furthermore, the unlimited pursuit of self-interest may conflict with community interest. Adam Smith's "invisible hand" of unregulated supply and demand assumed that high wages would lower infant mortality and lead to an increased labor supply. Wages would then drop, raising infant mortality. The Brazilian example cited in Chapter 7 certainly demonstrates the relationship between low wages and high infant mortality, but in this case the self-interest of the sugar barons hardly serves the public good. Daly and Cobb (1989:89) feel that the unrestrained personal gain-seeking of free-market theory needs to be tempered with "concern for justice, fairness, or the well-being of the community as a whole." As Daly and Cobb express it, self-interest depletes "moral capital" and undermines communities in the same way that it depletes "natural capital" and destroys ecosystems. The concept of moral capital also applies to the social support networks that have maintained peasants in small-scale cultures for centuries in the face of continuous exploitation by elites (Wolf 1957, Scott 1976).

Economists invoke inadequate classical theories and novel arguments for reducing all restraints to global trade, even though the unresolved human problems of free-market economics are magnified at a global scale. Economist Jagdish Bhagwati (1993), advisor to the Director-General of the General Agreement on Tariffs and Trade (GATT), the UN affiliate that sets world trade rules, supports the free trade, pro-growth position, and also points out that rich countries are more likely to worry about environmental issues. Therefore, according to Bhagwati, the world needs more growth and trade if the environment is to be protected. The GATT allows individual countries to set their own standards on the quality of imports, but they can only unilaterally regulate the domestic conditions of production. Under GATT rules one country cannot set up trade barriers based on another country's internal environmental destruction. Bhagwati rejects environmentalist concerns that such liberalized trade rules will unfairly encourage poor countries to lower their environmental standards to make their export products more competitive, a practice called "social dumping." He argues that rich country environmentalists have no right to impose their "ethical preferences" on other countries. Thus, a poor country might attempt to maintain clean drinking water rather than limiting deforestation. In Bhagwati's view it is "perfectly natural" for poor countries to have their own "preferences" and environmental standards. What he does not point out is that poverty itself is an unnatural product of culture.

The expected benefits of free trade would derive from the comparative advantage that different trading partners might enjoy in the production of different export products. This is Ricardo's nineteenth-century extension of Adam Smith's classic observation in *The Wealth of Nations*, that division of labor, or specialization, was the key to increasing industrial productivity. Tropical countries should enjoy a comparative trade advantage because they are more favorably situated to produce coffee and bananas than temperate countries. Thus, economic theory predicts that everyone would benefit if tropical countries traded commodities and raw materials for manufactured goods produced by Europe and North America. However, in the real world, risks and rewards and power and control are not equitably distributed. The market is not really free because the rich North exercises considerable control over the commodity markets and also controls the finance capital that promotes commodity production. Many poor countries are dependent on one or two export commodities and suffer enormously when prices drop on the world market. In contrast, price fluctuations yield rich returns for wealthy speculators on the commodity markets. Furthermore, the monetary rewards of global trade are very inequitably distributed. Thus, there may be hidden costs to free trade.

World Bank economist Herman Daly (1993), a critic of the assumed advantages of free trade, suggests that "deregulated international commerce" is a more accurate term than "free trade" to describe the liberalization of trade that is occurring under the GATT and other arrangements such as NAFTA (North American Free Trade Agreement). Daly does not question the basic logic of free trade as envisioned by Ricardo, but points out that Ricardo assumed that only goods, not finance capital and services, would move freely between nations. As shown in Chapter 7, free flowing finance capital has produced international debts that have intensified many social and environmental problems within certain countries. Highly mobile finance capital enjoys a major advantage over labor. Workers might seek the highest wages, but they are blocked by the physical difficulty of retraining and moving to better jobs, as well as by the presence of immigration barriers, while finance can move to the other side of the globe at the blink of an eye.

The trade specialization implied by free trade involves a contradiction because it means that countries are "no longer free not to trade, and that loss of independence can be a liability." Daly observes that community and national self-sufficiency in vital industries, and cultural services such as symphony orchestras, are public goods that are best not left to foreigners who have no stake in local affairs beyond commercial profit. Furthermore, international trade is objectively unsustainable to the extent that it is dependent on the petroleum subsides and tax credits that fuel the diesel tankers and cargo jets that move long-distance trade.

Daly's position on the public benefits of limiting international trade was argued in the nineteenth century by German-American economic theorist

Georg Friedrich List (1789–1846). In his 1837 book *The National System of Political Economy*, List maintained that the doctrine of free trade was simply an excuse for strong nations to dominate the domestic economies of weaker nations. Advocating free trade only within the boundaries of autonomous nation states, he understood that universal free trade implied a single world economy that only made sense in a nationless world of rootless individuals ruled by a single government. Speaking like a cultural anthropologist, he defined the "nation" as "a sovereign political body" that functioned to "develop its prosperity, culture, nationality, language, and freedom . . . its entire social and political position in the world" (List 1922:31). List maintained that nations needed national laws, and protective tariffs where necessary, to promote their own national economies. Unlike corporate business enterprises that seek commercial profit, nations are dedicated to the public good. The members of the nation, explained List:

> . . . share in the nation's glory and in its misfortunes; they share its wealth and its poverty. From the nation they draw all the benefits of civilization, enlightenment, progress, and social and political institutions, as well as advances in the arts and sciences. If a nation declines, the individual shares in the disastrous consequences of its fall.
>
> (LIST 1922:30)

In addition to social-cultural liabilities of the free market approach to global problems, Daly observes that economic scale has a critical influence on the human impact on the environment. When economic planners view the global-scale economy as a closed system in which nature is merely a subsystem, they treat natural capital and man-made capital as if they were interchangeable and thus see no practical limits to growth of the global economy. Daly finds it more realistic and adaptive to construct stationary economies as subsystems of stable ecosystems.

AGENDA 21 AND THE UNCED APPROACH

The massive report of the United Nations Conference on Environment and Development (UNCED), the UN Earth Summit held in Rio in 1992, is a comprehensive inventory and well-balanced analysis of global problems related to the environment. The UNCED Report, issued in five volumes, includes the Rio Declaration, the forty-chapter Agenda 21 action plan, and various annexes and resolutions all directed at implementing sustainable development. Agenda 21 is expected to lay the foundation for development planning well into the twenty-first century. The Earth Summit and the conferences that preceded it were an unprecedented search for solutions to global problems by government officials, UN agencies, scientists, and representatives of nongovernmental organizations, taking into account the often overlooked special needs of less developed countries and of the poor, women, and indigenous peoples.

The Rio Declaration ranked human welfare as the primary objective of sustainable development, asserting that all people "are entitled to a healthy and productive life in harmony with nature" (Principle 1). The eradication of poverty was seen as an "indispensable requirement for sustainable development" (Principle 5). Throughout the Report there are many laudable references to the need for holistic approaches to environmental problems and to the need for grassroots development and for empowering individuals and communities. These sentiments are difficult to fault. However, they are paralleled by what could be considered a contrary emphasis on global trade and free-market principles. Many of the provisions of Agenda 21 and related initiatives, such as the Biodiversity Treaty, seemed designed to facilitate the commercial exploitation of resources in the global market.

Indigenous peoples attending UNCED as representatives of small-scale cultures were pleased that their perspectives were incorporated in Agenda 21, but they astutely perceived the overarching power of economic forces and market principles in shaping the direction of the conference. This critical view was clearly expressed by indigenous UNCED participant Jose Dualok Rojas in the following bitterly cynical commentary downloaded in 1994 from the United Nations Environment Program Internet computer service:

> For us, the indigenous peoples, UNCED seemed to function like a commercial market. We perceived the poor countries of the South selling their natural resources, including human beings, to the highest bidder. The rich countries of the North impose conditions of exploitation for the natural resources of these poor countries. Indigenous peoples perceive that the Northern and Southern countries are functioning under a common denominator of complete exploitation of the natural resources by the accumulation of riches in the hands of a few. This is occurring as the indigenous peoples are dying of hunger and misery. This is equivalent to saying that human beings from rich countries can live well while those of poor countries can die. Consequently, UNCED only worked to guarantee the rights and positions for a few in regard to the natural resources that belong to all the world's peoples.

The concerns of indigenous peoples were borne out by the tone of the Biodiversity Treaty, which treated conservation as a financial investment and stressed the economic returns that could be made from biodiversity. For example, the wild plants used medicinally by indigenous people and their genetically unique indigenous cultigens could yield enormous profits for biotechnology and pharmaceutical companies when developed for the world market. Several special provisions of the treaty were drafted to ensure that outside corporate interests will have commercial access to genetic resources anywhere in the world on the basis of "equitable sharing of benefits" (Article

15). The traditional knowledge that local indigenous communities have accumulated over millennia will be treated as "intellectual property" and will be subject to ownership and control through commercial patents. The "contracting parties" to the Biodiversity Treaty are governments, but it is expected that biological resources and traditional knowledge will be developed with the "approval and involvement" of indigenous communities. These measures effectively convert natural resources and cultural knowledge from freely shared public goods into commercial commodities. An honorable attempt to "share benefits" may be inadequate compensation for the loss of community autonomy that might follow even if biodiversity is protected and resources are harvested sustainably.

SCALING DOWN: THE SMALL NATIONS ALTERNATIVE

Thus we see that a small-state world would not only solve the problems of social brutality and war: it would solve the equally terrible problems of oppression and tyranny. It would solve all problems arising from power.

(LEOPOLD KOHR 1978:79)

The most promising approaches to the future are those proposals by various anthropologists, ecologists, economists, and social activists for truly sustainable and humane cultural systems based on local communities, ecosystems, regions, and nationalities. In effect they would adapt the proven achievements of small-scale cultures to the contemporary world of market commerce and industrial technology. All of these approaches assume that most world problems are problems of scale. Global markets and multinational corporations are simply too large and too focused on profit-making to operate in the human interest. The alternative is to scale down the organization of cultural systems to make them responsive to human needs.

In 1957, in an obscure book entitled *The Breakdown of Nations*, economist Leopold Kohr modestly proposed a "new and unified political philosophy" based on a "theory of size" (Kohr 1978:xviii). This new theory contained the solution to all the world's problems, Kohr argued. According to Kohr, the basic problem underlying all forms of "social misery" was "bigness"—nations had become too large. Large nations simply could not prevent their power from becoming internally oppressive and they could not prevent devastating wars. Kohr identified precisely the problems in state organization that emerge when states are contrasted with small-scale tribal societies, even though he did not have a clear picture of what tribal societies were like. Kohr argued persuasively that a world divided into a global system of small nations of relatively equal power would be safer and more humane. His conclusions were so profound, and were applied to so many diverse world problems, that he was virtually ignored. The original edition of his book was published in England and only 500 copies reached the United States. The book was soon out of print and has now virtually disappeared. The work did inspire fellow economist E. F. Schumacher (1973) to write *Small Is Beautiful*, stressing the advantages of small-scale solutions and "appropriate technology" for economic problems. The popularity of *Small Is Beautiful* prompted a brief republication of Kohr's work, but few people appear to have appreciated its significance.

Kohr's proposal implies that world problems will not be solved by the United Nations or by deregulating international trade. Solutions require maximum cultural diversity. They must be worked out independently in each country and region of the world, preferably without regard to external economic or political interests and pressures. A world of small nations would, of course, still contain nations, and each nation would presumably still be stratified and hierarchical, but they could in theory be more responsive to the needs of their people. Furthermore, like tribes, they would be dependent on their own resources and would have an immediate interest in taking care of them. There would be room for great diversity in the kinds of solutions that might be developed to solve problems relating local culture to local environments. This is not to say that a small-nation world would be a utopia or totally free from war. There would still be internal conflicts and perhaps local wars, but both would be easier to contain and much less destructive than global wars of the sort fought twice in the twentieth century.

Kohr pointed out that the kind of small states that he envisioned already existed, as represented by local cultural and linguistic groupings. These "nations" simply needed to be granted political autonomy. He suggested that the large nations can break themselves down into appropriately sized small nations by providing local "nationalities" with equal voting power within a federal system which could then dissolve itself. Kohr felt that this would be a perfectly feasible way to create a small-nation world, but he was not optimistic about this ever coming about. The shortest chapter in his book was entitled "The Elimination of Great Powers: Can It Be Done?" The chapter contains one word: "No!" (Kohr 1978:197). Recent history suggests that the breakup of great powers may not be so difficult, given the experience of the former Soviet Union, which dissolved itself on December 26, 1991.

A BLUEPRINT FOR SURVIVAL

One of the most thorough outlines for a national-level cultural transformation for sustainable development was published in 1972 by the editors of the British science journal *The Ecologist* under the title *Blueprint for Survival* (Goldsmith et al. 1972). This work began with the assumption that the continuation of present trends would mean the ultimate collapse of industrial civilization. Pointing to the environmental crisis and related social system disruption, the *Blueprint* authors felt that radical change of some type would be inevitable. Their planning goal was the creation of a truly stable and sustainable society that would "give the fullest possible satisfaction to its members" (Goldsmith et al. 1972:21–23). Such a society would display the following characteristics:

1. Minimum disruption of ecological processes
2. Maximum conservation of materials and energy
3. A population in which recruitment equals loss
4. A social system in which the individual can enjoy, rather than feel restricted by, the first three conditions (Goldsmith et al. 1972:23)

The specific means by which this goal may be achieved do indeed represent a sweeping transformation of production, distribution, and society, and are so clearly spelled out that they deserve to be presented in full:

1. A control operation whereby environmental disruption is reduced as much as possible by technical means
2. A freeze operation, in which present trends are halted
3. A systematic substitution, by which the most dangerous components of these trends are replaced by technological substitutes whose effect is less deleterious in the short term and whose use over the long term will be increasingly ineffective
4. Systematic substitution, by which these technological substitutes are replaced by "natural" or self-regulating ones
5. The invention, promotion, and application of alternative technologies that are energy- and materials-conservative
6. Decentralization of polity and economy at all levels, and the formation of communities small enough to be reasonably self-regulating and self-supporting
7. Education for such communities (Goldsmith et al. 1972:23–24)

At the heart of the *Blueprint's* proposals to reduce ecological disruption was the reestablishment of natural as opposed to technological regulation of ecological processes. In agriculture, for example, the *Blueprint* envisioned heavy reliance on biological control of insect pests and on organic fertilizers. Resource management was to be accomplished by a tax system that would punish wasteful use of energy and raw materials and reward long-lived, labor-intensive products. Pressure on the natural environment was to be reduced by the establishment of a stationary population. In Britain, where population already exceeded the carrying capacity of local food production, the plan called for a reduction in population by 50 percent over 150 to 200 years.

Significantly, the key to the entire *Blueprint* transformation was in the social system. The *Blueprint* pointed out that within a small, relatively face-to-face and highly self-sufficient community individuals would be much more likely to organize and accept the cultural restraints that would be needed to maintain long-term stability. Borrowing freely on anthropological views of tribal communities, the authors emphasize that such small-scale societies would also provide abundant personal satisfactions and stimulation that would more than compensate for the reduction in consumption that stability would require. Decentralization, self-sufficiency, and self-regulation would greatly reduce the need for transportation—and many obvious costs of urbanization and massive centralized political systems. What they recommend is not a total abandonment of the nation-state concept, but rather the establishment of a new political system based on neighborhoods of 500 people as minimal units organized into communities of 5,000 and regions of 500,000 with national representation. The selection of 500 as the size of the minimal unit is surely no accident because, as has been indicated earlier, this is the mean size for many tribal societies and may represent the operation of some fundamentally human characteristics. Their plans call for well-integrated, carefully timed implementation stretching over many years.

Anthropologist Sol Tax made a strikingly similar proposal, suggesting that the world be divided into 10,000 relatively self-sufficient, politically autonomous "localities" averaging 500,000 people each (Tax 1977:229). These local territories were to be connected by an egalitarian global communication network that sounds very much like the Internet computer network.

Biologist Paul Ehrlich developed a scenario for an alternative future along similar lines (Ehrlich & Harriman 1971, Ehrlich & Ehrlich 1974). He argued that the most developed nations (overdeveloped in his terms) must undergo dedevelopment and he proposed a new constitution and complete political reorganization for the United States to help achieve such a goal. The presently underdeveloped areas must settle for semidevelopment in his scheme, emphasizing agrarian self-sufficiency, and a total restructuring of the world trade system would be required. The authors of the *Blueprint* gave the following response to critics who consider such proposals to be too drastic, if not totally unreasonable and politically impossible to implement: "If we plan remedial action with our eyes on political rather than ecological reality, then very reasonably, very practicably, and very surely we shall muddle our way to extinction" (Goldsmith et al. 1972:18).

BIOREGIONALISM, SUSTAINABLE COMMERCE, AND ECONOMIC COMMUNITIES

A decentralist alternative needs to evolve, in which people directly make the decisions that affect their lives. Politically independent bioregional communities can offer a setting in which people can carry on their affairs in an open face-to-face manner, offering everyone a full say in decisions that affect their lives. Such communities could form the underlying basis for an ecological society.

(TOKAR 1987:98)

To create an enduring society, we will need a system of commerce and production where each and every act is inherently sustainable and restorative. Business will need to integrate economic, biological, and human systems to create a sustainable method of commerce. As hard as we may try to become sustainable on a company-by-company level, we cannot fully succeed until the institutions surrounding commerce are redesigned.

(HAWKEN 1993:XIV)

Like the authors of the *Blueprint*, anthropologist Billie R. DeWalt (1988) argued that sustainable development requires an approach very different from that advocated by the world's major development agencies. His "precepts for survival" are moral principles for community and regional development goals. He proposes that sustainable development must emphasize the following:

1. Long-term community goals
2. Nature/culture balance
3. Local regions and ecosystems
4. Local resource self-sufficiency
5. Basic human needs
6. Decentralization, local autonomy
7. Local cultural integrity
8. Justice and equity
9. Reduction of resource competition
10. Gradual change, diversity

This development alternative would empower small- and large-scale cultures and would reduce the role of the global market economy and the international political hierarchy. The UNCED Report incorporated many of the above objectives, but did not envision the radical transformation that a full implementation of such an approach would require. However, many nonprofit organizations and activists such as the "Greens" advocate similar perspectives and are attempting to implement them. Greens are not opposed to market-based economics, but they argue that the power of large corporate business enterprises makes it difficult for local communities to effectively manage their own affairs. Vermont "Green" and community organizer Brian Tokar (1987) proposes that democratic community-based economies can be built around such innovative institutions as Community Land Trusts, Community Loan Funds, and food coops. As he explains:

> Mass industry would be replaced by decentralized, ecologically sound production geared toward local needs. The economy would be aimed at enhancing people's quality of life, rather than urging the endless consumption of goods. Unemployment would cease to be a problem, as the necessary work to sustain communities would be justly shared among all who wish to work.
>
> (TOKAR 1987:112)

Greens are not talking about isolated "communes." They envision diverse interconnected community economies operating within bioregions. Bioregional development or ecodevelopment focuses attention on naturally defined regions that often do not correspond to established political boundaries and are usually smaller than states. Bioregions define the limits of sustainability in reference to the "natural capital" of ecosystems and natural resources. Bioregionalism is being shaped by a network of organizations scattered throughout Europe and North America only loosely coordinated by occasional congresses and the publications of the San Francisco-based Planet Drum Foundation.

The "Buffalo Commons" proposed by regional planners Deborah and Frank Popper (1987, Matthews 1992) is a specific application of bioregional development, although not based in Green political economy philosophy. The Popper's argue that the shortgrass prairies of the Great Plains, from Texas to Montana and North Dakota, should never have been developed for large-scale, permanent commercial agriculture, because of the severe climate and lack of water resources in this region. It was the last major area of the country to be settled by farmers, and this only occurred and has been maintained because of continuous government subsidies. The Popper's predict that overgrazing and erosion will force the abandonment of the area within a few decades. They recommend that the government gradually buy back the private land, restore the shortgrass prairie, and turn the entire region into a vast commons for the bison, elk, deer, and antelope. It could then become a nature preserve for ecotourism and hunting much like the East African game parks. The Native Americans whose ancestors originally controlled the region might play a major role in the buffalo commons.

Herman E. Daly and John B. Cobb (1989:135–139) propose that a basis for an "economics for community" can be found in the formal distinction between *chrematistics,* a branch of political economy dealing with short-term profit maximization, and *oikonomia,* the study of household management for the long-term satisfaction of real needs, rather than abstract and fundamentally insatiable exchange values. They suggest that the household focus of oikonomia be expanded ". . . to include the larger community of the land, of shared values, resources, biomes, institutions, language, and history, then we have a good definition of 'economics for community'." Daly and Cobb suggest that sustainable economic communities would be based on the following values:

1. availability of satisfying and useful work for members of the community;
2. security for members of the community in access to biological and social necessities;
3. stability in the community;
4. access to the qualities that make life varied, stimulating, and satisfying; and
5. a thriving, vital community. (Daly & Cobb 1989:135)

Successful businessman Paul Hawken (1993) agrees with Daly and Cobb's critique of free-market economics and also believes that it is possible to incorporate workable market-based incentives within a sustainable "ecology of commerce." Like the Greens, Hawken maintains that small businesses are more sustainable than large corporations and they should be based on local and regional, not global, products. Local production and distribution by small local businesses means that communities can maintain more control over their capital and actually deplete fewer natural resources. Hawken also maintains that commerce should develop without "exotic sources of capital," thereby undermining the global financialization process. He points out that because venture capital is so speculative it creates instability through too rapid growth.

A balance between small-, large-, and global-scale cultural institutions would undoubtedly offer the most satisfying future for all peoples and would have the best chance of being sustainable. Implementing such change will require a reordering of cultural processes. The process of sapienization that originally produced humanity and small-scale culture must be given priority ahead of politicization. Political power must regulate the commercialization and financialization processes. The primary obstacle to such change will not be the concentrated political and economic power of governments and transnational corporations as such, but rather the ability of elites to control the cultural symbols that motivate human beliefs and behavior for their own interests. Political and economic democracy will help limit this power, thus making sustainable development possible. The rapidly evolving decentralized global communications and information networks could help to strengthen the autonomy of small-scale cultures and communities, if these technologies can remain noncommercial.

Bibliography

Alkire, William H. 1978. *Coral Islanders*. Arlington Heights, Ill.: AHM.

Alvarado, Anita L. 1970. "Determinants of Population Stability in the Havasupai Indians." *American Journal of Physical Anthropology* 33(1):9–14.

Alvard, Michael S. 1993. "Testing the 'Ecologically Noble Savage' Hypothesis: Interspecific Prey Choice by Piro Hunters of Amazonian Peru." *Human Ecology* 21(4):355–387.

Anderson, E. N., Jr. 1969. "The Life and Culture of Ecotopia." In *Reinventing Anthropology*, edited by Dell Hymes, 264–283. New York: Pantheon.

Anthropology Resource Center. 1978. *Native Americans and Energy Development*. Cambridge, Mass.: ARC.

Ardrey, Robert. 1966. *The Territorial Imperative*. New York: Atheneum.

Asimov, Isaac. 1971. "The End." Penthouse, January.

Bailey, Robert C., G. Head, M. Jenike, B. Owen, R. Rechtman, and E. Zechenter, 1989. Hunting and Gathering in Tropical Rain Forest: Is It Possible?" *American Anthropologist* 91:59–82.

Barclay, Harold. 1982. *People Without Government*. London: Kahn & Averill & Cienfuegos.

Barlett, Peggy F. 1987. "Industrial Agriculture in Evolutionary Perspective." *Cultural Anthropology* 2:137–154.

Barlett, Peggy F. 1989. "Industrial Agriculture." In *Economic Anthropology*, edited by Stuart Plattner, 253–291. Stanford: Stanford University Press.

Barnet, Richard J. and John Cavanagh. 1994. *Global Dreams: Imperial Corporations and the New World Order*. New York: Simon & Schuster.

Barnett, Harold, and Chandler Morse. 1963. *Scarcity and Growth: The Economics of Natural Resource Availability*. Baltimore: Johns Hopkins University Press.

Barney, Gerald O., ed. 1977–1980. *The Global 2000 Report to the President of the United States*, 3 vols. New York: Pergamon.

Bartlett, H. H. 1956. "Fire, Primitive Agriculture, and Grazing in the Tropics." In *Man's Role in Changing the Face of the Earth*, edited by William L. Thomas, Jr., 692–720. Chicago: University of Chicago Press.

215

Basso, Keith. 1972. "Ice and Travel Among the Fort Norman Slaves: Folk Taxonomies and Cultural Rules." *Language in Society* 1(1972):31–49.

Bayliss-Smith, Tim. 1974. "Constraints on Population Growth: The Case of the Polynesian Outlier Atolls in the Precontact Period." *Human Ecology* 2(4):259–295.

Beckerman, Stephen. 1983. "Does the Swidden Ape the Jungle?" *Human Ecology* 11(1):1–12.

Bell, Diane. 1982. *Aboriginal Women and the Religious Experience.* Young Australian Scholar Lecture Series, no. 3. Bedford Park, South Australia: Australian Association for the Study of Religions, South Australian College of Advanced Education.

Benedict, Ruth. 1959. *Patterns of Culture.* New York: Mentor. (Originally published in 1934.)

Bentley, Gillian R., Tony Goldbert, and Grazyna Jasienska. 1993. "The Fertility of Agricultural and Non-Agricultural Traditional Societies." *Population Studies* 47:269-281.

Bergman, Roland. 1974. *Shipibo Subsistence in the Upper Amazon Rainforest.* Ann Arbor, Michigan: University Microfilms.

Bern, John. 1979. "Ideology and Domination: Toward a Reconstruction of Australian Aboriginal Social Formation." *Oceania* 50(2):118–132.

Berndt, Catherine H. 1981. "Interpretations and 'Facts' in Aboriginal Australia." In *Woman the Gatherer,* edited by Frances Dahlberg, 153–203. New Haven: Yale University Press.

Berreman, Gerald D. 1981. "Social Inequality: A Cross-Cultural Analysis." In *Social Inequality: Comparative and Developmental Approaches,* edited by Gerald D. Berreman, 3–40. New York: Academic.

Bhagwati, Jagdish. 1993. "The Case for Free Trade." *Scientific American* 269(5):42–49.

Birdsell, J. B. 1953. "Some Environmental and Cultural Factors Influencing the Structure of Australian Aboriginal Populations." *American Naturalist* 87, 834:171–207.

—. 1971. "Ecology, Spacing Mechanisms, and Adaptive Behavior in Aboriginal Land Tenure. "In *Land Tenure in the Pacific,* edited by Ron Crocombe, 334–361. Melbourne: Oxford University Press.

—. 1979. "Ecological Influences on Australian Aboriginal Social Organization. "In *Primate Ecology and Human Origins: Ecological Influences on Social Organization,* edited by Irwin S. Bernstein and Euclid O. Smith, 117–151. New York: Garland STPM.

Birkeland, Janis 1993. "Some Pitfalls of 'Manstream' Environmental Theory and Practice." *The Environmentalist* 13(4):263–275.

Bluestone, Barry and Bennett Harrison. 1982. *The Deindustrialization of America.* New York: Basic Books.

Boas, Franz. 1928. *Anthropology and Modern Life.* New York: Norton.

Bodley, John H. 1975. *Victims of Progress.* Menlo Park, Calif.: Cummings.

—. 1981. "Inequality: An Energetics Approach." In *Social Inequality: Comparative and Developmental Approaches,* edited by Gerald D. Berreman, 183–197. New York: Academic.

—. 1988. *Tribal Peoples & Development Issues: A Global Overview.* Mountain View, Calif.: Mayfield Publishing.

—. 1990. *Victims of Progress,* 3rd edition. Mountain View, Calif.: Mayfield Publishing.

Boemma, Addeke H. 1970. "A World Agricultural Plan." *Scientific American* 223(2):54–69.

Bogue, Donald T. 1969. *Principles of Demography.* New York: Wiley.

Bohannan, Paul. 1971. "Beyond Civilization." *Natural History* 80(2):50–67.

Bongaarts, John. 1994. "Can the Growing Human Population Feed Itself?" *Scientific American* 270(3):36–42.

Borgstrom, Georg. 1965. *The Hungry Planet.* New York: Macmillan.

—. 1967. *The Hungry Planet.* New York: Macmillan.

Boserup, Ester. 1965. *The Conditions of Economic Growth*. Chicago: Aldine.

Boulding, Kenneth. 1966. "The Economics of the Coming Spaceship Earth." In *Environmental Quality in a Growing Economy: Essays from the Sixth Resources for the Future Forum*, edited by Henry Jarrett, 3–14. Baltimore: Johns Hopkins University Press.

Bowdler, S. 1977. "The Coastal Colonization of Australia." In J. Allen, J. Golson, and R. Jones (editors), *Sunda and Sahul: Prehistoric Studies in Southeast Asia, Melanesia and Australia*, 205–246. London: Academic Press.

Braun, Denny. 1991. *The Rich Get Richer: The Rise of Income Inequality in the United States and the World*. Chicago: Nelson-Hall.

Brooks, David J. 1993. *U.S. Forests in a Global Context*. USDA Technical Report RM-228. Fort Collins, Colorado: U.S. Department of Agriculture, Forest Service, Rocky Mountain Forest and Range Experiment Station.

Brown, Harrison. 1954. *The Challenge of Man's Future*. New York: Viking.

—. 1956. "Technological Denudation." In *Man's Role in Changing the Face of the Earth*, edited by William L. Thomas, Jr., 1023–1032. Chicago: University of Chicago Press.

Brown, Lester R. 1963. *Man, Land and Food*. U.S. Department of Agriculture FAE Report No. 11. Washington, D.C.: U.S. Government Printing Office.

—. 1994. "Facing Food Insecurity." In *State of the World, 1994*, edited by Lester R. Brown et al., 177–197. New York and London: W. W. Norton and Company.

Brown, Lester R. and Edward Wolf. 1984. "Food Crisis in Africa." *Natural History* 93(6):16–20.

Brown, Paula and H. C. Brookfield. 1963. *Struggle for Land*. Melbournee: Oxford University Press.

Cairncross, Frances. 1993. *Costing the Earth: The Challenge for Governments, the Opportunities for Business*. Boston, Mass: Harvard Business Press.

Campbell, Alastair H. 1965. "Elementary Food Production by the Australian Aborigines." *Mankind* (65):206–211.

Carmack, Robert M. 1988. *Harvest of Violence: The Maya Indians and the Guatemalan Crisis*. Norman, Oklahoma: University of Oklahoma Press.

Carneiro, Robert L. 1960. "Slash-and-Burn Agriculture: A Closer Look at Its Implications for Settlement Patterns." In *Men and Cultures*, edited by A. F. C. Wallace, 229–234. Philadelphia: University of Pennsylvania Press.

—. 1968. "The Transition from Hunting to Horticulture in the Amazon Basin." *Proceedings of the Eighth International Congress of Anthropological and Ethnological Sciences*, 244–248. Tokyo: ICAES.

—. "A Theory of the Origin of the State." *Science* 169(3947):733–738.

—. 1978. "The Knowledge and Use of Rain Forest Trees by the Kuikuru Indians of Central Brazil." *Anthropological Papers* (University of Michigan Museum of Anthropology), (67): 201–216.

—. 1981. "The Chiefdom: Precursor of the State." In *The Transition to Statehood in the New World*, edited by Grant D. Jones and Robert R. Kautz, 37–79. Cambridge: Cambridge University Press.

Carneiro, Robert L. and D. F. Hilse. 1966. "On Determining the Probable Rate of Population Growth During the Neolithic." *American Anthropologist* 68(1):177–181.

Casimir, Michael J., R. P. Winter, and Bernt Glatzer. 1980. "Nomadism and Remote Sensing: Animal Husbandry and the Sagebrush Community in a Nomad Winter Area in Western Afghanistan." *Journal of Arid Environments* 3(1980):231–254.

Caulfield, Mina Davis. 1981. "Equality, Sex, and Mode of Production." In *Social Inequality: Comparative and Developmental Approaches*, edited by Gerald D. Berreman, 201–219. New York: Academic.

Chagnon, Napoleon. 1968. *Yanomamo: The Fierce People*. New York: Holt, Rinehart & Winston.

—. 1988. "Life Histories, Blood Revenge, and Warfare in a Tribal Population." *Science* (26 February) 239:985–992.

Charbonnier, G. 1969. *Conversations with Claude Levi-Strauss*. London: Cape.

Chayanov, A. V. 1966. *The Theory of Peasant Economy*. Homewood, Ill.: Richard D. Irwin, for the American Economic Association.

Chomsky, Noam. 1989. *Necessary Illusions: Thought Control in Democratic Societies*. Boston, Mass.: South End Press.

—. 1991. *Deterring Democracy*. London, New York.: Verso.

—. 1993. *Year 501: The Conquest Continues*. Boston: South End Press.

Chomsky, Noam and Edward S. Herman. 1979. *The Washington Connection and Third World Fascism*. Boston: South End Press.

Clark, Colin. 1968. *Population Growth and Land Use*. London: Macmillan.

Clark, J. G. D. 1952. *Prehistoric Europe: The Economic Base*. New York: Philosophical Library.

Cleave, T. L. 1974. *The Saccharine Disease*. Bristol: Wright.

Coale, Ansley J. 1974. "The History of the Human Population." *Scientific American* 231(3):40–51.

Cobb, Ron. 1970. *Raw Sewage*. Los Angeles: Sawyer Press.

Cohen, Mark Nathan 1977. *The Food Crisis in Prehistory: Overpopulation and the Origins of Agriculture*. New Haven Conn.: Yale University Press.

—. (editor). 1982. "Paleopathology at the Origins of Agriculture." Conference on Paleopathology and Socioeconomic Change at the Origins of Agriculture, State University of New York College at Plattsburgh.

—. 1989. *Health and the Rise of Civilization*. New Haven: Yale University Press.

Cohen, Ronald and Elman R. Service, eds. 1978. *Origins of the State: The Anthropology of Political Evolution*. Philadelphia: ISHI.

Cohen, Yehudi, ed. 1974. *Man in Adaptation*. 2nd ed. Chicago: Aldine.

Cole, H. S. D., ed. 1973. *Models of Doom*. New York: Universe.

Colson, Elizabeth. 1979. "In Good Years and in Bad: Food Strategies of Self-Reliant Societies." *Journal of Anthropological Research* 35(1):18–29.

Commoner, Barry. 1971. *The Closing Circle*. New York: Knopf.

Comp, T. Allan (editor). 1989. *Blueprint for the Environment: A Plan for Federal Action*. Salt Lake City: Howe Brothers.

Conklin, Harold C. 1954. "An Ethnoecological Approach to Shifting Agriculture." *Transactions of the New York Academy of Sciences*, 2nd ser., vol. 17(2):133–142.

Cook, Earl. 1971. "The Flow of Energy in an Industrial Society." *Scientific American* 224(3):134–144.

Cooke, G. W. 1970. "The Carrying Capacity of the Land in the Year 2000." In *The Optimum Population for Britain*, edited by L. R. Taylor, 15–42. London: Academic.

Coon, Carleton S. 1971. *The Hunting Peoples*. Boston: Little, Brown.

Cotton, Steve, ed. 1970. *Earth Day: The Beginning*. New York: Amo, Bantam.

Coughenour, M. B., J. E. Ellis, D. M. Swift, D. L. Coppock, K. Galvin, J. T. McCabe, T. C. Hart. 1985. "Energy Extraction and Use in a Nomadic Pastoral Ecosystem." *Science* 230(4726):619–625.

Cowgill, George L. 1975. "Population Pressure as a Non-Explanation." In *American Antiquity* 40(2):127–131, Part 2, Memoir 30.

Cowlishaw, Gillian. 1978. "Infanticide in Aboriginal Australia." Oceania 48(4): 262–283.

Crystal, Graef S. 1991. *In Search of Excess: The Overcompensation of American Executives.* New York and London: W.W. Norton & Co.

Culbert, T. Patrick. 1974. *The Lost Civilization: The Story of the Classic Maya.* New York: Harper & Row.

Dakeyne, R. B. 1967. "Conflicting Interests on Bougainville." Pacific Viewpoint 8(2):186–187.

Dalton, George. 1961. "Economic Theory and Primitive Society." *American Anthropologist* 63(1):1–25.

—. 1965. "Primitive Money." *American Anthropologist* 67(1):44–65.

—. 1967. *Economic Development and Social Change: The Modernization of Village Communities.* Garden City, N.Y.: Natural History.

Daly, Herman E. 1993. "The Perils of Free Trade." *Scientific American* 269(5):50–57.

Daly, Herman E. and John B. Cobb. 1989. *For the Common Good: Redirecting the Economy toward Community, the Environment, and a Sustainable Future.* Boston: Beacon Press.

Dasmann, Raymond. 1976. "Future Primitive: Ecosystem People Versus Biosphere People." *CoEvolution Quarterly* 1(Fall): 26–31.

Davis, Shelton H. 1988. "Introduction: Sowing the Seeds of Violence." In Robert M. Carmack (editor), *Harvest of Violence: The Maya Indians and the Guatemalan Crisis.* Norman & London: University of Oklahoma Press.

Deevy, Edward S. 1960. "The Human Population." *Scientific American* 203(3):195–204.

Demarest. Arthur A. 1993. "The Violent Saga of a Maya Kingdom." *National Geographic* 183(2):94–111.

Demeny, Paul. 1990. "Population," in Turner, B. L. et al., *The Earth As Transformed by Human Action: Global and Regional Changes in the Biosphere Over the Past 300 Years,* 41–54. Cambridge, England: Cambridge University Press.

Dentan, Robert K. 1968. *The Semai: A Nonviolent People of Malaya.* New York: Holt, Rinehart & Winston.

DeWalt, Billie R. 1988. "The Cultural Ecology of Development: Ten Precepts for Survival." *Agriculture and Human Values* 5(1 & 2):112–123.

Dewhurst, J. Frederic and Associates. 1947. *America's Needs and Resources: A Twentieth Century Fund Survey Which Includes Estimates for 1950 and 1960.* New York: Twentieth Century Fund.

—. 1955. *America's Needs and Resources: A New Survey.* New York: Twentieth Century Fund.

Diamond, Stanley. 1974. *In Search of the Primitive.* New Brunswick, N.J.: Transaction.

—. 1968. "The Search for the Primitive." In *The Concept of the Primitive,* edited by Ashley Montagu, 96–147. New York: Free Press.

Divale, W. I. and Marvin Harris. 1976. "Population, Warfare, and the Male Supremacist Complex." In *American Anthropologist* 78(3):521–538.

Dole, Gertrude. 1978. "The Use of Manioc Among the Kuikuru: Some Implications." *Anthropological Papers* (University of Michigan Museum of Anthropology) (67): 217–247.

Dowling, John H. 1979. "The Goodfellows vs. the Dalton Gang: The Assumptions of Economic Anthropology." *Journal of Anthropological Research* 35(3):292–308.

Dumond, Don E. 1972. "Population Growth and Political Centralization." In *Population Growth: Anthropological Implications*, edited by Brian Spooner, 286–310. Cambridge: MIT Press.

Dumaine, Brian. 1994. "A Knockout Year for CEO Pay." *Fortune* July 25, 94.

Dye, Thomas R. 1983. *Who's Running America?: The Reagan Years*. Englewood Cliffs, N. J.: Prentice-Hall.

Eames, Edwin and Judith G. Goode. 1973. *Urban Poverty in a Cross-Cultural Context*. New York: Free Press.

Edwards, Mike. 1994. "Chernobyl: Living with the Monster." *National Geographic* 183(2):100–115.

Ehrlich, Paul. 1968. *The Population Bomb*. New York: Ballantine.

—. 1969. "Eco-Catastrophe." *Ramparts*, September, 1969, 24–28.

Ehrlich, Paul and Anne Ehrlich. 1972. *Population, Resources, Environment*. San Francisco: W. H. Freeman.

—. 1974. *The End of Affluence*. New York: Ballantine.

—. 1990. *The Population Explosion*. New York: Simon and Schuster.

Ehrlich, Paul and Richard L. Harriman. 1971. *How to Be a Survivor: A Plan to Save Spaceship Earth*. New York: Ballantine.

Ewen, Stuart. 1976. *Captains of Consciousness: Advertising and the Social Roots of the Consumer Culture*. New York: McGraw-Hill.

Fabun, Don. 1970. *Food: An Energy Exchange System*. Beverly Hills, Calif.: Glencoe.

Fairchild, Hoxie Neale. 1928. *The Noble Savage: A Study in Romantic Naturalism*. New York: Columbia University Press.

Falla, Ricardo. 1994. *Massacres in the Jungle: Ixcan, Guatemala, 1975–1982*. Boulder, Colorado: Westview.

FAO, Food and Agriculture Organization of the United Nations. 1987. *The Fifth World Food Survey*. Rome.

FAO, Food and Agriculture Organization of the United Nations. 1992. *The State of Food and Agriculture*. Rome.

FAO, Food and Agriculture Organization of the United Nations. 1993. *The State of Food and Agriculture 1993*. FAO Agriculture Series No. 26. Rome.

Fei, Hsiao-t'ung and Chih-i Chang. 1945. *Earthbound China: A Study of Rural Economy in Yunnan*. Chicago: University of Chicago Press.

Feshbach, Murray and Alfred Friendly, Jr. 1992. *Ecocide in the USSR: Health and Nature under Siege*. New York: Basic Books.

Finkel, A., ed. 1974. *Energy, the Environment, and Human Health*. Acton, Mass.: Publishing Sciences.

Firth, Raymond. 1957. *We the Tikopia*. New York: Barnes and Noble.

Flanagan, William G. 1987. "Fortress Fisher." *Forbes* (December):232–237.

Flannery, Kent V. 1969. "Origins and Ecological Effects of Early Domestication in Iran and the Near East." In *The Domestication and Exploitation of Plants and Animals*, edited by Peter J. Ucko and G. W. Dimbleby, 73–100. London: Duckworth.

Foster, George. 1969. *Applied Anthropology*. Boston: Little, Brown.

Fox, James. 1994. "Security." *Forbes FYI* (September 26):13–14.

Freeman, M. M. R. 1971. "A Social and Ecological Analysis of Systematic Female Infanticide." *American Anthropologist* 73(5):1011–1018.

Freydberg, Nicholas and Willis A. Gortner. 1982. *The Food Additives Book*. Toronto: Bantam.

Fried, Morton. 1967. *The Evolution of Political Society*. New York: Random House.

Friedman, Jonathan. 1974. "Marxism, Structuralism and Vulgar Materialism." *Man* 9(3):444–469.

——. 1979. "Hegelian Ecology: Between Rousseau and the World Spirit." In *Social and Ecological Systems*, edited by P. C. Burnham and R. F. Ellen, 253–270. ASA Monograph No. 18. London: Academic.

Geertz, Clifford. 1963. *Agricultural Involution: The Process of Ecological Change in Indonesia*. Berkeley: University of California Press.

George, Susan. 1977. *How the Other Half Dies: The Real Reasons for World Hunger*. Montclair, N.J.: Allanheld, Osmum & Co.

——. 1992. *The Debt Boomerang: How Third World Debt Harms Us All*. Boulder, Colorado: Westview Press.

Goldberg, Edward D. 1976. *The Health of the Oceans*. Paris: UNESCO.

Goldschmidt, Walter. 1978. *As You Sow: Three Studies in the Social Consequences of Agribusiness*. Montclair, N.J.: Allanheld, Osmum & Co.

Goldsmith, Edward, et al. 1972. *Blueprint for Survival*. Boston: Houghton Mifflin.

Goody, Jack. 1976. *The Domestication of the Savage Mind*. Cambridge: Cambridge University Press.

Gould, Richard A. 1971. "Uses and Effects of Fire Among the Western Desert Aborigines of Australia." *Mankind* 8(1):14–24.

——. 1978. "Comparative Ecology of Food-Sharing in Australia and Northwest California." In *Omnivorous Primates: Gathering and Hunting in Human Evolution*, 422–454. New York: Columbia University Press.

Goulet, Denis. 1971. *The Cruel Choice: A New Concept in the Theory of Development*. New York: Atheneum.

Grainger, A. 1980. "The State of the World's Forests." *The Ecologist* 10(1):6–54.

Great Britain. *Britain 1982: An Official Handbook*. London: Her Majesty's Stationery Office.

Great Britain, Ministry of Agriculture. 1990. *Agricultural Statistics United Kingdom 1988*. London: HMSO.

Greider, William. 1987. *Secrets of the Temple: How the Federal Reserve Runs the Country*. New York: Simon and Schuster.

Gross, Daniel R. and Barbara A. Underwood. "Technological Change and Caloric Costs: Sisal Agriculture 1971." *American Anthropologist* 73(2):725–740.

Gustafson, A. F., C. H. Guise, W. J. Hamilton, Jr., and H. Ries. 1939. *Conservation in the United States*. Ithaca, N.Y.: Comstock.

Gutkind, E. A. 1956. "Our World From the Air: Conflict and Adaptation." *In Man's Role in Changing the Face of the Earth*, edited by William L. Thomas, Jr., 1–44. Chicago: University of Chicago Press.

Haas, Jonathan. 1982. *The Evolution of the Prehistoric State*. New York: Columbia University Press.

Hagood, Mel A. 1972. "Which Irrigation System?" *Proceedings of the 11th Annual Washington Potato Conference and Trade Fair*, 83–86. Washington Potato Conference, Moses Lake, Washington.

Hallam, S. 1975. *Fire and Hearth*. Canberra: Australian Institute of Aboriginal Studies.

Hallpike, C. R. 1973. "Functionalist Interpretations of Primitive Warfare." *Man* 8(3):451–470.

—. 1979. *The Foundations of Primitive Thought*. Oxford: Clarendon.

Hamblin, Robert L. and Brian L. Pitcher. 1980. "The Classic Maya Collapse: Testing Class Conflict Theories." *American Antiquity* 45(2):246–271.

Hamilton, Annette. 1979. "A Comment on Arthur Hippler's Paper 'Culture and Personality Perspective of the Yolngu . . .'" *Mankind* 12(2):164–169.

Hardin, Garrett. 1968. "The Tragedy of the Commons." *Science* 162(3859):1243–1248.

—. 1991. "The Tragedy of the Unmanaged Commons: Population and the Disguises of Providence." In *Commons Without Tragedy*, edited by Robert V. Andelson, 162–185. London: Shepheard-Walwyn.

Harris, David R. 1972. "The Origins of Agriculture in the Tropics." *American Scientist* 60(2):180–193.

Harris, Marvin. 1971. *Culture, Man and Nature*. New York: Crowell.

—. 1975. *Culture, People and Nature*. New York: Crowell.

Harris, Marvin and Eric B. Ross. 1987. *Death, Sex, and Fertility: Population Regulation in Preindustrial and Developing Societies*. New York: Columbia University Press.

Hartmann, Betsy and James Boyce. 1982. *Needless Hunger: Voices from a Bangladesh Village*. San Francisco: Institute for Food and Development Policy.

Hassan, Fekri A. 1981. *Demographic Archaeology*. New York: Academic Press.

Hawken, Paul. 1993. *The Ecology of Commerce. A Declaration of Sustainability*. New York: HarperCollins.

Hayden, Brian. 1975. "The Carrying Capacity Dilemma: An Alternate Approach." *American Antiquity* 40(2):11–19, Memoir 30.

—. 1981a. "Research and Development in the Stone Age: Technological Transitions Among Hunter-Gatherers." *Current Anthropology* 22(5):519–548.

—. 1981b. "Subsistence and Ecological Adaptations of Modern Hunter/Gatherers." In *Omnivorous Primates: Gathering and Hunting in Human Evolution*, edited by Robert S. Harding and Geza Teleki, 344–421. New York: Columbia University Press.

Hazell, Peter B. R. 1994. "Rice in India." National Geographic Research & Exploration 10(2):172–183.

Hecker, Howard M. 1982. "Domestication Revisited: Its Implications for Faunal Analysis." *Journal of Field Archaeology* 9:217–236.

Heilbroner, Robert L. 1963. *The Great Ascent: The Struggle for Economic Development in Our Time*. New York: Harper & Row Torchbooks.

—. 1974. *An Inquiry into the Human Prospect*. New York: Norton.

Hemming, John. 1978. *Red Gold: The Conquest of the Brazilian Indians*. Cambridge: Harvard University Press.

Henry, Jules. 1963. *Culture Against Man*. New York: Random House.

Herskovits, Melville J. 1952. *Economic Anthropology*. New York: Knopf.

Hewlett, Barry. 1991. "Demography and Childcare in Preindustrial Societies." *Journal of Anthropological Research* 47(1):1–37.

Hickerson, Harold. 1965. "The Virginia Deer and Intertribal Buffer Zones in the Upper Mississippi Valley." In *Man, Culture and Animals: The Role of Animals in Human Ecological Adjustments*, edited by Anthony Leeds and Andrew P. Vayda, 43–65. Publication No. 78. Washington, D.C.: American Association for the Advancement of Science.

Hippler, Arthur E. 1974. "The North Alaska Eskimos: A Culture and Personality Perspective." *American Ethnologist* 1(3): 449–469.

—. 1977. "Cultural Evolution: Some Hypotheses Concerning the Significance of Cognitive and Affective Interpenetration During Latency." *Journal of Psychohistory* 4(4):419–460.

—. 1979a. "Comments on Causality Among Cross-Cultural Correlations, by Janet Reis, and Ideological Bias, by Walter Precourt." *Behavior Science Research* 14(4):293–296.

—. 1979b. Review of *Aborigines and Change*, edited by R. M. Berndt. *Journal of Psychological Anthropology* 2(4):507–510.

—. 1979c. Review of *The Mardudjara Aborigines*, by R. Tonkinson. *Journal of Psychological Anthropology* 2(4):493–494.

—. 1981. "The Yolngu and Cultural Relativism: A Response to Reser." *American Anthropologist* 83(2):393–396.

Hobbes, Thomas. 1958. *Leviathan*. New York: Liberal Arts. (Originally published in 1651.)

Homer-Dixon, Thomas F. 1991. "On the Threshold: Environmental Changes as Causes of Acute Conflict." *International Security* 16(2):76–116.

Horton, D. R. 1984. "Red Kangaroos: Last of the Australian Megafauna." In *Quaternary Extinctions: A Prehistoric Revolution*, edited by Paul S. Martin and Richard G. Klein, 639–680. Tucson, Arizona: The University of Arizona Press.

Hubert, M. King. 1969. "Energy Resources." In *Resources and Man*, ed. National Academy of Sciences, 157–242. San Francisco: W. H. Freeman.

Huey, John. 1993. "The World's Best Brand." *Fortune* (May 31):44–54.

Hunn, E. 1982. "Mobility as a Factor Limiting Resource Use in the Columbia Plateau of North America." In *Resource Managers: North American and Australian Hunter-Gatherers*, edited by N. Williams and E. Hunn, 17–43. Boulder, Colorado: Westview Press.

Hunter, Beatrice Trum. 1982. *Food Additives and Federal Policy: The Mirage of Safety*. Brattleboro, UT.: Greene.

IPCC (Intergovernmental Panel on Climate Change). 1991. *Climate Change: The IPCC Response Strategies*. Washington, D.C. and Covelo, Calif.: Island Press.

IWGIA. 1978. *Guatemala 1978: The Massacre at Panzos*. Copenhagen: International Work Group for Indigenous Affairs.

Jacobsen, Thorkild and Robert M. Adams. 1958. "Salt and Silt in Ancient Mesopotamian Agriculture." *Science* 128(3334):1251–1258.

Jannuzi, F. Tomasson and James T. Peach. 1977. *Report on the Hierarchy of Interests in Land in Bangladesh*. Washington, D.C.: Agency for International Development. September.

Johnson, Allen. 1975. "Time Allocation in a Machiguenga Community." *Ethnology* 14(3):301–310.

Johnson, Allen. 1985. "In Search of the Affluent Society." In *Anthropology: Contemporary Perspectives*, edited by David E. K. Hunter and Phillip Whitten, 201–206. Boston: Little, Brown & Co. (reprinted from *Human Nature* 1978 September).

Johnson, Allen and Clifford A. Behrens. 1982. "Nutritional Criteria in Machiguenga Food Production Decisions: A Linear-Programming Analysis." *Human Ecology* 10(2):167–189.

Kaberry, Phyllis M. 1939. *Aboriginal Woman: Sacred and Profane*. London: Routledge.

Kahn, Herman and B. Bruce-Briggs. 1972. *Things to Come: Thinking about the 70's and 80's*. New York: Macmillan.

Kahn, Herman and Anthony J. Wiener. 1967. *The Year 2000: A Framework for Speculation on the Next Thirty-three Years.* New York: Macmillan.

Kaplan, Robert D. 1994. "The Coming Anarchy." *The Atlantic Monthly* (February) 273(2):44–76.

Keenleyside, H. L. 1950. "Critical Mineral Shortages." In *Proceedings of the United Nations Scientific Conference on the Conservation and Utilization of Resources,* 17 August–6 September 1949, 38–46. Lake Success, N.Y.: United Nations.

Kelly, Raymond C. 1968. "Demographic Pressure and Descent Group Structure in the New Guinea Highlands." *Oceania* 38(1):36–63.

Kennedy, Paul M. 1993. *Preparing for the Twenty-First Century.* New York: Random House.

Kermode, G. O. 1972. "Food Additives." *Scientific American* 226(3):15–21.

Kirch, Patrick Vinton and D. E. Yen. 1982. *Tikopia: The Prehistory and Ecology of a Polynesian Outlier.* Bernice P. Bishop Museum Bulletin 238. Honolulu: Bishop Museum Press.

Klein, Richard G. 1979. "Stone Age Exploitation of Animals in Southern Africa. "*American Scientist* 67(2):151–160.

—. 1981. "Stone Age Predation on Small African Bovids." *South African Archaeological Bulletin* 36(1981):55–65.

—. 1984. "Mammalian Extinctions and Stone Age People in Africa." In *Quaternary Extinctions: A Prehistoric Revolution,* edited by Paul S. Martin and Richard G. Klein, 354–403. Tucson, Arizona: The University of Arizona Press.

Knudson, Bob. 1972. "Time Management—It Pays." *Proceedings of the 11th Annual Washington Potato Conference and Trade Fair,* 71–76. Washington Potato Conference, Moses Lake, Washington.

Knudson, Kenneth E. 1970. "Resource Fluctuation, Productivity, and Social Organization on Micronesian Coral Islands." Doctoral dissertation, University of Oregon.

Koch, Klaus-Friedrich. 1970. "Cannibalistic Revenge in Jalé Warfare." *Natural History* 79(2):41–50.

Kohr, Leopold. 1978. *The Breakdown of Nations.* New York: Dutton. (Originally published in 1957.)

Krantz, Grover S. 1976. "On the Nonmigration of Hunting Peoples." *Northwest Anthropological Research Notes* 10(2):209–216.

Kunstadter, Peter. 1971. "Natality, Mortality and Migration in Upland and Lowland Populations in Northwestern Thailand." In *Culture and Population,* edited by Steven Polgar, 46–60. Cambridge, Mass.: Schenkman.

Lancaster, P. A. et al. 1982. "Traditional Cassava-Based Foods: Survey of Processing Techniques." *Economic Botany* 36(1):12–45.

Landsberg, Hans H. 1964. *Natural Resources in America's Future: A Look Ahead to the Year 2000.* Baltimore: Johns Hopkins University Press.

Landsberg, Hans H., Leonard L. Fischman, and Joseph L. Fisher. 1963. *Resources in America's Future: Patterns of Requirements and Availabilities 1960–2000.* Baltimore: Johns Hopkins University Press.

Lappe, Frances Moore and Joseph Collins. 1977. *Food First: Beyond the Myth of Scarcity.* Boston: Houghton Mifflin.

Lathrap, Don W. 1970. *The Upper Amazon.* New York: Praeger.

—. 1977. "Our Father the Cayman, Our Mother the Gourd: Spinden Revisited, or a Unitary Theory for the Emergence of Agriculture in the New World." In *Origins of Agriculture,* edited by Charles A. Reed, 713–751. The Hague: Mouton.

Lee, Richard B. 1968. "What Hunters Do for a Living, or How to Make Out on Scarce Resources." In *Man the Hunter*, edited by Richard B. Lee and Irven De Vore, 30–48. Chicago: Aldine.

—. 1969. "!Kung Bushman Subsistence: An Input-Output Analysis." *Contributions to Anthropology: Ecological Essays*. National Museums of Canada Bulletin 230, 73–94.

Levin, M. G. and L. P. Potapov. 1964. *The Peoples of Siberia*. Chicago: University of Chicago Press.

List, Friedrich. 1922 [1837]. *The National System of Political Economy*. London: Longmans, Green and Co.

Lourandos, Harry. 1985. "Intensification and Australian Prehistory." In T. Douglas Price & James A. Brown (editors), *Prehistoric Hunter-Gatherers: The Emergence of Cultural Complexity*, 385–423. New York: Academic Press.

—. 1987. "Pleistocene Australia: Peopling a Continent." In Olga Soffer (editor), *The Pleistocene Old World: Regional Perspectives*, 147–165. New York: Plenum Press.

Lovering, T. S. 1968. "Non-Fuel Mineral Resources in the Next Century." *Texas Quarterly*. (summer), 127–147.

Luten, Daniel B. 1974. "United States Requirements." In *Energy, the Environment, and Human Health*, edited by A. Finkel, 17–33. Acton, Mass.: Publishing Sciences Group, Inc.

MacCannell, Dean and Jerry White. 1984. The Social Costs of Large-Scale Agriculture: The Prospects of Land Reform in California. In *Land Reform, American Style*, edited by Charles C. Geisler and Frank J. Popper, 35–54. Totawa, N.J.: Rowman & Allanheld.

MacNeish, Richard S. 1971. "Speculation About How and Why Food Production and Village Life Developed in the Tehuacan Valley, Mexico." *Archaeology* 24(4):307–315.

Madden, J. Patrick. 1967. *Economics of Size in Farming: Theory, Analytic Procedures, and a Review of Selected Studies*. Economic Research Service, USDA. Agricultural Economic Report No. 107.

Malinowski, Bronislaw. 1941. "An Anthropological Analysis of War." *American Journal of Sociology* 46(4):521–550.

—. 1944. *Freedom and Civilization*. New York: Roy.

Malthus, Thomas R. 1895. *An Essay on the Principle of Population* (parallel chapters from the [1st] and [2nd] editions). New York: Macmillan. (1st edition originally published 1798, 2nd edition originally published 1807.)

Mamdami, Mahmood. 1973. *The Myth of Population Control: Family, Caste, and Class in an Indian Village*. New York: Monthly Review Press.

Marple, Gary A. and Harry B. Wissmann, eds. 1968. *Grocery Manufacturing in the United States*. New York: Praeger.

Marsh, George P. 1864. *Man and Nature*. New York: Scribner's.

Martin, Paul S. 1967. "Prehistoric Overkill." In *Pleistocene Extinctions: The Search for a Cause*, edited by P. S. Martin and H. E. Wright, Jr., 75–120. Proceedings of the 7th Congress of the International Association for Quaternary Research. New Haven: Yale University Press.

—. 1984. "Prehistoric Overkill: The Global Model." In *Quaternary Extinctions: A Prehistoric Revolution*, edited by Paul S. Martin and Richard G. Klein, 553–573. Tucson, Arizona: University of Arizona Press.

Martin, Thomas L., Jr., and Donald C. Latham. 1963. *Strategy for Survival*. Tucson, Arizona: University of Arizona Press.

Mathews, Anne. 1992. *Where the Buffalo Roam*. New York: Grove Weidenfeld.

Mazur, Allan and Eugene Rosa. 1974. "Energy and Life Style." *Science* 186(4164):607–610.

McCarthy, F. D. and Margaret McCarthy. 1960. "The Food Quest and Time Factor in Aboriginal Economic Life." In C. P. Mountford (editor), *Records of the American-Australian Scientific Expedition to Arnhem Land, Vol. 2, Anthropology and Nutrition*, 145–194. Melbourne: Melbourne University Press.

McCay, Bonnie J. and James M. Acheson, editors. 1987. *The Question of the Commons: The Culture and Ecology of Communal Resources.* Tucson, Arizona: University of Arizona Press.

McDonald, David. 1977. "Food Taboos: A Primitive Environmental Protection Agency (South America)." Anthropos 72:734–748.

Mead, Margaret. 1940. "Warfare Is Only an Invention—Not a Biological Necessity." *Asia* 40:402–405.

Meadows, Donella H., Dennis L. Meadows, and Jorgen Randers. 1992. *Beyond the Limits: Confronting Global Collapse, Envisioning a Sustainable Future.* Post Mills, Vermont: Chelsea Green Publishing Co.

Meadows, Donella H., Dennis L. Meadows, Jorgen Randers, and William W. Behrens III. 1972. *The Limits to Growth.* New York: Universe.

Meggers, Betty J. 1971. *Amazonia: Man and Culture in a Counterfeit Paradise.* Chicago: Aldine.

—. 1995. "Judging the Future by the Past, The Impact of Environmental Instability on Prehistoric Amazonian Populations." In *Indigenous Peoples and the Future of Amazonia: An Ecological Anthropology of an Endangered World*, edited by Leslie E. Sponsel, 15–43. Tucson and London: The University of Arizona Press.

Meggers, Betty J. and Clifford Evans. 1957. *Archaeological Investigations at the Mouth of the Amazon.* Bulletin 167. Washington, D.C.: Bureau of American Ethnology, Smithsonian Institution.

Mellars, Paul. 1976. "Fire Ecology, Animal Populations and Man: A Study of Some Ecological Relationships in Prehistory." *Proceedings of the Prehistoric Society* 42:15–45.

Mining Magazine. 1971. "Bougainville Project Nearing Completion." *Mining Magazine* 124(5): 377–381.

Modjeska, Nicholas. 1982. "Production and Inequality: Perspectives from Central New Guinea." In *Inequality in New Guinea Highlands Societies*, edited by Andrew Strathern, 50–108. Cambridge: Cambridge University Press.

Montagu, Ashley. 1972. "Sociogenic Brain Damage." *American Anthropologist* 74(5):1045–1061.

Moore, Andrew M. T. 1983. "The First Farmers in the Levant." In *The Hilly Flanks and Beyond: Essays on the Prehistory of Southwestern Asia*, 91–111. Studies in Ancient Oriental Civilization No. 36. Chicago: The Oriental Institute of the University of Chicago.

Moran, Emilio. 1993. *Through Amazonian Eyes: The Human Ecology of Amazonian Populations.* Iowa City: University of Iowa Press.

Morgan, Dan. 1979. *Merchants of Grain.* New York: The Viking Press.

Morgan, Lewis Henry. 1877. *Ancient Society.* New York: Holt.

Morris, David M. 1979. *Measuring the Condition of the World's Poor: The Physical Quality of Life Index.* New York: Pergamon.

Mosley, Michael Edward. 1975. *The Maritime Foundations of Andean Civilization.* Menlo Park, Calif.: Cummings.

Murdock, George P. 1963. "Human Influences on Ecosystems of High Islands." In *Man's Place in the Island Ecosystem*, edited by F. R. Fosberg, 145–152. Bishop Museum Press.

Myers, Fred R. 1982. "Always Ask: Resource Use and Land Ownership Among Pintupi Aborigines of the Australian Western Desert." In *Resource Managers: North American and Australian Hunter-Gatherers*, edited by Nancy M. Williams and Eugene S. Hunn, 173–195. AAAS Selected Symposium No. 67. Boulder, Colorado: Westview.

Naisbitt, John. 1994. Global Paradox: The Bigger the World Economy, the More Powerful Its Smallest Players. New York: William Morrow.

Naisbitt, John and Patricia Aburdene. 1990. *Megatrends 2000.* New York: William Morrow.

Naroll, R. 1966. "Does Military Deterrence Deter?" *Trans-Action* 3(2):14–20.

Nash, June. 1989. *From Tank Town to High Tech: The Class of Community and Industrial Cycles.* Albany: State University of New York.

—. 1994. "Global Integration and Subsistence Insecurity." *American Anthropologist* 96(1):7–30.

Nash, Manning. 1966. *Primitive and Peasant Economic Systems.* San Francisco: Chandler.

National Academy of Sciences. 1969. *Resources and Man.* San Francisco: W. H. Freeman.

National Research Council, Committee on Mineral Resources and the Environment. 1975. *Mineral Resources and the Environment.* Washington, D.C.: National Academy of Sciences.

Neel, James V. 1968. "Some Aspects of Differential Fertility in Two American Indian Tribes." *Proceedings of the Eighth International Congress of Anthropological and Ethnological Sciences* 1(1968): 356–361. Tokyo: ICAES.

—. 1970. "Lessons from a Primitive People." *Science* 170(3960):815–821.

Nelson, Richard K. 1969. *Hunters of the Northern Ice.* Chicago: University of Chicago Press.

Netting, Robert McC. 1993. *Smallholders, Householders: Farm Families and the Ecology of Intensive, Sustainable Agriculture.* Stanford, Calif.: Stanford University Press.

Newcomb, W. W., Jr., 1960. "Toward an Understanding of War." In *Essays in the Science of Culture,* edited by Gertrude Dole and Robert L. Cameiro, 317–336. New York: Crowell.

Newman, Katherine S. 1988. *Falling from Grace: The Experience of Downward Mobility in the American Middle Class.* New York: The Free Press.

—. 1993. *Declining Fortunes: The Withering of the American Dream.* New York: Basic Books.

Nicklin, Flip. 1984. "Krill: Untapped Bounty From the Sea?" *National Geographic* 165(5): 626–643.

Nietschmann, Bemard. 1973. *Between Land and Water: The Subsistence Ecology of the Miskito Indians, Eastern Nicaragua.* New York: Seminar Press.

Nordhaus, William D. 1974. "Resources as a Constraint on Growth." *American Economic Review* 64:22–26.

Nougier, Louis-Rene. 1954. Essai sur le peuplement prehistorique de la France. *Population* (Paris) 9:241–273.

Nulty, Leslie. 1972. *The Green Revolution in West Pakistan.* New York: Praeger.

Odum, Howard T. 1971. *Environment, Power, and Society.* New York: Wiley, Inter-Science.

Oliver, Douglas L. 1973. *Bougainville: A Personal History.* Honolulu: University of Hawaii Press.

Olsen, Mary Kay Gilliland. 1993. "Bridge on the Sava: Ethnicity in Eastern Croatia, 1981–1991." *Anthropology of East Europe Review* 11(1–2):54–62.

Otterbein, Keith. 1970. *The Evolution of War: A Cross-Cultural Study.* New Haven: Human Relations Area Files.

Paddock, William and Paul Paddock. 1967. *Famine—1975!* Boston: Little, Brown.

Payne, Roger. 1968. "Among Wild Whales." New York Zoological Society Newsletter, November, 1–6.

Pearce, David W. and Jeremy J. Warford. 1993. *World Without End: Economics, Environment, and Sustainable Development.* New York: Published for the World Bank by Oxford University Press.

Peoples, James G. 1982. "Individual or Group Advantage? A Reinterpretation of the Mating Ritual Cycle." *Current Anthropology* 23(3):291–310.

Peters, C. M., A. H. Gentry, and R. Mendelsohn. 1989. "Valuation of an Amazonian Rain Forest." *Nature* 339 (June 29).

Phillips, Kevin. 1990. *The Politics of Rich and Poor: Wealth and the American Electorate in the Reagan Aftermath.* New York: Random House.

—. 1994. *Arrogant Capital: Washington, Wall Street, and the Frustration of American Politics.* Boston: Little, Brown and Company.

Pimentel, David, et al. 1973. "Food Production and the Energy Crisis." *Science* 182(4110): 443–449.

Platt, John. 1969. "What We Must Do." *Science* 166(3909):1115–1121.

Polgar, Steven. 1972. "Population History and Population Policies from an Anthropological Perspective." *Current Anthropology* (132):203–211.

Political Risk Services. 1994. *Political Risk Yearbook.* Syracuse, New York: Political Risk Services.

Popper, Deborah Eppstein and Frank J. Popper. 1987. "The Great Plains: From Dust to Dust." *Planning* 53(12):12–18.

Porter, Bernard. 1968. *Critics of Empire.* London: Macmillan.

Powell, Douglas S., Joanne L. Faulkner, David R. Darr, Zhiliang Zhu, and Douglas W. MacCleery. 1993. *Forest Resources of the United States, 1992.* Rocky Mountain Forest and Range Experiment Station, General Technical Report RM-234. Fort Collins, Colorado.

Power, Thomas Michael. 1988. *The Economic Pursuit of Quality.* Armonk, N.Y.: Sharp.

Quilter, Jeffrey and Terry Stocker. 1983. "Subsistence Economies and the Origins of Andean Complex Societies." *American Anthropologist* 85(3):545–562.

Radin, Paul. 1971. *The World of Primitive Man.* New York: Dutton.

Rambo, A. Terry. 1985. "Primitive Polluters: Semang Impact on the Malaysian Tropical Rain Forest Ecosystem." Anthropological Papers no. 76. Museum of Anthropology, University of Michigan.

Rappaport, Roy A. 1971. "The Flow of Energy in an Agricultural Society." *Scientific American* 224(3):117–132.

—. 1968. *Pigs for the Ancestors: Ritual in the Ecology of a New Guinea People.* New Haven: Yale University Press.

—. 1979. *Ecology, Meaning, and Religion.* Richmond, Calif.: North Atlantic.

—. 1977. "Maladaptation in Social Systems." In *The Evolution of Social Systems,* edited by J. Friedman and M. J. Rowlands, 49–71. London: Duckworth.

Rathje, William L. and Cullen Murphy. 1992. *Rubbish!: The Archaeology of Garbage.* New York: HarperCollins Publishers.

Redfield, Robert. 1947. "The Folk Society." *American Journal of Sociology* 52(4):293–308.

—. 1953. *The Primitive World and Its Transformations.* Ithaca, N.Y.: Cornell University Press.

Redford, K. 1991. "The Ecologically Noble Savage." *Orion* 9:24–29.

Reichel-Dolmatoff, Gerardo. 1971. *Amazonian Cosmos: The Sexual and Religious Symbolism of the Tukano Indians.* Chicago: University of Chicago Press.

Reid, W. V. 1992. "How Many Species Will There Be?" In *Tropical Deforestation and Species Extinction,* edited by T. C. Whitmore and J. A. Sayer, 55–73. London: Chapman & Hall.

Reisner, Marc. 1986. *Cadillac Desert: The American West and Its Disappearing Water.* New York: Viking Penguin.

Reser, Joseph. 1981. "Australian Aboriginal Man's Inhumanity to Man: A Case of Cultural Distortion." *American Anthropologist* 83(2):387–393.

Reynolds, Vernon. 1972. "Ethology of Urban Life." In *Man, Settlement, and Urbanism,* edited by Peter J. Ucko, R. A. Tringham, and G. W. Dimbleby, 401–408. London: Duckworth.

Ribeiro, Darcy. 1968. *The Civilizational Process,* translated by Betty J. Meggers. Washington, D.C.: Smithsonian Institution Press.

Richards, Paul W. 1973. "The Tropical Rain Forest." *Scientific American* 229(6):58-67.

Riches, David. 1974. "The Netsilik Eskimo: A Special Case of Selective Female Infanticide." *Ethnology* 13(4):351–361.

Robey, Bryant, Shea O. Rutstein, and Leo Morris. 1993. "The Fertility Decline in Developing Countries." *Scientific American* 269(6):60–67.

Rojas, Jose Dualok. 1994. "UNCED: Ethics & Development from the Indigenous Point of View." United Nations Environment Programme (UNEP).

Ryan, Peter, ed. 1972. "Bougainville Copper Project." In *Encyclopedia of Papua New Guinea* 1:92–102. Melbourne: Melbourne University Press.

Sahlins, Marshall. 1960. "Evolution: Specific and General." In *Evolution and Culture,* edited by Marshall Sahlins and Elman R. Service, 12–44. Ann Arbor: University of Michigan Press.

—. 1961. "The Segmentary Lineage: An Organization of Predatory Expansion." *American Anthropologist* 63(2), pt. 1, 322–345.

—. 1968. "Notes on the Original Affluent Society." In *Man the Hunter,* edited by Richard B. Lee and Irven DeVore, 85–89. Chicago: Aldine.

—. 1972. *Stone Age Economics.* Chicago: Aldine.

Sahlins, Marshall and Elman R. Service, eds. 1960. *Evolution and Culture.* Ann Arbor: University of Michigan Press.

Samuels, Michael. 1982. "Popreg 1: A Simulation of Population Regulation Among the Maring of New Guinea." *Human Ecology* 10(2):78–84.

Sapir, Edward. 1964. "Culture, Genuine and Spurious." In *Culture, Language and Personality,* edited by David G. Mandelbaum, 78–119. Berkeley and Los Angeles: University of California Press. (Originally published 1924.)

Saucier, Jean-Francois. 1972. "Correlates of the Long Postpartum Taboo: A Cross-Cultural Study." *Current Anthropology* 13(2)38–49.

Schele, Linda and David Freidl. 1990. *A Forest of Kings: The Untold Story of the Ancient Maya.* New York: William Morrow & Co.

Scheper-Hughes, Nancy. 1992. *Death Without Weeping: The Violence of Everyday Life in Brazil.* Berkeley: University of California Press.

Schneider, David. 1955. "Abortion and Depopulation on a Pacific Island: Yap." In *Health, Culture, and Community,* edited by B. D. Paul, 211–235. New York: Russell Sage Foundation.

Schrire, C. and W. L. Steiger. 1974. "A Matter of Life and Death: An Investigation into the Practice of Female Infanticide in the Arctic." *Man* 9(2):161–184.

Schumacher, E. F. 1973. *Small Is Beautiful: Economics As If People Mattered.* New York: Harper & Row.

Scott, James C. 1976. *The Moral Economy of the Peasant: Subsistence and Rebellion in Southeast Asia.* New Haven: Yale University Press.

Scott, James C. 1985. *Weapons of the Weak*. New Haven: Yale University Press.

Sen, Amartya. 1981. *Poverty and Famines: An Essay on Entitlement and Deprivation*. Oxford: Clarendon Press.

Sengel, Randal A. 1973. "Comments." *Current Anthropology* 14(5):540–542.

Service, Elman R. 1962. *Primitive Social Organization*. New York: Random House.

Sewell, Tom. 1992. *The World Grain Trade*. New York: Woodhead-Faulkner.

Shaler, Nathaniel S. 1905. *Man and the Earth*. New York: Duffield.

Shantzis, Steven B. and William W. Behrens III. 1973. "Population Control Mechanisms in a Primitive Agricultural Society." In *Toward Global Equilibrium*, edited by D. H. Meadows and D. L. Meadows, 257–288. Cambridge, Mass.: Wright-Allen.

Shweder, Richard A. 1982. "On Savages and Other Children." *American Anthropologist* 84(2): 354–366.

Simon, Julian. 1981. *The Ultimate Resource*. Princeton, New Jersey: Princeton University Press.

Sklair, Leslie. 1991. *Sociology of the Global System*. Baltimore: The Johns Hopkins University Press.

Smith, Adam. [1759] 1976. *The Theory of Moral Sentiments*. Indianapolis, Indiana: Liberty Classics.

Smith, E. A. and S. A. Smith. 1994. "Inuit Sex-Ratio Variation: Population Control, Ethnographic Error, or Parental Manipulation?" *Current Anthropology* 35:595–614.

Smith, Philip E. 1972. *The Consequences of Food Production*. Module in Anthropology no. 21. Reading, Mass.: Addison-Wesley.

Sofer, Cyril. 1965. "Buying and Selling: A Study in the Sociology of Distribution." *Sociological Review* (July):183–209.

Solow, Robert M. 1974. "The Economics of Resources or the Resources of Economics." *American Economic Review* 64(2):1–14.

Spaulding, Willard M., Jr., and Ronald D. Ogden. 1968. *Effects of Surface Mining on the Fish and Wildlife Resources of the United States*. Bureau of Sport Fisheries and Wildlife Resources Publication 68. Washington, D.C.: U.S. Government Printing Office.

Spoehr, Alexander. 1956. "Cultural Differences in the Interpretation of Natural Resources." In *Man's Role in Changing the Face of the Earth*, edited by William L. Thomas, Jr., 93–102. Chicago: University of Chicago Press.

Spooner, Brian. 1973. *The Cultural Ecology of Pastoral Nomads*. Module in Anthropology no. 45. Reading, Mass.: Addison-Wesley.

Steinhart, John S. and Carole E. Steinhart. 1974. "Energy Use in the U.S. Food System." *Science* 184(4134):307–316.

Stover, Leon N. and Takeko Kawai Stover. 1976. *China: An Anthropological Perspective*. Pacific Palisades, California: Goodyear Publishing Co.

Sussman, Robert W. 1972. "Child Transport, Family Size, and Increase in Human Population During the Neolithic." *Current Anthropology* 13(2):258–259.

Suttles, Wayne. 1960. "Affinal Ties, Subsistence, and Prestige Among the Coast Salish." *American Anthropologist* 62:296–305.

Sweet, Louise. 1965. "Camel Pastoralism in North Arabia and the Minimal Camping Unit." In *Man, Culture and Animals: The Role of Animals in Human Ecological Adjustments*, edited by Anthony Leeds and Andrew Vayda, 129–152. Publication No. 78. Washington, D.C.: American Association for the Advancement of Science.

Talburt, William F. and Ora Smith. 1967. *Potato Processing*. Westport, Conn.: Avi.

Tax, Sol. 1977. "Anthropology for the World of the Future: Thirteen Professions and Three Proposals." *Current Anthropology* 36(3):225–234.

Taylor, Gordon Rattray. 1972. *Rethink: A Paraprimitive Solution*. London: Secker & Warburg.

Toffler, Alvin. 1971. *Future Shock*. New York: Bantam.

Tokar, Brian. 1987. *The Green Alternative: Creating an Ecological Future*. San Pedro, Calif: R. & E. Miles.

Toth, James. 1992. "Doubts About Growth: The Town of Carlisle in Transition." *Urban Anthropology* 21(1):2–44.

Trowell, Hugh C. 1954. "Kwashiorkor." *Scientific American* 191(6):46–50.

Turnbull, Colin. 1968. "The Importance of Flux in Two Hunting Societies." In *Man the Hunter*, edited by Richard B. Lee and Irven DeVore, 132–137. Chicago: Aldine.

Underwood, Jane H. 1973. "The Demography of a Myth: Abortion in Yap." *Human Biology in Oceania* 2(2):115–127.

UNESCO. 1968. *Tropical Forest Ecosystems: A State-of-Knowledge Report*. Natural Resources Research XIV. Paris.

United Kingdom, Department of the Environment. 1990. *This Common Inheritance: Britain's Environmental Strategy*. (September). House of Commons Cm. 1200.

United Nations, Department of Economic Affairs. 1950. *Proceedings of the United Nations Scientific Conference on the Conservation and Utilization of Resources, 17 August–6 September 1949*. Lake Success, N.Y.

United Nations, Food and Agriculture Organization. 1963. *Third World Food Survey*. Freedom from Hunger Basic Study No. 11. Rome.

United Nations, Trusteeship Council. 1968. "Report of the United Nations Visiting Mission to the Trust Territory of New Guinea, 1968." *Trusteeship Council Official Records: Thirty-fifth Session* (27 May–19 June 1968). Supplement No. 2. New York.

—. 1971. "Report of the United Nations Visiting Mission to the Trust Territory of New Guinea, 1971." *Trusteeship Council Official Records: Thirty-eighth Session* (25 May–18 June 1971). Supplement No. 2. New York.

U.S. Bureau of the Census. 1983. *Statistical Abstract of the United States: 1984*, 104th ed. Washington, D.C.: U.S. Government Printing Office.

U.S. Department of Commerce, Bureau of the Census. *1982 Census of Agriculture*, Volume 1, *Geographic Area Series*, Part 5. California.

U.S. Department of Commerce. 1969a. *Census of Agriculture*. Vol. 1, *Area Reports*, pt. 46, [state of] Washington. Washington, D.C.: U.S. Government Printing Office.

—. 1969b. *Census of Agriculture*. Vol. 5, pt. 4, "Sugar Crops, Potatoes, Other Specified Crops." Washington, D.C.: U.S. Government Printing Office.

U.S. Department of the Interior, Bureau of Land Management. 1974. *Draft Environmental Impact Statement: Proposed Federal Coal Leasing Program*. 2 vols. Washington, D.C.: U.S. Government Printing Office.

U. S. Environmental Protection Agency. 1973. *Legal Compilation: Statutes and Legislative History, Executive Orders, Regulations, Guidelines, and Reports (General)*, vol. 1. Washington, D.C.: U.S. Government Printing Office.

U.S. National Advisory Commission on Civil Disorders. 1968. [Kerner Report.] Washington, D.C.: U.S. Government Printing Office.

U.S. National Commission on the Causes and Prevention of Violence 1969. *Justice: To Establish Justice, to Ensure Domestic Tranquility*. Final Report. Washington, D.C.: U.S. Government Printing Office.

U.S. President's Materials Policy Commission. 1952. *Resources for Freedom* [Paley Commission Report]. Washington, D.C.: U.S. Government Printing Office.

U.S. President's Science Advisory Committee. 1967. *The World Food Problem: A Report of the Panel on the World Food Supply*. 3 vols. Washington, D.C.: U.S. Government Printing Office.

Vanek, Joann. 1974. "Time Spent in Housework." *Scientific American* 23(15):116–120.

Vayda, Andrew P. 1968. "Primitive Warfare." In *International Encyclopedia of the Social Sciences* 16:473–498. New York: Macmillan, Free Press.

Wagley, Charles. 1951. "Cultural Influences on Population." Revista do Museu Paulista 5:95–104.

Walker, B. H., et al. 1981. "Stability of Semi-Arid Savanna Grazing Systems." *Journal of Ecology* 69:473–498.

Wallerstein, Immanuel. 1990. "Culture as the Ideological Battleground of the Modern World-System." *Theory, Culture & Society* 7:31–55.

Walter, Edward. 1981. *The Immorality of Limiting Growth*. Albany: State University of New York Press.

Washington Potato Commission. 1962. *Proceedings of the Annual Washington Potato Conference and Trade Fair*. Moses Lake, Washington: Washington Potato Commission.

WCED (World Commission on Environment and Development). 1987. *Our Common Future*. Oxford: Oxford University Press.

Webster, David. 1981. "Late Pleistocene Extinction and Human Predation: A Critical Overview." In *Omnivorous Primates: Gathering and Hunting in Human Evolution*, edited by Robert S. Harding and Geza Teleki, 556–595. New York: Columbia University Press.

Weiss, K. M. 1973. "Demographic Models for Anthropology." *American Antiquity* 38(2), Part 2, Memoir 27.

Western, David and Virginia Finch. 1986. Cattle and Pastoralism: Survival and Production in Arid Lands. *Human Ecology* 14(1):77–94.

White, Leslie A. 1949. *The Science of Culture*. New York: Grove.

—. 1959. *The Evolution of Culture*. New York: McGraw-Hill.

White, Lynn, Jr. 1967. "The Historical Roots of Our Ecological Crisis." *Science* 155(3767):1203–1207.

Whiting, John M. 1969. "Effects of Climate on Certain Cultural Practices." In *Environment and Cultural Behavior: Ecological Studies in Cultural Anthropology*, edited by A. P. Vayda, 416–455. New York: Natural History Press.

Willey, Gordon R. and Demitric B. Shimkin. 1971. "The Collapse of Classic Maya Civilization in the Southern Lowlands: A Symposium Summary Statement." *Southwestern Journal of Anthropology* 27(10):1–18.

Winterhalder, B. and F. A. Smith, eds. 1981. *Hunter-Gatherer Foraging Strategies: Ethnographic and Archaeological Analyses*. Chicago: University of Chicago Press.

Wolf, Eric R. 1957. "Closed Corporate Peasant Communities in Mesoamerica and Central Java." *Southwest Journal of Anthropology* 13(1):1–18.

—. 1982. *Europe and the People Without History*. Berkeley: University of California Press.

Woodburn, James. 1968a. "An Introduction to Hadza Ecology." In *Man the Hunter*, edited by Richard B. Lee and Irven DeVore, 49–55. Chicago: Aldine.

—. 1968b. "Stability and Flexibility in Hadza Residential Groupings." In *Man the Hunter*, edited by Richard B. Lee and Irven DeVore, 103–110. Chicago: Aldine.

World Bank. 1983. *World Development Report 1983*. New York: Oxford University Press.

World Bank. 1994. *World Development Report 1994: Infrastructure for Development.* New York: Oxford University Press.

Wright, Quincy. 1942. *A Study of War.* 2 vols. Chicago: University of Chicago Press.

Yde, Jens. 1965. "Material Culture of the Waiwai. Nationalmuseets Skrifter." *Etnografisk Roekke* 10. Copenhagen: National Museum.

Yengoyan, Aram A. 1981. "Infanticide and Birth Order: An Empiricial Analysis of Preferential Female Infanticide Among Australian Aboriginal Populations." In *The Perception of Evolution: Essays Honoring Joseph B. Birdsell,* edited by Larry L. Mai, Eugenia Shanklin, and R. W. Sussman, *Anthropology UCLA* 7:255–273.

Young, Vernon R. and Nevin S. Scrimshaw. 1971. "The Physiology of Starvation." *Scientific American* 225(4):14–21.

Zubrow, Ezra B. 1975. *Prehistoric Carrying Capacity.* Menlo Park, Calif.: Cummings.

Index

Abortion
  Australia, 151
  state intervention, 162
  village farmers, 156
Aburdene, P., 7
Acheson, J., 44
Adams, R., 32
Advertising, food, 130–131,
  132
Affluent society, 17
Afghanistan, 45
Africa, 45
  food production, 109
Agenda 21, 40, 206–208
Agribusiness
  California, 123–125
  green revolution, 139
Agricultural development,
  137–139
Agricultural systems, 49
Agriculture, 60
  Soviet, 29
  sustainable, 210–211
Alkire, W., 136
Alvarado, A., 159
Alvard, M., 57
Amazon
  Amazon River, 31
  Colombian, 56

rain forest, 48, 50, 57
  Peruvian, 57
Amazonia, 56
  Indians, 16
  manioc, 131–133
  Amazonian peoples, 57
  societies, 15
America
  crime rates, 168
  energy efficiency, 114–115
  Guatemala policy, 191–192
  incarceration rate, 170
  protein consumption, 126
  violence and insecurity,
    167–170
American Association for the
  Advancement of
  Science, 7
  Guatemala, 193
American Dream, 197
American, food marketing,
  128–130
Anarchy, 183
Anthropology
  definition of, 8–9
  cross-cultural approach, 9
Anthropology Resource
  Center, 79
Appropriate technology, 209
Aral Sea, 29–30

Architectural Digest, 196
Arctic, foragers, 146
Armaments companies, 195
Arms Trade News, 195
Asimov, I., 25, 143
Australia, meat exports, 135
Australia Northern Territory,
  51
Australian aboriginal culture,
  equality, 18, 65, 173
Australian Aborigines, 55
  clan territories, 136
  infanticide, 148, 150–151
  population equilibrium,
    149–151
  subsistence, 90, 91
  women, 68
Austronesian expansion, 154

Bailey, R., 95
Band organization, 148, 149
Bangladesh
  childhood malnutrition,
    107–108
  hunger, 110–112
Bantu expansion, 154
Barclay, H., 171
Barlett, P., 120
Barnet, R., 195

Barnett, H., 74
Barney, G., 35, 62, 85
Bartlett, H., 56
Basso, K., 50
Bayless-Smith, T., 145, 160
Beckerman, S., 94
Beedham, B., 182–183
Behrens, C., 89
Behrens, W., 156–159
Belgium, food self-
    sufficiency, 136–137
Bell, D., 173
Benedict, R., 14
Bentley, G., 162
Bern, J., 173
Berndt, C., 18
Bhagwati, J., 204
BIFAD (Board for
    International Food
    and Agricultural
    Development), 137
Big-man system, 100
Biodiversity, 26
Biodiversity Treaty, 207–208
Biological engineering, 113
Biomass, 25
Bioregionalism, 212–214
Biosphere, 48
Birdsell, J., 97, 136, 148,
    149–151
Birth spacing, 148–149
    village farmers, 156
Blueprint for Survival,
    209–211
Blueprint for the
    Environment, 203
Bluestone, B., 196
Board for International Food
    and Agricultural
    Development
    (BIFAD), 137
Boas, F., 1, 8
Bodley, J., 1, 65, 79, 112, 163
Bogue, D., 147–148
Bohannan, P., 199
Bongaarts, J., 140, 143

Borgstrom, 103, 104,
    134–137
Borlaug, N., 138
Borneo, shifting cultivators,
    155
Boserup, E., 89, 100, 152
Bougainville Island, New
    Guinea, 80
Boulding, K., 66
Bowdler, S., 151
Boyce, J., 110–111
Braun, D., 198
Brazil
    debt, 186
    meat exports, 135
    sisal and malnutrition,
        135–136
    Nambikuara, 174–175
    wages, 194
Breakdown of nations, 208
Bretton Woods Conference,
    185
Britain
    population growth, 85–88
    population reduction, 211
Brookfield, H., 97
Brooks, 72
Brown, H., 33, 71
Brown, L., 85, 106, 109
Brown, P., 97
Brundtland Commission, 39,
    75, 202
Budiansky, S., 27
Buffalo Commons, 213
Bushman, 17, 55, 95
    Bantu expansion, 154
    energy efficiency, 114–115
    leadership, 175
    violence, 171, 172
    workload, 97

Cairncross, F., 202
California, agribusiness,
    123–125
Caloric requirements, 105
Campbell Soup Co., 129
Campbell, A., 90

Canada, 49
Carlisle, Pennsylvania, 196
Carmack, R., 193
Carneiro, R., 50, 55, 96,
    153, 175
Carrying capacity, 144–145
    Australia, 150
    foragers, 97
    shifting cultivators, 97
Carter Commission, 39
Carter, President J., 35
Casimir, M., 45
Cattle, feedlots, 128
Caulfield, M., 52
Cavanagh, J., 185, 195
Cereal production, world,
    109
Ceremonial systems,
    Australia, 150
CGIAR (Consultative Group
    on International
    Agricultural
    Research), 137
Chagnon, N., 171, 174
Chang, C., 112
Charbonnier, G., 15
Chayanov, A., 98–99
Chernobyl, 29
Chiefdoms, 31
    defined, 175
    northwest coast, 136
    Pacific Island, 57–58
Child labor, 6
Chimbu, 97
China, 69
    childhood malnutrition
        107–108
    Ch'ing dynasty, 101–102,
    energy efficiency, 114–115
    famine, 103
    food self-sufficiency,
        136–137
    land ownership, 112
Chomsky, N., 191, 192
Chrematistics, 213
Christian, influence, 56
    missionaries, 57

Christianity, 42–43
Citibank, 196
Clark, C., 142
Clark, G., 31
Cleave, T., 200
Climate change, 47
Coal, leasing program, 77
Coale, A., 146, 152
Cobb, J., 75, 76, 203–206, 213–214
Coca-Cola, 130–131
Cohen, M., 152
Cohen, Y., 24, 24
Cold War, 5, 39, 201
Cole, H., 34
Collins, J., 110
Collins, Joseph, 83
Colombia, 56
Colson, E., 91
Comfort level, deprivation, 176
Commerce, sustainable, 212–214
Commercialization 3–4, 19, 21, 184
    political power, 214
    scale increases, 201
Commoner, B., 9, 42
Communities, economic, 212–214
Community Land Trusts, 213
Community Loan Funds, 213
Comp, T., 203
Conference on Overcoming Global Hunger, World Bank, 109
Conflict resolution, small-scale societies, 174
Conklin, H., 50
Consultative Group on International Agricultural Research (CGIAR), 137
Consumer culture, 67

Consumerism, 67
Consumption culture, 82
Contraception
    Australia, 151
    village farmers, 156
Contraceptive technology, 164
Cook, E. 61, 63, 69
Cooke, G. 87, 88
Coon, C., 14, 16
Copper mining, 79–82
Core, world system, 184
Coughenour, M., 45
Counterinsurgency, Guatemala, 190
Cowgill, G., 144–145
Cowlishaw, G., 148–149
Crime, American rates, 168
Crisis, environmental, 31, 32, 40, 42
Crystal, G., 194
Cuba, 67
    infant mortality, 190
Culbert, T., 32
Cultural change, 31
    ecology, 49
    evolution, 1, 24
    hegemony, 176
Cultural-materialist perspective, 43
Culture scale, 10–12, 23
Culture
    definition, 2
    evolution, 1, 60
    global-scale, 19–21, 33–34, 42, 59, 65
    global commercial, 40–41
    high- and low-energy, 61
    small-scale, 40, 44, 59
    tribal, 43
Culture of consumption, 65, 68, 69, 73–74

Dakeyne, R., 81
Dalton, G., 52, 53, 55
Daly, H., 75, 76, 203–206, 213–214

Dasmann, R., 48
Davis, S., 192
DDT, 7, 29
Deevy, E., 146, 152
Deforestation, 57
    debt, 186–187
    tropical, 27–28, 72
Deindustrialization, 194–198
Demarest, A., 32
Demeny, P., 146
Democracy, economic, 198
Demographic transition, 143–144, 164
Dentan, R., 171
Deprivation, material, 176
Desana, 56–57
Desert Tradition, Southwest, 154
Despicable savage, 18
Development, sustainable, 75, 76
Development decades, UN, 108, 137–138
DeVore, I., 17, 47
DeWalt, B., 212
Dewhurst, J., 70–72
Diamond, S., 11
Dioxin, 29
Distribution system, energy costs, 125–131
Divale, W., 148
Dole, G., 132–133
Domestic mode of production, 95–99
Domestication, 90–93
    population growth, 152
Dowling, J., 52
Dumaine, B., 195
Dummond, D., 145
Dye, T., 21

Eames, E., 170
Earth Day, 7
Earth Summit, UN, 206–208
Ecocide, 28

Economic development, 33

Economics for community, 213

Economists
classical, 74
consumption, 66
"cowboy," 66
scale, 52
tribal, 53, 55

Ecosystem, 48
manipulation, 93

Edwards, M., 30

Egalitarian societies, social order, 170–175

Ehrlich, P., 141–143, 147, 211

Eisenhower, M., 167

Elites, economic, 195

Energy costs, distribution system, 125–131

Energy crisis, 79

Energy efficiency, 114–115

Energy flow analysis, 115–120

Energy use, United States, 126–128

Energy utilization, 60–62

England, food self-sufficiency, 136–137

Entitlement, food, 111–112

Environmental crisis, 31

Environmental deterioration conflict, 183–184
factory farming, 116–117

Environmental Impact Statement, coal-leasing program, 77

Equality, 172–174

Equilibrium mechanisms, 98

Eskimo, 18, 49
song duels, 174

Ethnic conflict, 183

Evolution
cultural, 1
general, 24
specific, 24

Ewen, S., 67

Executive compensation, 194

Exploitation, definition, 176

Externality, economic, 202

Fabun, D., 138–139

Factory food production, 114–120

Fairchild, H., 16

Falla, R., 190–193

Family farm, disappearance, 123

Famine, modern world, 103–104

FAO (UN Food and Agricultural Organization)
agricultural development, 137
fisheries statistics, 135
food surveys, 105–109

Farmers, peasant, 45

Farming
reliability, 90
subsistence, 32
systems, 44
village, 32

Fei, H., 112

Feshbach, M., 29

Finance capital, 205
GATT, 135

Financialization
debt crisis, 184–187
deindustrialization, 196
political power, 214
scale increases, 201

Finch, V., 45

Firth, R., 161

Fisher Island, Florida, 196–197

Fishing, 134–137

Flanagan, W., 197

Flannery, K., 92, 101, 153

Food additives, 134

Food collecting, 94

Food consumption patterns, American, 131

Food coops, 213

Food packaging, 128

Food production, 94
limits, 137–140
social costs, 123–125
technological advances, 99–101

Food processing, 131–134

Food shortage, 90–91

Food surveys, FAO, 105–109

Food systems
evolution of, 88–95
definition of, 83
state-level, 101–103

Foragers
arctic, 146
demography, 152
energy efficiency, 114–115
infant mortality, 147
migration, 148
population control, 146–149

Foraging, 1
reliability, 90

Ford Foundation, agricultural research, 137

Forests, depletion of Western, 72

Formalist approach, 52, 54

Forrester, J., 34

Fortune 500, 21

Fortune, 21

Fossil fuel, 77
in food system, 116–119

Foster, G., 53

Fox, J., 197

France, Neolithic population growth, 152

Free market, global, 202–205

Freedom from hunger campaign, United Nations, 103–104

Freeman, M., 148–149

Freidel, D., 32

Freydberg, N., 134

Fried, M., 172, 175–176

Friedman, J., 46, 158

Friendly, A., Jr., 29

Gambia, energy efficiency, 114–115

GATT (General Agreement on Tariffs and Trade), 135, 204

Geertz, C., 49, 162

General Agreement on Tariffs and Trade (GATT), 135, 204

General Electric, 195, 198

General Motors, 21, 195

Genetic engineering, 138

Genieri, energy efficiency, 114–115

Genocide, Guatemala, 190–193

Gentry, A., 202

George, S., 110, 112, 128, 181, 184–187

Ghost acres, 134–137

Glatzer, B., 45

Global 2000 Report, 38, 62

Global biomass, 25

Global crisis, definition of, 2–4

Global culture, 49, 50

Global disequilibrium, 33

Global free market, 202–205

Global-scale culture, instability of, 34

Global system, 35, 66

Global trade, food, 134–137

Goldberg, G., 162

Goldschmidt, W., 123–124

Goldsmith, E., 209–211

Goode, J., 18, 170

Goody, J., 18

Gortner, W., 134

Gould, R., 51, 89, 144

Goulet, D., 55

Grain trade, developing countries, 107

Gramcsci, A., 20, 176

Great Britain, Ministry of Agriculture, 88

Green revolution, 138–139

Green taxes, 203

Greens, political party, 212–213

Greider, W., 185

Gross, D., 108, 135–136

Guatemala, state terrorism, 190–193

Gustafson, A., 7

Gutkind, E., 55

Guyana, Waiwai, 132

Hagood, M., 122

Hallam, S., 51

Hallpike, C., 18

Hamilton, A., 18

Hanunoo, Mindoro Island, 50

Hardin, G., 43, 44

Harriman, R., 211

Harris, D., 93, 102

Harris, M., 46, 91, 114–115, 118, 144, 148, 176–177

Harrison, B., 196

Hartman, B., 110–111

Hassan, F., 144–147, 152

Havasupai, population equilibrium, 159

Hawkens, P., 214

Hayden, B., 47, 89, 96, 144, 152

Hazell, P., 139

Health, 30
    Soviet, 29

Hecker, H., 90

Heilbroner, R., 5, 34, 201–202

Hemming, J., 15

Henry, J., 53

Herding society, 44-45

Herman, E., 191

Herskovits, M., 52, 54, 55

Hewlett, B., 152

Hicks, J., 76

Hicksonian Income (HI), 76, 96

Hilse, D., 153

Hippler, A., 18

Hobbes, T., 17, 171

Hoe farmers, energy efficiency, 114–115

Homer-Dixon, T., 183–184

Horton, D., 47, 151

Hubert, K., 64

Huey, J., 131

Hunger
    Bangladesh, 110–112
    measuring, 105–110
    population, 84–85

Hunn, E., 57

Hunter, B., 134

Hunters, tribal, 26

Iban, raiding, 155

Ideological systems, 55

IFAD (International Fund for Agricultural Development), UN, 108

IMF (International Monetary Fund), structural adjustments, 186, 187

India
    childhood malnutrition, 107–108
    food self-sufficiency, 136–137
    malnutrition, 108
    population and labor, 162

Indigenous peoples
    Australia, 51
    Canada, 51
    UNCED, 207

Indo-European expansion, 154

Industrial civilization, 34

Industrial Revolution, 5–6, 33, 64

Industrial society, 6

Inequality, 41
    hunger, 86

income, 194
wealth, 169
Infant mortality, 67, 107
Brazil, 187–190
foragers, 147
state intervention, 163
Infanticide, 148
village farmers, 156
Institutionalized inequality, 41
Intellectual property, 208
Intergovernmental Panel on Climate Change, 203
International Monetary Fund (IMF), 20
structural adjustments, 186, 187
Investor confidence, 191
Invisible Hand, Adam Smith, 204
IPCC, 64, 203
Ireland, potato famine, 103
IWGIA, 192

Jacobsen, T., 32
Jannuzi, F., 111
Japan
executive compensation, 194
ghost acres, 134
Jasienska, J., 162
Johnson, A., 68, 89, 173
Johnson, President L., 104
food marketing commission, 128–131
National Commission on Violence, 167

Kaberry, P., 173
Kakadu National Park, 51
Kaplan, R., 165, 182
Keenleyside, H. L., 70
Kellogg Foundation, agricultural research, 137
Kelly, R., 145
Kennedy, P., 7
Kermode, G., 134
King, H., 62, 73

Kirch, P., 58, 161–162
Klein, R., 47, 48
Knudson, K., 161
Kohr, L., 208–209
Krantz, G., 148
Kuikuru, 50, 96
Kung, leadership, 175
Kunstadter, P., 155
Kwashiorkor, 107

Lancaster, P., 132
Landsberg, H., 69, 72
Lappe, F. M., 83, 110
Large-scale cultures, social order, 175–177
Lathrap, D., 28, 57, 93, 155
Law of the Minimum, 65
Leadership, small-scale societies, 174–175
Lee, R., 17, 47, 55, 91, 95, 97, 173, 175
Leisure, 97
Levin, M., 55
Levintanus, A., 30
Levi-Strauss, C., 15, 174–175
Lewis, H., 51
Libya, 67
Limits to Growth, 34, 65
List, G., 206
Lourandos, H., 151
Lovering, T., 80
Luddites, 6
Luten, D., 64

MacCannell, D., 125
Machigenga, 95
Mack, M., 193
MacNeish, R., 92
Madden, J., 123
Male supremacist complex, 148
Malinowski, B., 178, 181
Malnutrition, Brazil, 136, 188–189

Malthus, T., 33, 74, 83, 103, 138
Malthusian controls, 134
Malthusian dilemma, 84, 88, 99
food production limits, 137
Mamdani, M., 162
Manioc, 131–133
Maquiladora zone, 187
wages, 188
Marajo Island, 31
Marketing practices, American food system, 128–131
Marple, G., 128–131
Marsh, G., 33
Martin, P., 46–47
Martire d'Anghiera, P., 15
Marx, K., 6, 52
Matthews, A., 213
Maximum good, 43
Mayan civilization, 32
Mazur, A., 67
McArthur, M., 55, 68
McCarthy, F., 55, 68
McCay, B., 44
McDonald, D., 56
Mead, M., 181
Meadows, D. and D., 32, 34–35, 38, 65, 80, 85
Meggers, B., 28, 49
Mellars, P., 50
Menarche, age, 153
Mendelsohn, R., 202
Mesoamerica, domestication, 92
Mesolithic, subsistence, 90
Mesopotamian civilization, 32, 65
Ziggurat labor, 102
Mexico
debt crisis, 187
green revolution, 138–139
Maquiladora zone, 187, 188

Micronesia
    food aid, 136
    population, 160–161, 163
Middle East, domestication, 92
Millionaires, 194
Mineral resources, 70
Modjeska, N., 173
Money fetishism, 75
Montagu, A., 107
Moore, A., 92
Moran, E., 28
Morgan, D., 125
Morgan, H., 13
Morris, M., 164
Morse, C., 74
Mosely, M., 60
Murdock, G., 57–58
Murphy, C., 66
Myers, F., 28, 172

NAFTA (North American Free Trade Agreement), 205
Naisbitt, J., 7
Nambikuara, leadership, 174–175
Naroll, R., 177, 178
Nash, M., 55
Nash, J., 198
National Academy of Sciences, mineral resource and environment study, 73
National Advisory Commission on Civil Disorders, 169
National Commission on Food Marketing, 128–131
National Commission on Violence, 167
Native American lands, destruction of, 79
Near East, Neolithic population, 153

Neel, J., 15, 16, 151
Nelson, R., 49
Neolithic
    population growth, 151–153
    shifting cultivators, 31
    transition, 152
Netherlands, food self-sufficiency, 136–137
Netting, R., 44, 49, 120
New Guinea, 49, 56
    Chimbu, 97
    population pressure, 145
    sweet potatoes, 120–121
    Tsembaga equilibrium model, 156–159
New Zealand
    meat exports, 135
    shifting cultivators, 155
Newman, K., 197
Nicklin, F., 74
Noble savage, 13, 171
Nomadic pastoralism, 45
Nonprofit organizations, 212–213
Nordhaus, 65
North American Free Trade Agreement (NAFTA), 205
Northwest coast chiefdoms, potlatch, 136
Norway
    crime rates, 168
    farmland ownership, 123
    incarceration rate, 170
Nuer, expansion, 155
Nulty, L., 138

Odum, H., 59, 65, 115–120
Ogden, R., 79
Oikonomia, 213–214
Oil, price rises, 139
Olsen, M., 183
Optimization Model, 89
Optimum
    carrying capacity, 97
    population, 144

Opulence, 194–198
Otterbein, K., 178–182
Overconsumption, 40, 59, 96
    resources, 82
Overpopulation
    root of environmental problems, 141
    security crisis, 182–184

Pacific, 57
    Pacific islander, population, 160–162
Paddock, W., 104, 106
Paleolithic
    population equilibrium, 152
    subsistence, 89
Panzos, massacre, 192
Papua New Guinea, 82
Pastoral nomads, 46
Payne, R., 74
Peach, J., 111
Pearce, D., 75
Peoples, J., 158
Periphery, world system, 184
Peru, 60
    fish meal, 135
Peruvian Amazon, 57
Pesticides, 117
Peters, C., 202
Petroleum resources, 64
Pharmaceuticals, 27
Philippines, 50
Phillips, K., 185, 194, 195
Physical Quality of Life Index, 67
Pig feasting, 156–159
Planet Drum Foundation, 213
Platt, J., 2, 5
Pleistocene extinction, 46–48
Point Four Program, 137
Polgar, S., 152
Political Risk Yearbook, 191, 193
Political system, 100

Politicization process, 3, 19, 21, 32
  population expansion, 162
  scale increases, 201
  social order, 165–166
Polynesia, 57
  chiefdoms, 58
  population, 160–162
Popper, D. and F., 213
Population
  bomb, 141–143, 147
  equilibrium, 153
  hunger, 84–85
  policy, 163–164
  reduction, 211
  world projections, 163
Population growth
  Britain, 85–88
  food production, 99
  Neolithic, 151–153
  village farmers, 154–155
Population pressure, 142, 144–145
  model 88–89
Porter, B., 6
Post-partum taboo, state intervention, 162
Potapov, L., 55
Potato chips, 131–134
Potatoes, production and processing, 120–123
Poverty, deprivation, 176
Powell, D., 72
Power, T., 76
PQLI (Physical Quality of Life Index), 67
President's Materials Policy Commission, 71
President's Science Advisory Committee, 104, 108
Price signals, 202
Protein deficiency, 107
Protein consumption, American, 126

Quality of life, 67–68
  and population, 142
Quilter, J., 60

R-species, 90
Radin, P., 53
Raiding, shifting cultivators, 155
  state intervention, 162
Rambo, T., 46
Rappaport, R., 24, 55, 56, 49, 95, 120–121, 156–159
Rathje, W., 66
Redfield, R., 13, 53
Reichel-Dolmatoff, G., 56
Reid, W., 48
Reisner, M., 120
Religion, state, 177
Reser, J., 18
Resource consumption in the United States, 68
Resources
  depletion, 71, 74
  deterioration, 96
  limits, 74–75
  mineral, 70
  national requirements for, 70
RFF (Resources for the Future), 71–72
Ribeiro, D., 60
Ricardo, D., 33, 74, 205
Richards, P., 26
Riches, D., 148
Rio Conference, 40
Rio Declaration, 206
Robey, B., 164
Rockefeller Foundation, agricultural research, 137–138
Rojas, J., 207
Romanticism, 15–16, 18
Rosa, E., 67, 91
Ross, E., population growth, 144
Rousseau, J., 13, 17
Rousseauean romanticism, 14
Ruling elite, legitimacy, 166
Russia, peasants, 98–99
Rutstein, O., 164

Ryan, P., 81

Saccharine disease, 200, 201
Sacred sites, Australia, 150
Sahlins, M., 17, 23, 24, 55, 60, 96, 97, 98, 99, 136, 155
Samuels, M., 158
San
  Bantu expansion, 154
  leadership, 175
  violence, 171, 172
  workload, 97
Sapienization, 2, 21
Sapir, E., 14
Saucier, J., 156
Saudi Arabia, 67
Scale, economic, 206
  cause and effect, 200
Scaling down, 208–209
Schele, L., 32
Scheper-Hughes, N., 187–190
Schneider, D., 163
Schrire, C., 148
Schumacher, E., 209
Scotland, farmland ownership, 123
Scott, J., 189, 204
Scrimshaw, N., 108
Security crisis, overpopulation, 182–184
Segmentary lineage, 100, 155
Self-sufficiency, agrarian, 211
Sen, A., 111
Sengel, R., 153
Service, E., 13, 24, 25, 175
Sewell, T., 125
Shaler, N., 103
Shaman, 57
Shantzis, S., 156–159
Shifted farmers, 28, 186
Shifting cultivation, 93–94, 100
  systems, 55

Shifting cultivators, 96–97
  energy efficiency, 114–115
  New Zealand, 155
  raiding, 155
Shimkin, D., 32
Shweder, R., 18
Simon, J., 19–20, 34, 75, 143
Sklair, L., 66, 67
Small Is Beautiful, 209
Small nations alternative, 208–209
Small-scale culture, 11, 23, 48, 49
  demographic change, 162–163
  economics of, 51
Smith, Adam, 33
  invisible hand, 43, 204
  Wealth of Nations, 205
Smith, E., 53, 89
Smith, E. and S., 146–147, 148
Smith, O., 120, 132
Snow, C., 193
Social costs, food production, 123–125
Social dumping, 204
Social order, large-scale cultures, 175–177
Social responsibility, 44, 46
Socioeconomic reorganization, 43
Sofer, C., 131
Soft drink consumption, American, 126–128, 131
Solow, R., 74
Southwest Asia, 45
Southwest, Desert Tradition, 154
Soviet Union, 28–30
Spaulding, W., 79,
Specialization, labor, 201
Spoehr, A., 55
Spooner, B., 45
Sri Lanka, 67

Starvation, sugar, 187–190
Steiger, W., 148
Steinhart, J. and C., 113, 126–128
Stocker, T., 60
Stover, L., 102
Stratification, scale increases, 201
Stratified societies, 175–176
Structural adjustments, 186
Subsistence, 55
  farming, 80
  security, 89
  systems, 88–95
  technologies, 51
Substantivist, 52
Sugar production, Brazil, 187–190
Sumerian civilization, 32
Sumpturary regulations, chiefdoms, 175
Super-consumers, 196
Surplus, food, 97
Survival level, deprivation, 176
Sussman, R., 149
Sustainable society, 210
Suttles, W., 136
Swidden, sweet potatoes, 120–121

Talburt, W., 120, 132
Tax, S., 211
Taxes, green, 203
Thailand, hill tribes, 155
This Common Inheritance, United Kingdom, 202
Tikopia, 58
  population, 161–162
Tiv, expansion, 155
Toffler, A., 2, 3
Tokar, B., 212–213
Toth, J., 196
Trade
  commercial, 41
  intercultural, 41

Tragedy of the Commons, 43
Transnational agents, 20
Transnational corporations, 20, 21, 67
Transnational elite, 67
Tribal cultures, 10, 46
  definition of, 11
  destruction of, 79
  hunters, 26, 47
  peoples, 23
  religion, 43
Tropical rain forest, 26, 57
Tropical deforestation, 27–28
Tropical hardwoods, 73
Trowell, H., 107
Tsembaga, 95
  energy efficiency, 114–115
  equilibrium model, 156–159
  sweet potatoes, 120–121
Tupi, expansion, 155
Turnbull, C., 172

U.S.D.A. (United States Department of Agriculture), potatoes, 132
UN, 28, 64
UNCED (United Nations Conference on Environment and Development), 206–208, 213
  report, 212
Underproduction, in small-scale cultures, 96
Underwood, B., 108, 135–136
Underwood, J., 163
Unemployment, and violence, 169
United Kingdom
  Digest of Agricultural Census Statistics, 123
  ghost acres, 134
  This Common Inheritance, 202

United Nations, 20
  Brundtland Commission,
    free market, 202
  Conference on
    Environment and
    Development, 39,
    206–208, 213
  development decades, 108,
    137–138
  Environment Program,
    203
  freedom from hunger
    campaign, 103–104
  General Assembly, 39
  International Fund for
    Agricultural
    Development, 108
  mission in New Guinea,
    81–82
  resource conservation
    conference, 70, 104
  World Food Council, 108
  World Food Program, 108
United States
  Bureau of the Census, 122
  coal development, 77–79
  consumption of copper, 80
  Department of
    Commerce, 122, 125
  Department of the
    Interior, 78
  energy use, 126–128
  farmland ownership, 123
  food system labor, 121
  Geological Survey, 65
  National Advisory
    Commission on Civil
    Disorders, 169
  National Commission on
    Violence, 167–170
  President's Science
    Advisory Committee,
    104, 108
United States Department
  of Agriculture,
  Agricultural Statistics,
  128
  potatoes, 132
United States Agency for
  International
  Development
  (USAID), 137

Urbanization, 41
USAID (United States
  Agency for
  International
  Development), 109,
  137

Vanek, J., 68
Village farmers, population
  control, 153–156
von Liebig, J., 65

Wage competition, global
  market, 188
Wagley, C., 163
Waiwai, Guyana, 132
Walker, B., 45
Wallerstein, I., 66, 184
Walter, E., 34
War
  cross-cultural
    perspectives, 177–182
  definitions, 178
Warford, J., 75
Wealth distribution, Erhlich,
  143
Wealth of Nations, Adam
  Smith, 205
Weapons, nuclear, 195
Webster, D., 47
Weiss, K., 147
Wenner-Gren symposium, 17
West Africa, anarchy, 183
West Germany, food self-
  sufficiency, 136–137
Western, D., 45
Western Samoa, 67
Wet-rice growers, energy
  efficiency, 114–115
WFC (World Food
  Council), UN, 108
WFP (World Food
  Program), UN, 108
White, J., 125
White, L., 13, 14, 24, 65
White, L., Jr., 42, 43, 55
Whiting, J., 156
Williams, M., 27

Winter, R., 45
Winterhalder, B., 53, 89
Wissman, H., 128–131
Wolf, Edward, 109
Wolf, Eric, 204
Woodburn, J., 91, 172
Work, concept of, 97
World Bank, 20, 62, 69, 107
  Conference on
    Overcoming Global
    Hunger, 109
  grain import statistics, 135
  hunger, 109, 110
  structural adjustments, 186
  sustainable growth study,
    75
World Commission on
  Environment and
  Development, 39
World Development Report,
  21
World Food Council, UN,
  108
World Food Conference, 104
World Food Program, 108
World Health Organization,
  30
World, population projec-
  tions, 163
World Resources Institute, 48
World system theory, 184
Worldwide Fund for Nature,
  141
Wright, Q., 178, 181

Yanomamo
  conflict resolution, 174
  violence, 171
Yde, J., 132
Yen, D., 58, 161–162
Yengoyan, A., 148
Young, V., 108
Yugoslavia, conflict, 183

Zimbabwe, childhood
  malnutrition, 108
Zubrow, E., 145, 154
Zulu, 154–155